Redefining Shakespeare

Redefining Shakespeare

Literary Theory and Theater Practice
in the German Democratic Republic

Edited by
J. Lawrence Guntner and
Andrew M. McLean

Newark: University of Delaware Press
London: Associated University Presses

Associated University Presses
440 Forsgate Drive
Cranbury, NJ 08512

Associated University Presses
16 Barter Street
London WC1A 2AH, England

Associated University Presses
P.O. Box 338, Port Credit
Mississauga, Ontario
Canada L5G 4L8

The paper used in this publication meets the requirements of the American National Standard for Permanence of Paper for Printed Library Materials Z39.48–1984.

Library of Congress Cataloging-in-Publication Data

Redefining Shakespeare : literary theory and theater practice in the German Democratic Republic / edited by J. Lawrence Guntner and Andrew M. McLean.
    p.   cm.
Includes bibliographical references and index.
ISBN 0-87413-604-0 (alk. paper)
    1. Shakespeare, William, 1564–1616—Appreciation—Germany (East) 2. Shakespeare, William, 1564–1616—Criticism and interpretation—History—20th century.   3. Shakespeare, William, 1564–1616—Stage history—Germany (East)   4. English drama—Appreciation—Germany (East)—History—20th century.   5. English drama—History and criticism—Theory, etc.   6. Germany (East)—Civilization—English influences.   7. Criticism—Germany (East)—History—20th century. 8. Theater—Germany (East)—History—20th century. I. Guntner, J. Lawrence, 1941–   . II. McLean, Andrew M., 1941–   .
PR2971.G3R43   1998
822.3'3—dc21   96-40037
                                                              CIP

PRINTED IN THE UNITED STATES OF AMERICA

We dedicate this book to Daniela, Luciane, and Stephen Guntner, who have borne this enterprise with patience and general good humor, and to Morgan McLean and Cory Rayala, who love the theater and have grown up with this book.

Contents

List of Illustrations

Preface

In the fall of 1989, Günther Klotz visited America for the first time. He spoke idiomatic English and had translated and edited numerous British and American authors in the course of his professional career as an editor for Aufbau-Verlag and staff member of the Academy of the Sciences of the German Democratic Republic (GDR). It had taken much bureaucratic maneuvering for him to obtain a travel visa for his visit, and when he had finally reached America, ironically, his troubled homeland was about to fall apart. It became the morning joke for him to inquire whether he still had a country to return to before scanning the headlines for the latest news. Political events moved quickly; not long after his return the GDR ceased to exist. Klotz had served in the German army during World War II, and had been wounded and taken prisoner by the Russians. After the war he remained in the East. He, like Maik Hamburger, who later left England voluntarily, wanted to build a new Germany, solidly antifascist and democratically socialist. In hindsight their efforts were doomed from the start. Initially, at least, belief in the larger benefits of a socialist society provided an excuse for tolerating what many recognized as totalitarian aberrations in this emerging social order; things would get better, they thought, given time. But they did not.

The theater became a way to criticize the system and for the audience to find a release for their frustrations about a social experiment that continually impinged on their personal freedoms and way of life. On 11 September 1961 students at the State Institute for Economics in Karlshorst, an outlying district of East Berlin, performed Heiner Müller's play *Die Umsiedlerin oder das Leben auf dem Lande* (*The Refugee, or Life in the Country*). It is a play about the industrialization and collectivization of agriculture in East Germany in the fifties. Müller and the director, B. K. Tragelehn, had rehearsed and reworked the script for over two years. It was to be their contribution to a socialist society and culture; however, after the performance the student performers were interrogated until they "confessed" to having performed an "anti-communist play." Tragelehn, interrogated to find out who was behind this "anti-communist plot," was expelled from the Socialist Unity Party and sent to an open-face coal mine for two years to learn about the working class through manual labor. Müller was subjected to party disciplinary measures, expelled from the Writers' Union, and prohibited

11

from having anything published or performed for the next two years. He and his wife, Inge, were made persona non grata in an attempt to isolate them. When Müller sought advice from composer Hanns Eisler, Bertolt Brecht's companion in exile, Eisler quipped ironically: "Müller, you ought to be happy that you live in a country that takes literature seriously. And if you want my advice, think about Schiller. An Austrian tyrant is murdered in Switzerland. That's the kind of play you want to write in Germany."[1] It is not without reason that Müller, arguably the most important German dramatist since Brecht, spent much of his professional career reworking and rewording theater classics, including Shakespeare, and that Tragelehn has also spent much of his career since then translating and directing Shakespeare, albeit more often in West Germany than in East Germany.

In April 1964, to celebrate the four hundredth anniversary of Shakespeare's birth, Adolf Dresen and his ensemble performed *Hamlet* in Greifswald, a small town on the Polish border near the Baltic Sea. The farmers and workers in the audience were pleased, the theater elite from Berlin were enthusiastic, but party officials smelled sedition. Party functionaries disrupted performances, and after only twelve performances, the head of the Theater cancelled the show on the grounds that the performance was "a destruction of the classical heritage and the humanistic view of mankind," that it exemplified "left-wing radicalism," and that it contained "influences of absurd theater."[2] Dresen was dismissed and went to an oil refinery to learn, like Tragelehn, about the working class through manual labor; cast members who protested Dresen's treatment were fired. The exciting new translation by Maik Hamburger and Dresen was labeled "inadequate." In his autobiography, *Krieg ohne Schlacht* (*War without Battle*), Müller claims: "A dictatorship is more colorful for a playwright, more colorful than democracy. Shakespeare is unthinkable in a democracy."[3] Müller reminds us that the political relevance of Shakespeare's plays to contemporary politics becomes more readily visible when the plays are performed against a clearly defined political backdrop.

This book explores the relationship between Shakespeare and East German politics and cultural policy. It tells the story of how Shakespeare was performed, translated, criticized, and understood within the context of East German social history. East German theater people, literary historians, audiences, and the ruling Socialist Unity Party always believed that culture in general and theater in particular had something to do with politics.

Those involved in the theater felt their work would help to change people as well as society. Alexander Weigel's reason for working in the theater makes the point: "I wanted to teach them [the audience] how they could change the world and lead a better life."[4] In order to teach well, educators respond to changing conditions. So, too, the theater and its approach to staging Shakespeare, was defined officially, redefined in performance, and then done differently later when political conditions changed. What makes this process interesting is that theater was in a continual state of change despite the fact that the GDR developed more and more into a closed society. Yet it was precisely this contradiction that provided East German directors, translators, set designers, dramaturgs, and performers with the dramatic materials they needed to redefine their understanding of Shakespeare for contemporary East German audiences.

In a state where for all practical purposes a "public sphere" did not exist, the stage came to assume the role of a public forum where cultural ideology and, by extension, the East German socialist state, could be staged, debated, and criticized. Performance of theater classics, ancient and modern, frequently took over the function of critical journalism, history books, or political commentary. Audiences came to expect, and party cultural functionaries came to suspect, that Shakespeare productions might just contain gift-wrapped critiques of the GDR's socialist system (and they often did). Thus, Shakespeare performance became instrumental in shaping a political awareness and new self-confidence among the people that led to the 1989 bloodless revolution and the fall of the Berlin Wall.

Since the implosion of the German Democratic Republic and its ingestion into the Federal Republic of Germany, a cultural as well as a material levelling has taken place. Infamous landmarks demarking the frontier have been razed, and once well-defined contours differentiating the cultural landscape of East and West Germany have become blurred,[5] even in Shakespeare performance.

This collection of essays and interviews retraces those contours. In this restaging of Shakespeare in East Germany the principal actors speak for and about themselves. The story line runs from the affirmation of Shakespeare as the major representative of a "humanist view of mankind" ("*humanistisches Menschenbild*") to the subversion and radical deconstruction of this doctrine and even of the plays themselves. Our examination of Shakespeare is representative rather than comprehensive; there were some sixty public theaters in the GDR outside of Berlin. Yet what happened on stage in Berlin, the cultural and political nerve center of the country, was soon felt elsewhere.

Our focus explores how one socialist society appropriated Shakespeare. But this focus may also be seen as a paradigm for what happened to Shakespeare and other classics, to a certain degree, in other East European socialist societies. In the GDR it led to the evolution of a unique relationship between critical theory, literary history, and theater practice, which requires an understanding of the cultural matrix that produced it.

As actors and the theater audience learned to look at Shakespeare's plays in a new way, critics and scholars set about rewriting English literary history. Shakespeare's plays, which had always been a mainstay of the German theater and an integral part of German education, were redefined in light of a Marxist perspective and historiography. The result was a fruitful and sometimes heated dialogue between critical theory and theatrical practice that led to a new understanding of Shakespearean dramaturgy and theater. Later this dialogue cooled as the political class became disinterested and the players disillusioned. Robert Weimann's work is a critical keystone for understanding the theoretical debate that affected GDR theatrical productions. It moves from Shakespeare's use of the popular staging traditions to the question of authority as both a textual and an existential issue linking or dividing the forces of society and the standards of writing.

We call this book "redefining Shakespeare" to emphasize that Shakespeare on the GDR stage, in translation, in criticism, and in the mind of the spectator, was not ideologically fixed but assumed different forms and functions according to the time, the place, the players, and the audience who were interacting with each other. In fact, it constituted a highly divisive, ununified space in the cultural landscape of the country. Attempts to appropriate Shakespeare for an official cultural ideology are not at the center of our concern. Rather, we focus on the scholars, directors, and translators who worked at what Heiner Müller called "the difference,"[6] that is, at the contradictions in the reception of Shakespeare which involved conflict with official pronouncements on Shakespeare.

Most of the essays and interviews in this volume were completed before the GDR ceased to exist as a sovereign state; interestingly, there was no reason to redo them. They tell their own story, provide insights into life in the GDR, and reflect the theatrical and political concerns that engaged some of the country's best minds. Interviews done after the GDR's demise confirm the insights of the earlier pieces, add details about women's roles in the GDR theater, and illustrate the workings of different levels of censorship. Taken together, the early and later pieces might be read as an oral history of Shakespeare in the GDR. While their country is gone, their work in the theater and their redefinition of Shakespeare in the theater and in scholarship will remain.

Acknowledgments

THIS book has been a long time in the making and many people have helped us along the way. The contributors and especially those interviewed have indulged us generously with their time, patience, and hospitality. A special word of thanks must be given to Robert Weimann for steady support and constructive criticism from the beginning to the end, and to Maik Hamburger for his suggestions as to whom to talk to and where to look. In the early stages of this project Heinz-Uwe Haus and Günter Klotz were generous with their time and firsthand experiences. For their generous hospitality, time, and personal insights into the complexities of GDR history and politics, we thank Christa and B. K. Tragelehn as well as Armin-Gerd and Juttka Kuckhoff. A special word of appreciation is due to Gisela Schlösser of the Brecht Archive at the Berliner Ensemble. For providing photo materials, we thank Ludwig Böhme of the Staatstheater Dresden, Ute Echte of the Berliner Ensemble, Margrit Lenk of the Neues Theater in Halle, Sigrid Meixner of the Mecklenbürgisches Staatstheater in Schwerin, Manfred Möckel of the Maxim Gorki Theater, Lothar Schirmer of the Berliner Musuem, Brigitte Spiegel of the Volksbühne, Wolfhard Theile of the Deutsches Theater, and B. K. Tragelehn. For permission to reproduce their photographs of Shakespeare productions we also thank Adelheid Beyer, Peter Festersen, Henschel Verlag, Wolfram Schmidt and Vera Tenschert. Marina Halbas delivered typescripts in times of emergency, Sabine Hake and Zehra Khan-Owald helped translate interviews, and Astrid Zaunick checked transcriptions. Johannes Heyer at the German end and Dave Datta, Sandy Duveneck, and Jeff Shaub at the North American end of the Internet managed the logistics of transporting manuscripts across the Atlantic. We also thank the following people who contributed to completing this book: Jay Halio, Donna Hamilton, Renate Kosmalla, Sylvia McClain, Abigail Streblow, Katarina Stein, Günter Walch, and Wolfgang Wicht.

Chronology: Shakespeare and the GDR, 1945–1990

1945

30 April: "Gruppe Ulbricht" enters Berlin; includes Gustav von Wangenheim later Head of Deutsches Theater.

8 May: German Army surrenders.

11 June: Berlin municipal authorities grant theater licenses.

9 July: "Chamber of Cultural Activists" under direction of Paul Wegener to renew theater.

17 July—3 August: Potsdam Conference divides Germany into four occupational zones.

3—11 September: Land reform in Soviet Zone.

7 September: Deutsches Theater reopens with Lessing's *Nathan der Weise* with Paul Wegener as Nathan (Dir. Fritz Wisten).

October: Section for acting founded at Music Academy in Weimar under Maxim Vallentin; beginning of Stanislavsky method as dominant norm for GDR theater.

1 December: Bruno Henschel Verlag founded; monopoly for distribution of stage plays in GDR.

Hamlet (Dir. Gustav von Wangenheim, Deutsches Theater).

1946

21—22 April: Formation of Socialist Unity Party (Communists and Social Democrats).

May: First issue of *Theater der Zeit* edited by Fritz Erpenbek; becomes official and sole theater journal of GDR; propagates Stanislavsky method.

May: DEFA, East German film company, founded.

1947

"Socialist Realism" (Andrey Zhdanov) is made norm for theater performance.

17

October: First (and last) pan-German Writers Congress.

Gustav von Wangenheim, *Die Maus in der Falle.*

1948

March: Socialist Unity Party convention proclaims "Unity and Purity of the Party," and suppresses criticism, especially of those emigrants returning from Western countries.

15 April: *Measure for Measure* (Dir. Wolfgang Langhoff, Deutsches Theater).

5 June: Soviet Zone rejects participation in Marshall Plan.

20 June: Currency reform in Allied Zones dooms hope of a reunited Germany; followed by currency reform in Soviet Zone.

24 June: Berlin Blockade begins.

21 October: Bertolt Brecht returns to Berlin.

1949

11 January: *Mutter Courage* (Dir. Bertolt Brecht/Erich Engel, Deutsches Theater).

5 May: Berlin Blockade lifted.

1 September: Berliner Ensemble under direction of Helene Weigel begins its first season.

7 September: Federal Republic of Germany established.

7 October: German Democratic Republic established.

1950

8 February: Ministry for State Security founded.

4—6 July: Writers Union founded.

20—24 July: Third Party Congress elects Walter Ulbricht general secretary and lays down doctrine of planned economy and class struggle. detonation of Berlin Castle (residence of the Hohenzollerns and symbol of Junker Prussia).

1951

15—17 March: Stanislavsky conference at Academy of Arts; debate over Brecht and Stanislavsky methods.

Twelfth Night (Dir. Wolfgang Heinz, Deutsches Theater).

1952

Maxim Gorki Theater founded in Berlin (emphasis on "Stanislavsky Method" for contemporary Soviet drama).

1952

Maxim Gorki Theater opens (emphasis on the plays of Maxim Gorki, contemporary Soviet and Eastern European drama, and the Stanislavsky method).

Helene Weigel/Berlin Ensemble, *Theaterarbeit* contains the photographs and practical details from model productions by the Berliner Ensemble.

1953

5 March: Stalin dies.

17 June: Workers uprising in East Berlin and other cities.

Third Art Exhibition in Dresden: "Soviet Realism" and the socialist "Menschenbild" ("vision of humanity") are made standard for graphic art; art proclaimed a "Weapon for Socialism."

Othello (Dir. Wolfgang Heinz, Deutsches Theater).

Heiner Kipphardt, *Shakespeare dringend gesucht* ("Shakespeare desperately wanted") (Dir. R. Herwart Grosse, Deutsches Theater).

1954

7 January: Ministry for Culture established, headed by Johannes R. Becher (1954–58).

1955

25 March: Soviet Union recognizes GDR as sovereign nation.

1956

East German National People's Army established.

February: Khrushchev denounces Stalin; "de-Stalinization" also in GDR.

14 August: Brecht dies.

October: GDR approves suppression of uprising in Budapest.

A Midsummer Night's Dream (Dir. Fritz Wisten, Volksbühne Berlin).

A Midsummer Night's Dream (Dir. Rudi Kurz, Leipzig).

1957

Fifth Cultural Congress: guidelines for cultural dogma that will be known as the "Bitterfeld Way" are offered.

King Lear (Dir. Wolfgang Langhoff, Deutsches Theater).

1958

27 November: Khrushchev issues ultimatum for Western Allies to leave Berlin.

Robert Weimann's *Drama und Wirklichkeit in der Shakespearezeit.* ("Drama and Reality in the Age of Shakespeare").

1959

First Bitterfeld Conference. "The Bitterfeld Way" slogans: "Pick up your pen and write, mate! Our socialist national culture needs you!" "Socialist Realism" becomes official cultural policy; aesthetic principles subjugated to economic principles.

1960

Collectivization of agriculture and remaining private industry and business; Wilhelm Pieck, President of GDR since 1949, dies and no successor is elected.

1961

13 August: Berlin Wall erected.

Heiner Müller and B. K. Tragelehn censored, punished, and banned from working for *Die Umsiedlerin: oder das Leben auf dem Lande* (*The Refugee,* Dir. B. K. Tragelehn, Karlshorst).

Twelfth Night (musical) (Dir. Günther Deicke/Klaus Fehmel, Berlin).

Peter Hack's *Die Sorgen und die Macht* (*The Cares and the Power*, Dir. Wolfgang Langhoff, Deutsches Theater) subjected to harsh official criticism.

1962

Troilus and Cressida (Dir. Hannes Fischer, Dresden).

1963

Sixth Party Congress: Kurt Hager named Ideological Head of the Central Committee; continues hard-line course of "Bitterfeld Way" cultural policy.

Wolfgang Langhoff removed as Head of Deutsches Theater.

Two Gentlemen of Verona (Dir. Benno Besson, Deutsches Theater).

West German members withdraw from German Shakespeare Society to found Deutsche Shakespeare-Gesellschaft (West) in Bochum.

1964

April: Resumption of German Shakespeare Society activities in Weimar. Shakespeare-Tage attended by Walter Ulbricht; Cultural Minister Alexander Abusch's programmatic keynote address, "Shakespeare: Realist and Humanist, Genius of World Literature," broadcast live to the nation. "Appropriation of the Cultural Heritage" propagated.

Second Bitterfeld Conference: "Shakespeare the Great Innovator" to be example for GDR drama, with emphasis on "folk characters" and "folk scenes."

Brezhnev replaces Khrushchev.

Hamlet (Dir. Adolf Dresen, tr. Maik Hamburger/Adolf Dresen, Greifswald); production canceled after twelve performances

Coriolanus (Dir. Manfred Wekwerth/Joachim Tenschert/Ruth Berghaus, Berliner Ensemble).

Hamlet (Dir. Hans-Dieter Mäde, Karl-Marx-Stadt).

Hamlet (Dir. Wolfgang Heinz, Deutsches Theater).

Armin-Gerd Kuckhoff, *Das Drama William Shakespeares.*

1965

15—18 December: Eleventh Plenary Session of the Central Committee: Erich Honecker attacks "harmful tendencies" in culture. Wolf Biermann banned from public performance. Rock music denounced as fascist and its fans as Hitler Youth.

1966

Measure for Measure (Dir. Adolf Dresen, Deutsches Theater; tr. Maik Hamburger); a critique of the cultural oppression of 1965 Plenary Session.

1967

Robert Weimann: *Shakespeare und die Tradition des Volkstheaters: Soziologie. Dramaturgie. Gestaltung.* ("Shakespeare and the Popular Tradition in the Theater. Studies in the Social Dimension of Dramatic Form and Function").

1968

Faust (Dir. Adolf Dresen/Wolfgang Heinz, Deutsches Theater): radical departure from official versions of the character of Faust.

20—21 August: Prague Spring suppressed with help of GDR troops.

1969

As You Like It (Dir. B. K. Tragelehn; tr. Heiner Müller, Film School Potsdam).

Willy Brandt elected chancellor of West Germany.

1970

A Midsummer Night's Dream (Dir. Fritz Bennewitz, Weimar).

19 March: First meeting of heads of the two German states, Willy Brandt and Prime Minister Willi Stoph, in Erfurt, followed by return visit in Kassel.

1971

3 May: Erich Honecker replaces Walter Ulbricht as general secretary.

15—19 June: Eighth Party Convention of the Socialist Unity Party under slogan "Already Existing Socialism" (*realexistierender Sozialismus*); liberalization of cultural policy announced.

A Midsummer Night's Dream (Dir. Christoph Schroth; tr. Maik Hamburger, Halle).

A Midsummer Night's Dream (Dir. Werner Freese, Magdeburg).

1972

21 December: "Basic Treaty" *(Grundvertrag)* governing relations between East and West Germany signed.

The Life and Death of King Richard the Third (Dir. Manfred Wekwerth; tr. Manfred Wekwerth, Deutsches Theater).

Macbeth (Dir. Bernd Bartoszewski; tr./adaptation Heiner Müller, Brandenburg).

1973

Rock music and western television officially tolerated. The roundtable discussions at Shakespeare-Tage's "The Work of Shakespeare: Interpretation,

Adaptation, Reworking, New Creation" signals end of cooperation between literary historians and theater people.

1 August: Walter Ulbricht dies.

Theater playbills require Ministry of Culture approval.

Hamlet (Dir. Gert Jurgons, Schwerin)

1974

A Midsummer Night's Dream (Dir. Klaus-Dieter Kirst, Dresden).

The Tempest (Dir. Friedo Solter, tr. Maik Hamburger, Deutsches Theater)

1975

Conference on Security and Cooperation in Europe (Helsinki Agreement): door for regime's critics opened.

1976

11 November: Expatriation of Wolf Biermann after a concert in Cologne; over 100 prominent artists, writers, and singers sign protest petition in solidarity; many later emigrate. Leads to a steady drain of GDR theater talent.

King Lear (Dir. Friedo Solter, Deutsches Theater).

A Midsummer Night's Dream (Dir. Klaus Fiedler, Rudolstadt).

1977

Hamlet (Dir. Benno Besson; tr. Heiner Müller/Matthias Langhoff, Volksbühne) and Heiner Müller's *Hamletmaschine.*

1979

Writers Congress stages tribunal and expels critical writers.

Measure for Measure (Dir. B. K. Tragelehn; tr. B. K. Tragelehn, Stuttgart).

1980

A Midsummer Night's Dream (Dir. Alexander Lang, Deutsches Theater/Dir. Thomas Langhoff, Maxim Gorki Theater).

King John (Dir. Fritz Bennewitz, Weimar).

Christa Wolf awarded West Germany's Georg Büchner Prize for German literature.

1981

A New Midsummer Night's Dream (Dir. Tom Schilling, Comic Opera Berlin).

Measure for Measure (Dir. Peter Schroth/Peter Kleinert, Weimar).

Twelfth Night (Dir. Martin Meltke, Brandenburg).

Romeo and Juliet (Dir. Peter Schroth/Peter Kleinert, Theater im Palast Berlin).

1982

Weimar symposium on "Theatrical Practice and Shakespeare Scholarship" signals new critical approach to Shakespeare performance.

Macbeth (according to Shakespeare) (Dir. Heiner Müller/Ginka Tscholokowa; tr.-adaptation Heiner Müller, Volksbühne).

Othello (Dir. Frank Castorf, Anklam) (Taken off program after one performance).

1983

Luther Year initiates study of crisis in authority and its representation in Shakespeare's England.

1984

"Monday Peace Prayers" begin in Leipzig's St. Nicholas Church and the "Initiative for Peace and Human Rights."

4 September: Honecker cancels visit to West Germany under Soviet pressure.

Troilus and Cressida (Dir. Manfred Wekwerth/Joachim Tenschert, Berliner Ensemble).

1985

Restored Semper Opera reopens in Dresden.

Hamlet (Dir. B. K. Tragelehn; tr. H. Müller/M. Langhoff, Munich).

The Merchant of Venice (Dir. Thomas Langhoff, Deutsches Theater).

War; Peace; Love—A Rehearsal of Shakespeare [Troilus and Cressida] (Theaterwürfel Berlin tr. B.K. Tragelehn.).

1986

International Shakespeare Association World Congress in West Berlin with theater performances in East Berlin.

Romeo and Juliet (Dir. Christoph Schroth, Schwerin; part 1 of Shakespeare project).

1987

Tenth Writers Congress demands end of licensing for publication.

A Winter's Tale (Dir. Christoph Schroth, Schwerin; part 2 of Shakespeare project).

Anatomy Titus Fall of Rome. A Shakespeare Commentary (Dir. Wolfgang Engel, Dresden; Dir. F.P. Steckel; Bochum, tr.-adaptation Heiner Müller).

Twelfth Night (Dir. Martin Meltke, Greifswald).

Puck (Dir. Tom Schilling; Music, Bernd Köllinger, Comic Opera Berlin).

Weimar symposium on "Gender, Power, Humanity" opens window for new theoretical discourses by international participants.

1988

17 January: human rights and peace movement dissidents protest during the annual march commemorating the murders of Rosa Luxemburg and Karl Liebknecht.

Robert Weimann, *Shakespeare und die Macht der Mimesis*.

1989

Mass exodus through Hungary and the West German embassy in Prague. September: massive "Monday Demonstrations" in Leipzig.

4 November: a million demonstrators for democracy in East Berlin are organized by theater people.

9 November: Berlin Wall falls.

Hamlet Material from Shakespeare (Dir. Frank Castorf, Cologne).

1990

18 March: first free elections in East Germany.

24 March: *Hamlet/Maschine* (Dir. Heiner Müller; tr. Heiner Müller, Deutsches Theater).

1 July: Currency Union.

3 October: German Democratic Republic joins Federal Republic of Germany.

2 December: First all-German general elections won by Christian Democrats led by Helmut Kohl.

Redefining Shakespeare

Introduction:
Shakespeare in East Germany: Between Appropriation and Deconstruction

J. LAWRENCE GUNTNER

I
Die Stunde Null: **Starting from Scratch (1945–1949)**

BY the end of the Second World War eighty-nine German theaters lay in ruins, and at least four thousand theater people had fled Nazi Germany. Many of them never returned. They took with them a vital share of a rich German theater tradition: the critical avant-garde theater of the Weimar Republic: Max Reinhardt, Leopold Jessner, and Erwin Piscator.[1] Goebbels had ordered German theaters to close on 1 September 1944 in support of "the total war," and German audiences, in both East and West, were thirsty for theater.[2] More serious than the damage to the buildings was the damage done to the minds of the remaining actors and actresses, directors and audiences by what Brecht called "Göring Theater," that is, a theater of pomp and circumstance.[3] On occasion it was technically brilliant, yet it generally lacked any reference to the social context of the audience. Socialists and Communists saw this situation as the chance to cast off the ballast of the previous twelve years and begin anew. For them Germany was in the midst of a *Zeitenwende*[4] in which the stage would play an important role as a political-pedagogical force, "a weapon and a tool" for educating the masses for social change.[5] Of course, any appropriation of the German classic theater tradition for the development of a *socialist* national theater would have to take Shakespeare, the greatest stimulating force in the development of this tradition, into account.

When the Communist exiles in the "Gruppe Ulbricht" entered Berlin on the heels of the Soviet Army on April 30, eight days before the German Wehrmacht unconditionally surrendered, they brought with them from their Moscow exile a Stalinist system steeped in suspicion and paranoia. They

29

**Entrance to the Chamber Theater of the Deutsches Theater Berlin, 1945.
Photo: Eva Kemlein, courtesy of the Berlin Museum.**

also brought with them "socialist realism," a version of theater propagated by Stalin and his cultural mouthpiece Andrey Zhdanov. Ulbricht and other Communist leaders had little understanding for the developments on the stage of the Weimar Republic and no truck with Brecht's ideas about how realism in the modern theater should be stylized through "alienation" (*Verfremdungseffekt*). For them theater was simply a chapter in the formation of a socialist society. "Socialist realism" was an extension of the critical treatment of social ills characteristic of the great bourgeois, realistic nineteenth-century novelists, such as Dickens, Zola, and Tolstoy. However, since the ills had been ostensibly corrected under socialism, the task of twentieth-century "socialist realism" was not to criticize but to affirm the positive nature of contemporary socialist society—a society in harmony with the socialist *"Menschenbild."* A resolution by the Central Committee of the Soviet Union's Communist Party makes this clear:

> Dramatic literature and theater must reflect in plays and performances the life of Soviet society in its incessant surge forward, and contribute fully to the further development of the best sides of Soviet Man's character, . . . [must] make Soviet youth spirited, optimistic, devoted to their country, believing in the victory of our cause, unafraid of obstacles, and capable of overcoming any difficulty, . . . [and] must also show that such qualities belong, not only to a few elect ones or to heroes, but to many millions of Soviet citizens.[6]

The approach to acting was to be the Stanislavsky method, and the enemy in this *"Kulturkampf"* was bourgeois "formalism." A favorite target would be Brecht's Berliner Ensemble and its theater of portrayal, which emphasized the story, as opposed to Stanislavsky's theater of experience, which emphasized character.[7]

Hardly had the armistice been signed when the heavily damaged Deutsches Theater Berlin reopened on 7 September 1945 with Lessing's *Nathan der Weise,* a play banned under the Nazis because of Nathan, its tolerant Jewish protagonist. Three months later on 11 December 1945, a production of *Hamlet* directed by Gustav von Wangenheim, recently returned from Soviet exile, opened with a first-class cast of established German actors: Horst Caspar as Hamlet, Walther Richter as Claudius, Gerda Müller as Gertrude, Paul Wegener as Polonius, and Heinrich Greif as Hamlet. It included both darlings of the Nazi period (Caspar), Soviet exiles (Greif), and "internal emigrants" who had refused to cooperate with the Nazis (Müller).

Wangenheim saw Hamlet, like Germany in 1945, as caught between two historical epochs. Hamlet was portrayed as a man who acts against "the sea of troubles" for the sake of a more humane world that would eventually culminate in a socialist society, in a sense, a prerevolutionary hero. Special attention was lavished on Fortinbras, played by Heinrich Greif. He was tall

Gustav von Wangenheim rehearsing *Hamlet*, 1945. Photo: Willi Saeger, courtesy of the Deutsches Theater.

and blond, with a mellifluous voice, and as Fortinbras he embodied Germany's bright future. He wore a luminescent costume and all of the few spotlights available were focused on him when he entered. Wangenheim moved the scene downstage close to the audience to make Fortinbras— the human embodiment of an optimistic socialist future—tangible for the audience, especially the younger generation.[8] Attention to Fortinbras became a GDR tradition and its staging a convention frequently imitated. It is also one source of Heiner Müller's comment forty-five years later that the central concern of any *Hamlet* performance in the GDR was: "Who is Fortinbras?" Just as central for Wangenheim were Hamlet's instructions to The Players ("to hold a mirror up to nature") and the function of "The Mousetrap" in the play.[9] Hamlet's remarks on *how* to perform and *what* to perform became the official credo for Shakespeare reception in the GDR, and the play within the play became a metaphor for the role of the theater in building up a socialist state. For Wangenheim, the central message of the play was Shakespeare's humanism—"what a piece of work is man"—that anticipated socialism. Thus, he saw Hamlet as a role model. In a speech to young members of the audience on 3 February 1946, he called out, "Be radical like Hamlet. Think things through to the end. Act with decision! We are more fortunate than Shakespeare's Hamlet because we know the way out. We understand the purpose of our struggle."[10]

II
Toward an East German Shakespeare (1949–1964)

"Arisen out of the ruins, facing toward the future" ("Auferstanden aus Ruinen und der Zukunft zugewandt") was the opening line of the East German national anthem. It contains a phoenixlike image with which the founders of the German Democratic Republic, the first socialist state on German territory, liked to compare themselves: as the torchbearers of a German intellectual, political, and moral tradition reborn after its misuse and abuse by the Nazis. Intent on avoiding the mistakes made between 1929 and 1933, the Communist, Wilhelm Pieck, and the Social Democrat, Otto Grotewohl, joined hands to establish an "antifascist" united front in July 1945. In April 1946 Communists and Social Democrats merged to become the Socialist Unity Party. The handshake of Pieck and Grotewohl became the party logo.[11] Later, the fellow-traveling Christian Democrats and the Liberals joined the alliance. However, it was a coalition soon to be dominated by the Communists and their general secretary, Walter Ulbricht. The decision dictated by Moscow not to participate in the Marshall Plan in favor of a planned economy cut East Germany off from the economic developments of Western capitalism and from the massive financial support West Germany received from the West. It was only a matter of time before economic pressures would force the ruling Socialist Unity Party, burdened by oppressive reparations to the Soviet Union, to falsify economic progress reports and to erect a system of state control to eliminate criticism. On 8 February 1950 the "Ministry for State Security" was founded on the model and with the assistance of the Soviet secret police. Ulbricht and his associates had neither time nor patience for the democratic forms of socialism championed by German emigrants returning from Western countries or by those who had been incarcerated in Nazi prison camps. The ministry, "Shield and Sword of the Party," soon turned into the feared "Stasi," a seemingly omnipotent state within the state. It transgressed its legislative legitimation. Neither its responsibilities nor its limits were ever clearly defined. It would also be used to influence cultural uniformity in the area of Shakespeare performance and criticism.

Although the GDR was founded on 7 October 1949, one month after the founding of the Federal Republic of Germany, it was not recognized as a sovereign state until 1955. In 1955 the Soviet Union proposed a unified Germany with free elections if West Germany would agree not to ratify the Paris Agreements and not to join NATO. Chancellor Adenauer refused and the Soviet Union recognized the German Democratic Republic as a sovereign state. However, the fate of the GDR had already been sealed two years earlier by the workers' uprising on 17 June 1953. In the years that followed, an ever-increasing economic gap between East and West Germany led to an ever-increasing flow of skilled workers and professionals to the West and more political repression. On 13 August 1961, the infamous Berlin Wall was erected. The "material" Wall soon became a "cultural wall" against unwanted cultural developments and an instrument of oppression to keep dissidents in line and to enforce a hard-line cultural policy laid down in 1959 at the so-called Bitterfeld Conference.

In April 1959 the Party organized a national conference to develop a socialist cultural policy. Artists, intellectuals, writers, and theater people attended the meeting, which was held in a chemical processing plant near Bitterfeld. The purpose of the conference was to encourage worker-writers and to appropriate "the positive cultural heritage" of the German national tradition for a new socialist tradition. The conference guidelines, meant to develop identification with the first "Workers's and Farmers's State" on German soil as well as cultural activity among workers, farmers, and artists, became known as "the Bitterfeld Way" (der Bitterfelder Weg). However, aesthetic principles were clearly subjugated to party ideology.[12] The month before, the Central Committee itself had censored Wolfgang Langhoff, director of the Deutsches Theater, his dramaturg Heiner Kipphardt, and Hans-Dieter Mäde, head of the Maxim Gorki Theater, for choosing their repertory on "aesthetic principles." They were told bluntly: "We think it is about time for you and your colleagues to consider your responsibility to the Farmers' and Workers' State."[13] To the party, theater meant "socialist realism" and plays dealing with the contemporary reality of the GDR. It rejected any "decadent," "bourgeois" influences from "the West" such as "Absurd Theater." It is no wonder, therefore, that Shakespeare had a difficult time of it in the early years of the GDR. The German classics—Lessing, Schiller, Goethe—remained the preferred subjects for redefinition and appropriation. When Shakespeare was performed, it was mainly the comedies as regular thigh slappers; the histories or tragedies were performed as conventional character studies.

Wolfgang Langhoff's King Lear (Deutsches Theater, 1957) broke with the early GDR Shakespeare tradition of Stanislavskian character studies. This production was one of the most important Shakespeare productions of the fifties, and it set a standard and example for later Shakespeare performances.[14] Heinrich Kilger's set cleared the stage of any socialist realist trappings. The hexagonal performing area, an obvious reference to Shakespeare's Globe Theater, was enclosed by H-shaped wooden structures that framed the stage and provided an upper gallery on which the actors could also perform. The bare stage gave the actors more space to develop their character in line with the story line: a struggle to the death between human passions and a decaying social order. Following Brecht, Langhoff's dramaturgical concept called for Lear's character to be located within the plot, keeping Lear's character out of the dramatic foreground as was the German tradition for this "tragedy of character." Lear was shown to be just as much a victim of forces struggling for control of a decaying social order as he was of his own volcanic passions. For Langhoff, Lear was never insane but simply unwilling to move with the times. Through emotional restraint rather than passionate gesticulation, Willy Kleinau, and later Wolfgang Heinz, as Lear emphasized the workings of Lear's psyche. This, plus the lack of naturalistic scenery, dampened the emotional pathos that spectators and cultural functionaries had come to associate with Shakespeare performance. Despite Brecht's work, and that of the Berliner Ensemble, to develop an epic style and a dialectic approach to character portrayal, audience expectations and official taste were still rooted in the pathos of conventional bourgeois theater of the thirties. The "ruins in the minds of the audience" Brecht had called attention to had still not been cleared away. The harsh critique of Langhoff's *Lear* made by Fritz Erpenbek, head editor of *Theater der Zeit*, the official theater journal, and a leading proponent of socialist realism and the Stanislavsky method, was predictable: "bloodless."[15] Nevertheless, the production ran for 129 performances and set off a lively discussion on how to redefine classical drama from a socialist perspective.

III
The East German Shakespeare (1964–1980)

The year 1964 marked the 400th anniversary of Shakespeare's birth and the centennial of the German Shakespeare Society, the oldest literary society in Germany. The year also marked the beginning of an East German Shakespeare tradition that emphasized the plebeian characters and their view of the action from below and the links between the German classics, Shakespeare's humanistic "Menschenbild," Renaissance, and socialist ideals.[16] In April of 1964 the Shakespeare Society resumed its activities in Weimar from which many West Germans had withdrawn to set up their own headquarters in Bochum in 1963. The Central Committee tried to use the occasion to stake out a claim on Shakespeare and to appropriate him for their socialist national culture. The importance of the occasion for party cultural policy was clear when the keynote address was given by Cultural Minister Alexander Abusch, who was also deputy chairman of the Council of Ministers. Walter Ulbricht himself attended, and the speech was televised live to the nation from Weimar.

Abusch's speech in Weimar, "Shakespeare, Realist and Humanist, Genius of World Literature," traced the seminal influence of Shakespeare on Schiller and Goethe, and Marx and Engels. Abusch defined Shakespeare as the anticipator of a German humanistic and realistic theater tradition that reached back to the eighteenth century and which had now culminated in present socialist culture. Shakespeare's dramas affirmed a positive view of

King Lear, **DIR. W. Langhoff, 1957. 1.1: Lear divides his kingdom. Photo: Dietlind Krönig, courtesy of the Deutsches Theater.**

humanity that transcended class bounds and anticipated a socialist culture that combined theory and practice and could therefore be appropriated as an element of the "positive national heritage."[17] This was not simply an extension of party politics onto the stage, but a welcome message for theater people that the German classical heritage, including Shakespeare, had been officially rehabilitated. At the Second Bitterfeld Conference held immediately afterward on 24–25 April, Shakespeare was set up as the "the great innovator" (*Der grosse Erneuerer*), an example to be emulated, a normative standard to be imitated, and a mortgage impossible for any aspiring dramatist to meet. This is partially behind Müller's cryptic remark in Weimar twenty-four years later: "We have not arrived at ourselves as long as Shakespeare is still writing our plays."[18]

A milestone for international Shakespeare performance was Manfred Wekwerth's and Joachim Tenschert's staging of Brecht's adaptation of *Coriolanus* at the Berliner Ensemble in 1964. It used Shakespeare's parable of *Coriolanus* to explore the relationship between the individual's hunger for power and the interests of the masses, or the state. For domestic Shakespeare reception in East Germany, however, two very different productions of *Hamlet* in 1964 signaled that East German Shakespeare performance, translation, and criticism had reached a turning point. The one was performed in Karl-Marx-Stadt (again called Chemnitz), directed by Hans-Dieter Mäde, and the other in Greifswald, directed by Adolf Dresen. Altogether there were eight *Hamlet* performances in the festival year.[19]

Mäde, in the tradition of socialist realist drama, used *Hamlet* to explore the relationship between the classical humanistic ideals of Shakespeare's Renaissance past and the socialist society of the present. For Mäde, Hamlet had been destroyed by the contradictions and political interests in an archaic social order, but Hamlet's ideals had been realized in the socialist present. Hamlet's mission to "set the world aright" had simply been postponed until a later day, and with the advent of the Bolshevik revolution in the twentieth century, this day had arrived. Performed in the small Karl-Marx-Stadt Civic Theater, the stage was extended by a ramp into the auditorium. Peter Friede's stage design was dark and confined. There was no curtain, and the background was grayish and dark, symbolizing the past. Mäde used lighting rather than scenery to accentuate the performers, but he also resorted to rows of mute soldiers with spears to separate the dark English Renaissance upstage from the brighter modern present downstage. This resulted in occasional absurdities such as cloddish soldiers visible in the background of the "closet scene." The masses were kept in gray, the court wore costumes in various shades of red, and Hamlet wore the traditional black, as did Fortinbras. Jürgen Hentsch as Hamlet—slender, melancholic, hypersensitive, introverted, intellectual—committed his bloody deeds in the dark gray background but held his monologues with their ideals spotlighted on the ramp close to the audience, that is, projected *into* the socialist present. Yet rather than directed *at* the audience, they were overheard *by* the audience. This performance was the opposite of a plebeian, "folk theater" approach to Shakespeare performance because it relegated the audience to passive eavesdroppers rather than interacting with them to constitute the "meaning" of the play. The performance implied both a continuity between the Renaissance Elizabethan past of Hamlet and the socialist present of the audience[20] and a consensus between audience and actors in their interpretation of the play.[21] Predictably Mäde's production was praised in all the official organs as an example to be emulated and as an antidote to Jan Kott's view in *Shakespeare Our Contemporary,* not the least because of Hentsch's outstanding performance as the Prince of Denmark.[22]

Adolf Dresen's production in Greifswald put its finger on a contradiction ignored in Mäde's production: the contradiction between Hamlet's lofty abstract ideals and the reality of his concrete bloody deeds, between Ham-

Hamlet, DIR. Mäde, 1964. 5.1: Hamlet (Hentsch) "confined": Marcellus and Horatio hold him back. Photo courtesy of Henschel Verlag.

let, the moralizing humanist, and Hamlet, the revenger.[23] Hamlet invents all kinds of reasons for not revenging his father right off, and as a consequence he murders six innocent victims before he finally gets around to "the bloody business" of killing Claudius. For Dresen,[24] Hamlet's hesitation may be understandable as the reaction of a Wittenberg student of humanism, but the consequences were disastrous. This reading of the play contradicted both the bourgeois Romantic tradition that viewed Hamlet's delay as an irrational character weakness (Freud) as well as the socialist realist tradition that viewed Hamlet's hesitation as justifiable given the historical situation in which he finds himself (Marx). For Dresen, it was difficult to interpret Hamlet as a revolutionary hero, or even the forerunner of one. In the program notes, Hamlet was described as "The Fall of the mind, with many victims."[25] For Dresen it was not sufficient to use the play simply to exemplify the discrepancy between theory and practice; he needed to show the consequences of this kind of behavior. "In his age, Hamlet had no other choice," Dresen concluded. "But no age will excuse those of us in power today for not using our reason."[26] Summing up the dramaturgical concept behind the production as "Buchenwald is not far from Weimar" (*"Buchenwald liegt nahe bei Weimar"*) took this idea to its logical conclusion. If *"Deutschland ist Hamlet"* (Freiligrath), "poor in deeds and rich in thought" (*tatenarm und gedankenvoll;* Hölderlin), then recent German history could be compared to a deranged Hamlet who had willfully put aside the Weimar heritage of enlightened reason and transformed Europe into a heap of smoldering ruins. This, in effect, questioned an official cultural policy that insisted on a continuity and harmony between Shakespeare's past and present socialist ideals and actions.

This break with both the Romantic and the socialist realistic *Hamlet* traditions was underlined by the appearance and dramatic portrayal of the characters. Jürgen Holtz as Hamlet was on the corpulent side and often out of breath, yet extroverted, straightforward, and always in motion.[27] With gusto he rattled off his monologues down front close to and at the audience. Holtz's Hamlet obviously enjoyed playing the merry madman killer and frequently let out a bleating laugh. Ursula Schöne-Makus's Gertrude was a buxom and femininely rounded woman and Rupert Ritzi's Claudius was a realistic and competent administrator. Balding, slight of build, and dressed in black knee pants, Ritzi resembled more an aged yet traditional German Hamlet and less the traditional German Claudius, who is often overweight and overconfident. The performance worked at making visible and obvious to the audience every possible hidden or ambiguous aspect and contradiction. In the "nunnery scene," for example, Hamlet's abrasive upbraiding of Ophelia was provoked by the very visible movement of the curtain behind which Polonius and Claudius were eavesdropping. This mode of performance—"artistic yet natural, realistic yet stylized"[28]—realized Brecht's plan to apply the tradition of the "Volkstheater" to Shakespeare five months *before* the Berliner Ensemble opened with *Coriolan.* However, it was taken by official commentators as a direct critique of the officially proclaimed socialist utopia. Except for reviews in *Theater der Zeit,*[29] it has been ignored by official theater histories. This radically fresh approach to Shakespeare's *Hamlet* in provincial Greifswald preceded by four years Dresen's production of Goethe's *Faust* at the Deutsches Theater in 1968, a production usually heralded as the turning point in the East German treatment of theater classics.

The Greifswald *Hamlet* used a completely new *gestus*-oriented German translation in contemporary vernacular geared to the needs of actors rather than to the interests of philologists or literary critics. Just as the performance disturbed or inspired directors, actors, and critics, the translation by Maik Hamburger and Adolf Dresen disturbed or inspired members of the East German Shakespeare Society. Some labeled it "inaccurate" or "unclassical," but others welcomed its fresh and down-to-earth rendering of Shakespeare's English into German. The Hamburger-Dresen translation aimed at conveying meaning through the performing actors and actresses, through spoken word in conjunction with the body—the gestures, stance, pitch, and tempo of the performing player. This approach to Shakespeare translation privileged the plays as scripts for performance rather than as

Hamlet, **DIR. Dresen, 1964. Hamlet (Holtz) "berserk." Photo courtesy of Henschel Verlag.**

literature to be read and questioned the validity of interpreting Shakespeare according to any ideological stencil.

The Greifswald *Hamlet* initiated a new epoch in German Shakespeare translation. Convinced that every historical age requires its own Shakespeare translation, Maik Hamburger, Heiner Müller, and B. K. Tragelehn, approached Shakespeare's script as a performance score rather than as a purely literary text. They attempted to free German blank verse translations of Shakespeare from the Romantic airs of Schlegel-Tieck and make them more accessible to a contemporary theater audience. Redefinitions of Shakespeare's drama in terms of the contemporary East German cultural politics can be traced in the translations and reworkings of Heiner Müller. In the belief that the closer a translation is to the historical original, the more contemporary it is, Müller's translation of *As You Like It* (1969) tries to approximate Shakespeare's English as closely as possible, including English syntactical patterns. His *Hamletmaschine* (1977), a radical abbreviation and revision of the play, relocates Hamlet, the character, and *Hamlet*, the play, in a postmodern society where there are no social, moral, or cultural lynch pins of authority. Plans made for "A New German Shakespeare" with translations by Müller and Tragelehn, unfortunately never materialized.[30]

At the reinaugural meeting of the Shakespeare Society in 1964 Robert Weimann spoke on "*Shakespeares Volkstümlichkeit*" and published "*Shakespeare's Publikum und Plattformbühne im Spiegel klassizistischer Kritik*" in the first issue of the East German *Shakespeare Jahrbuch*.[31] They contain the germs of a seminal approach to Shakespeare later published as *Shakespeare und die Tradition des Volkstheaters* (1967), which, with the exception of Jan Kott's *Shakespeare Our Contemporary*, is the only book to have an impact on Shakespeare performance in Germany.[32] Marxist Shakespeare scholarship up to then had concentrated on the authority of the word, that is, on the written text, to demonstrate the continuity between Shakespeare's early humanism and socialist ideals. Weimann, taking a cue from proletarian theater and inspired by performances of Brecht at the Berliner Ensemble, demonstrated that the representation of the word in performance by the body of the player undermined the authority of any attempt to validate a particular signification in a given historical situation. Whereas East German Marxist criticism up to then had accepted the word as given and excluded the player and the spectator in the construction of meaning, Weimann showed that the player and the spectator were, in fact, the essential elements in this process.

To demonstrate this, Weimann pays close attention to the dramatic *gestus* of the text, to the popular tradition in English drama which informed Shakespeare's staging practices, and to the position of the actors in relationship to the spectators (*Figurenposition*) as a running commentary on the action.

For Weimann, the meaning negotiated during performance is not constituted for all time, but, like translations, varies according to the historical
situation. On the one hand, Weimann shows the direct relationship between
historicity and performance—the subtitle of the English language edition is
"Studies in the Social Dimension of Dramatic Form and Function"—and on
the other, he denies the transcendent validity of this historical signification
at a later point in history. Weimann's starting point, which he had begun
to develop as early as 1955,[33] was that sixteenth-century English society
was in a state of "mingle-mangle," "gallimaufry," or "hodge podge" as a
consequence of revolutionary changes that had preceded the Elizabethan
settlement, a compromise, or alliance, of diverse forces, both old and new.
For him, Elizabethan social relations were in a state of balance, transition,
or relative unity which did not privilege one group or social force over the
other. Similarly, he pointed out that Shakespeare's drama can be characterized as "mingling kinges and clownes" and as providing what he called a
"complementary perspective" of the world.[34] This concept of "complemen-
tarity" stood in direct contrast to Lenin's two culture theory, which defined
the social relationships in Elizabethan society as antagonistic and determined by class struggle with one ultimately defeating, i.e., burying, the
other. It was, however, in line with Brecht's dialectical approach to Shakespeare and provided scholarly support for Dresen's staging and Hamburger's translation of *Hamlet*. For literary scholars, especially in the West,
it broke down the artificial distinction between textual form and cultural
history, and it pointed beyond the then still dominant New Criticism and
anticipated similar positions that would be taken up by the "New
Historicism."[35]

The Berlin Wall, which split Germany in 1961, also split the Shakespeare
Society, one of the few remaining pan-German organizations. Up until 1963
the *Shakespeare Jahrbuch* had included contributions from both East and
West German scholars, but since the editorship lay in the hands of West
Germans it rarely, if ever, included a Marxist essay. After 1964 the Shakespeare Society (West) began publishing its own *Jahrbuch (West)*, and the
East Germans continued publishing the original *Jahrbuch* in Weimar. Its
editorial policy favored a Marxist approach to Shakespeare and scholarship
dedicated to documenting how Shakespearean drama contained and sus-
tained "peace, humanism, and realism." There was a strong emphasis on
studies of plebeian characters and on scenes in the popular tradition as a
commentary from below on the dramatic action. The close relationship
between poetic theory, cultural history, and theater practice was always
stressed. Interesting recent Shakespeare productions from all over the GDR
and Eastern Europe formed a focal point for discussion, and the Weimar
National Theater regularly staged for the "Shakespeare-Tage" Shakespeare
plays directed by Fritz Bennewitz in cooperation with Anselm Schlösser, a

longtime influential member of the Society's board of directors. Directors such as Bennewitz, Benno Besson, Hans-Dieter Mäde, Horst Schönemann, and Manfred Wekwerth received particular attention, and some even addressed the plenary session, as did also Heiner Müller, Gerhard Wolfram, and Volker Braun. A high point and a substantial core of the Shakespeare Society's revitalizing approach to Shakespearean dramaturgy is Robert Weimann's work on the popular tradition. After 1985, when he succeeded Martin Lehnert as president, Weimann initiated a discussion of fundamental critical and theoretical issues such as authority, representation, discourse and power, gender, character and subjective agency through internationally oriented and internationally attended symposia. The annual Weimar symposia brought together scholars from all over the world who were on the cutting edge of theoretical discussion and as such provided an open window through which current international critical discourse entered East Germany.[36] Not only scholars but also East German English teachers, students, and interested citizens made use of the Weimar meeting as an intellectual and social occasion. It was a time for many to reassess positions and perspectives and to reorient one's outlook before returning to a cultural climate dominated until the end by both pro-Slavic and pre-Althusserian versions of cultural policy.

The Second Bitterfeld Conference, 24–25 April 1964, was mainly self-congratulatory in tone: Ulbricht repeated his familiar attacks on "abstract realism" and "alienation." However, the tone of the notorious Eleventh Party Plenary Session one and a half years later in December 1965, was cold and bitter. Erich Honecker, future head of the party, attacked subjective, "decadent" and "bourgeois" tendencies in culture, singling out the singer Wolf Biermann, the dramatists Heiner Müller, Peter Hacks, and Volker Braun, and the writer Stefan Heym. Adolf Dresen's production of *Measure for Measure* at the Deutsches Theater (1966) was a direct reaction to this repressive cultural policy. Angelo (Jürgen Holtz) was portrayed as a single-minded fanatic who sweeps the state clean of any critical elements and at the same time brings down his own damnation.[37] East Germany's participation in crushing the Prague Spring (August, 1968) was the material extension of this hard line cultural policy. It crushed any hope of reform-minded dissidents and intellectuals that Ulbricht would someday lead East Germany to socialism with "a human face."

IV
Subversive Shakespeare (1965–1980)

With Moscow's approval, Erich Honecker staged a coup in May 1971 that forced Walter Ulbricht to step down. In December Honecker announced: "In practice there is nothing which restricts the creative activity of our artists. If one proceeds from the solid premises of socialism, there can in my opinion be no taboos in art and literature."[38] Obviously the socialist revolution was not going to spread any further in Europe in the near future, so Honecker turned to consolidating *real-existierender Sozialismus* in the GDR. This meant accepting the status quo. In the sixties and seventies control over cultural policy lay in the hands of hard-liners such as head party ideologist Kurt Hager and Minister for Culture Klaus Gysi. After 1973 theater repertories had to be approved beforehand by the "Direktion für das Bühnenrepertoire" set up by Gysi's successor Hans-Joachim Hoffmann. This policy remained in effect until 1986 when Gorbachev's ideas about perestroika and glasnost began to influence some members of the Central Committee.

Honecker's "liberalization," however, failed to provide an impetus for a genuine GDR drama or performance. On the contrary, it lured the ensembles and their audience into a preference for the private sphere and an unwillingness to deal with political issues. Heiner Müller, repeatedly censored and persecuted during the sixties, quit writing plays about contemporary East German society and turned to translations and idiosyncratic adaptations of classical drama, such as Shakespeare's *Hamlet*, Aeschylus's *Prometheus Bound* or Sophocles' *Oedipus Rex*, and to dramatic adaptations of prose, such as Gladkov's novel *Cement.* Likewise the director B. K. Tragelehn, in perpetual hot water since the *Umsiedlerin* affair, turned to translating Shakespeare as a kind of occupational therapy and as means of earning a livelihood.[39] The biggest stage hit of the seventies was a dramatization of Ulrich Plenzdorf's *Die neuen Leiden des Jungen W.,* a novel about the private lives of young people in the GDR with a direct reference to Goethe's *Die Leiden des Jungen Werthers* (*The Sorrows of Young Werther*). This trend toward privatizing in society was reflected in a new trend in the Shakespeare repertory. In the sixties the focus had been on the public person and his political responsibilities, as found in *Hamlet* or *Coriolanus.* In the seventies the swing was toward private lives and plays that dealt with personal and sexual problems, desires, hopes, and fears, in *A Midsummer Night's Dream* or *Romeo and Juliet,* for example.[40]

If in the sixties theater suffered under censorship and reprisals, in the seventies it eventually stagnated under the disinterest of a cultural bureaucracy. Ulbricht, for all his dogmatism, was interested in the theater; Honecker could not have cared less. The affirmative role of theater and the consensus between stage and auditorium on the role of theater in preparing for a truly socialist society, which had existed to a great extent during the sixties, had been terminated by the Eleventh Plenary Session and the events in Prague. The gap between official pronouncements and everyday reality had become too great to ignore. Theater people took less and less interest in theoretical pronouncements and critical discussion, and their attendance in Weimar became less frequent.

But the seventies were not without reprisals; the most spectacular and serious was the expatriation of Wolf Biermann in November 1976 while he was on a concert tour in West Germany. Over one hundred artists, writers, and public personalities spontaneously signed a petition demanding the government reverse its decision and published it in West German newspapers. Honecker's reaction was not ideological confrontation but administrative reprisals: arrests, fines, and jail. In 1979 the Writers' Congress, now headed by Hermann Kant, a popular writer loyal to the party, staged a tribunal against eight writers who were excluded from the Congress and threatened with criminal prosecution if they were to publish in the West. The Biermann affair initiated an exodus of disappointed and disillusioned creative talent, intellectuals, and theater people which did not ebb until 1989: Manfred Krug, Hilmar Thate, Angelika Dömrose, Armin Müller-Stahl, Jutta Hoffmann, Adolf Dresen, and Alexander Lang, to name but a few.

During the seventies Manfred Wekwerth and Benno Besson, two distinguished disciples of Brecht, applied Weimann's ideas about Elizabethan performance to Shakespeare: Wekwerth to *Richard III* at the Deutsches Theater (1972) and Besson to *Hamlet* at the Volksbühne (1977). Weimann served as consultant to both productions, and the English language edition of *Shakespeare and the Popular Tradition in the Theater* (1978) is dedicated to these two "friends in the theater who have come closest to a modern Shakespeare in the popular tradition." Both performances privileged the performing actor interacting with his audience to construct meaning. By turning the audience into a cultural court of appeals, such an approach undermined notions of preordained authority and particularly Besson's *Hamlet* challenged the notion of a direct continuity between Elizabethan England and socialist East Germany. This performance showed little concern for the "anticipation" of a socialist social order in Shakespeare's humanistic ideals.

Wekwerth mobilized Weimann's theory of the "complementary perspective" to allow Richard Gloucester (Hilmar Thate) to exhibit his fascination as a character by playfully, in terms of sheer theatricality, inviting the audience to assist in moralizing on two meanings in the play.[41] The scenic background consisted of gallows and torturers' equipment that symbolized the brutal feudal social order which had spawned such a creature. As the historical Richard, Thate stomped out of this background to the roll of drums, and then as the comic Vice figure, he hopped down off the ramp stage, which jutted out into the auditorium of the Deutsches Theater, to chat familiarly to and with the audience. Wekwerth's staging of *The Life and Death of Richard III* explored the contradictory character and career of the appealing and appalling Elizabethan Overreacher. Richard traps himself

Richard III, **DIR. Wekwerth, 1972. Opening scene with Richard Gloucester (Thate) and torturers' tools in the background. Photo courtesy of Henschel Verlag.**

because he seeks to appropriate for himself the power of "divine right" after he himself has so brilliantly circumvented and debunked it. The production rejected interpretations of Shakespeare's play as either a neoclassical romantic "tragedy of character" or as a socialist realist parable of how "man" is mechanistically formed by "society"; instead, it demonstrated how a ruthless power is able to shape the course of history under specific circumstances.

Although Wekwerth utilized the contradictions in the character of Richard to raise questions about the validity of interpreting Shakespearean drama through character, he raised few if any questions concerning issues of moral complexity in the world since Richard's age. For all of the ambivalence in Richard's character, there was little, if any, ambivalence in the dramaturgical concept underlying the production or in the role of theater in conveying it. Besson, on the other hand, allowed the contradictions in the character of Hamlet to gain the upper hand and to undermine any ideas of dramaturgical closure. Ezio Tofolutti's stage design—a bare stage enclosed by gray rectangular screens, the ceiling hung with grayish-blackish cloth, and front lighting to cast long shadows—suggested an impenetrable labyrinth with no easily discernible contours through which Hamlet could navigate to discover "the truth" of his story. Hamlet, like his time, "is out of joint," and there are still many questions to be answered.

Besson's dramaturgical concept revolved thematically around the mother and the grave and was entitled *The Tragical History of Hamlet, Prince of Denmark.*[42] Hamlet's revenge on Claudius and his treatment of Ophelia were motivated entirely by his frustrated desire for loving affection from his mother. Whenever Hamlet (Manfred Karge) tried to embrace his mother or vice versa, Claudius (Dieter Montag) immediately stepped between them. Gertrude (Ursula Karusseit) was reduced to an object of Claudius's lust and was unable to respond emotionally to Hamlet or to Ophelia, whose death she announced with a tone of cold satisfaction. This Hamlet, like his Elsinore, was a mixture of clowning and brutality, a play actor at once ridiculous and ruthless. Like Jürgen Holtz in the Greifswald *Hamlet,* Manfred Karge as Hamlet had a childlike enthusiasm for playacting the "antic disposition" with face smeared red, knee britches open, shoes and socks in one hand, and a *wooden* sword, recalling the laughable weapon of the Tudor Vice, in the other. He delivered his "To be, or not to be" soliloquy while doing push-ups over a dagger pointed at his breast. The high point of his clowning came after the "mousetrap" when he "played" king by putting on a satin robe and paper crown. Karge's Hamlet was neither melancholic prince nor premature revolutionary, nor was he even given a chance to hesitate in killing Claudius since act 3, scene 3, was omitted. The one-time cornerstone in the neoclassical poetics of "realism," his dilettante remarks on how to perform and hold "a mirror up to nature," were endured by the First Player with barely disguised impatience and boredom. It was an obvious parallel to the situation of GDR professional actors at the mercy of dilettante party cultural functionaries. Ophelia (Heide Kipp) portrayed the contradiction between the patriarchal discourse of the dramatic text she was forced to speak at the behest of her father and her frustrated feelings for Hamlet expressed in her body language. This was especially obvious in the "nunnery scene." The effect of this conflict became visual when after going insane she ripped open her disheveled nightshirt to reveal her bare breasts, an act of feminist revolt against the restricting corset imposed on her by a patriarchal society.[43] As in the Greifswald *Hamlet,* thirteen years earlier, Fortinbras was played by a child (Pierre Besson), which undermined the tradition of Fortinbras initiating a golden socialist future. In the final scene, Fortinbras had the corpses stood up on end for the audience to see and his final words "shoot," were not to announce a salute to the dead, but signaled a new round of violence.

At least three aspects of this production broke directly with the official GDR *Hamlet* tradition begun by Wangenheim's 1945 production: the characterization of Hamlet as motivated by oedipal urges, the scornful rejection of a theory of mimesis that held a mirror up to nature, and a pessimistic

Hamlet, DIR. Besson, 1977. Gravedigger, Hamlet, and Horatio with labyrinth setting visible in background. Photo: Adelheid Beyer, courtesy of the Volksbühne Berlin.

Hamlet, DIR. Besson, 1977. 3.2: Hamlet (Karge) "playing" king. Photo: Adelheid Beyer, courtesy of the Volksbühne Berlin.

conclusion. It was a lesson in Brechtian "alienation" that emphasized material theatricality to de-psychologize *Hamlet* and lay bare the dramatic fable.
Such an approach obstructed facile closure for ideological reasons and left
many aesthetic and ideological questions open. It owed a debt to Dresen's
earlier *Hamlet,* yet bore the handwriting of Heiner Müller. In fact Müller and
Matthias Langhoff served as dramaturgs for the production and developed
a performance script which was essentially a reworking of the Hamburger-
Dresen translation.[44] Finally, Besson's production initiated a tradition of
using Shakespeare performance to comment on the contemporary *theater
situation* in the GDR. It staged the end of any form of consensus between
theater and official cultural ideology or between the performer and the
official spectator. Besson's *Hamlet* was in a sense East German theater's
"declaration of independence" from any moralizing responsibilities for creating a socialist society.

In 1980 two very different productions of *A Midsummer Night's Dream*—
one by Alexander Lang at the Deutsches Theater and the other by Thomas
Langhoff at the Maxim Gorki—reaffirmed and took for granted the end of
the "didactic" role of theater in socialist society.[45] For Lang, Shakespeare's
dream was in reality a nightmare. Athens and the woods were the flipside
of the same coin; a disinterested technocracy, lacking feeling or fantasy,
had forcibly injected the youth of Athens with a narcotic that left them
confused and separated from each other and themselves. The Athenian
courtiers were bored by the performance and fondled their fiancees before
falling asleep while the rude mechanicals struggled with "Pyramus and
Thisbe." Lang inverted the traditional theme of man and society to suggest
that socialist society had consciously abused its youth. The performance
corresponded to the theater situation under Honecker, who thought that
because a level of socialism had been realized in the GDR, art no longer
had to be viewed as a weapon in the struggle to achieve a socialist culture.[46]
For all his suppression of artistic fantasy in the name of creating a "socialist"
culture, Walter Ulbricht, at least, had been interested in books and occasionally attended the theater; Honecker preferred to go hunting.

Thomas Langhoff's staging of the play at the Maxim Gorki Theater took
a different approach. Although the world of the woods was not a nightmare
it was, nevertheless, a metaphor for the human subconscious. It was a
threatening, brutal, and bizarre world populated by odd creatures, indeed—
a bald-headed Titania, a masked wrestler Puck, naked midgets, and punkish
fairies—and ruled by uncontrolled Eros. In this performance, the world of
Athens and the woods were separated only by a paper wall suggesting that
the veneer of social order was thin indeed and that youth were willing and
able to tear it down when it came to fulfilling their own erotic fantasies.

V
Shakespeare Deconstructed (1980–1990)

Despite East German success in international politics and athletics, improvements in the relationship with West Germany as a result of the "Ostpolitik" initiated by Willy Brandt, and a "thaw" in some areas of culture (such as the tolerance of jazz and rock music, the alternative cultural scene in Berlin's Prenzlauer Berg, or the publication of plays by Plenzdorf and Müller), the eighties were also a decade of protest against censorship, travel restrictions, and a senile and immobile bureaucracy. The unresolvable social contradictions and the grassroots protests, in which theater people played a central role, culminated in a mass exodus in 1989 through Hungary and Czechoslovakia, the fall of the Berlin Wall, and the peaceful dissolution of the German Democratic Republic as a sovereign state in 1990.

East German Shakespeare reception in the eighties was characterized by its own version of deconstruction. This was visible on stage in Heiner Müller's Shakespeare translations-adaptations and in Robert Weimann's critical theory, which reassessed the relations between discourse and power and pointed out significant areas of conflict between the signs of authority and the authority of signs.[47] In the eighties the ban on Müller's plays was progressively lifted and his Shakespeare renditions were allowed to be performed on major East German stages: *Macbeth* (directed by Heiner Müller/Ginka Tscholakowa at the Volksbühne Berlin, 1982), *Anatomy Titus Fall of Rome. A Shakespeare Commentary* (directed by Wolfgang Engel, Dresden, 1987), and *Die Hamletmaschine* as a part of *Hamlet/Maschine* (directed by Müller himself at the Deutsches Theater, 1990). After the Biermann affair, the Honecker regime seemed to lose interest in potential political subversion in the theater. The removal of the acute political pressure of the Ulbricht era, and the theater's loss of its role as an agent for—or critic of—the socialist utopia, resulted in the deconstruction of Shakespeare as an icon of official cultural policy.

Controversy followed Müller's idiosyncratic rendition of *Macbeth nach Shakespeare ("according to/after Shakespeare")* (adapted 1971, staged 1972 in Brandenburg by Bernd Bartoszewski). Müller's text was published in *Theater der Zeit* (8/1972), and a general furor followed in the GDR. Anselm Schlösser attacked the notion that *Macbeth* might be relevant to contemporary socialist society—after all, 1971 was Lenin's 100th birthday, and there are obvious parallels between Macbeth and Stalin—but above all Schlösser objected to Müller's "emendations."[48] Wolfgang Harich berated Müller's notorious pessimism that recognized no epochal "improvements" in society since the 1917 Bolshevik revolution.[49] Müller was again in hot water with the cultural bureaucracy, which had yet another reason to keep his plays off the East German stage. In 1982 Müller and Ginka Tscholokowa were allowed to direct his version of *Macbeth* at the Volksbühne. The message was that violence begets violence. Character and setting were deconstructed: Macbeth was played by three different actors (Dieter Montag, Hermann Beyer, and Michael Gwisdek), bald-headed witches dressed in evening gowns waltzed to the tune of "The Blue Danube," and Lady Macbeth (Corinna Harfouch) resembled a young housewife from the East German provinces; the setting resembled the inner courtyard of an East Berlin tenement including a bar for beating rugs. Into this courtyard a telephone booth was raised out of the stage floor on various occasions. Lady Macduff sought sanctuary in the booth only to be stabbed to death there in slow motion by the murderers—recognizable as Macbeth 2 (Hermann Beyer) and Macbeth 3 (Michael Gwisdek) while Macbeth 1 (Dieter Montag) looked on. Any desire for naturalistic historicizing was denied the audience. The actors who played various roles occasionally wore the names of the characters on the their back, and brutality and violence were acted out with clowning and exaggerated realism, that is, using red paint for blood that was not wiped up after the performance, or using sausages for sexual organs that were cut off. The exaggerated theatricality of the performance, in the tradition of Besson's *Hamlet* production five years earlier, insisted that theater was an independent reality in itself. As such it denied the validity of any official "interpretation" from outside which substantiated any particular ideology. For Müller brutal power does not wear a particular mask.[50]

In *Anatomy Titus Fall of Rome. A Shakespeare Commentary,* Müller deconstructs Shakespeare's plot by injecting his own commentary, which becomes the dramatic fable itself in the first third of the play. Wolfgang Engel, the director of the first East German performance (Dresden 1987), set the play in a classroom in which the actors played pupils who were acting out a history lesson supplemented by Müller's interjected commentaries. In *Hamletmaschine,* Müller deconstructs Shakespeare's dramaturgy, characters, and text to replace them with a theater of images that defy interpretation. Written in 1977 during his work on the Besson production of *Hamlet,* it was not available in print in the GDR until 1988. Even the playwright himself is deconstructed before the audience's eyes when a photo of playwright Müller is torn up on stage. In a conversation with Ruth Berghaus, Müller observes, "Personality has disappeared, dissolved in the snare or in the party or whatever you want."[51] In doing so he broke with a long-standing GDR Shakespeare tradition: neither Hamlet nor Fortinbras could henceforth be presented, or taken for granted, as revolutionary heroes.

If the inspiration for Wangenheim's *Hamlet* might have been the opening lines of the final stanza of Freiligrath's 1844 poem *"Deutschland ist Hamlet"* ("Make a decision! Jump into the fight— / Kick open the gate, be daring and bold"),[52] the inspiration for Müller's *Hamlet/Maschine* (1990) was the

Macbeth, DIR. Müller/Tscholakowa, 1982. Macbeth learns of Lady Macbeth's death. From left to right: Macbeth (Montag), Macduff/Macbeth 2 (Beyer), Seyton (Mühe) on telephone booth. Photo: Adelheid Beyer, courtesy of the Volksbühne Berlin.

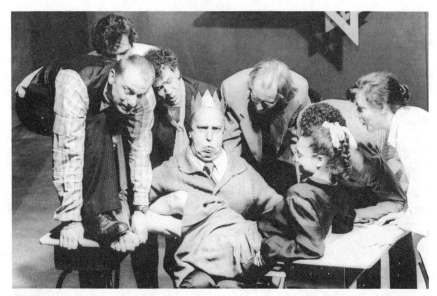

Titus Andronicus, **DIR. Engel, 1987. Titus stamps on Saturninus's hand while Lavinia sits on his lap. Photo: Hans-Ludwig Böhme.**

refrain of a song by the punk band, "The Stranglers" ("No more heroes, no more Shakespearos"). If Wangenheim's purpose was to reclaim *Hamlet,* Müller's was to deconstruct it for a postmodern world which corresponded to his personal motto: "No hope, no despair." Hamlet, played by Ulrich Mühe, was a young hero of the theater's political opposition to the repressive policies of the state; he repeatedly uttered Müller's lines from *Hamlet-maschine:* "I was Hamlet. I stood on the coast talking to the breakers, blah-blah, behind me the ruins of Europe." This was neither an optimistic nor a critical vision of a better future in a united Germany, but a ritual wake for a country and its cultural dogma which viewed Shakespeare's Hamlet as the epitome of human culture. Müller's Hamlet was incapable of active and willful resistance, and the climax decelerated to a slow motion slapstick in the final duel with Laertes, as if two wound-up puppets were slowly running down. Müller's Fortinbras, a robotlike metallic figure with a golden mask, a golden right hand, and a briefcase recited not Shakespeare but Zbigniew Herbert's poem "Fortinbras' Lament": "You had to fail this or that, you were not fit to live / you believed in the crystalline terms and not in the human clay."[53] Müller's *Hamlet,* like Wangenheim's, was also directed at the audience, but as Maik Hamburger put it: "If Shakespeare's *Hamlet* is one huge question, Müller's *Hamlet/ Maschine* is one huge statement."[54] The audience was overwhelmed by Erich Wonder's scenery (the most expensive set in GDR history), the monumental length of the performance (7 1/2 hours), and

Hamlet/Maschine, **DIR. Müller, 1990. "The Mousetrap." Photo: Wolfhard Theile.**

the lack of any kind of dialogic interaction between the performers and the spectators.[55] By the time the performance ended, both the audience and the actors were exhausted. This Hamlet simply had waited too long and time ran out on him as it did on Claudius and Gertrude. By the end of the play all of the protagonists seemed to be happy that it was finally time to die, and Jörg Gudzuhn as Claudius greedily gulped down the poisoned chalice.

In 1987, two years before the Wall came down, Müller had told the German Shakespeare Society that "we have not arrived at our destination as long as Shakespeare is still writing our plays." To arrive at where he was going, Müller deconstructed not only the "socialist national culture" but also tried his hand at deconstructing Shakespeare. In *Hamlet/Maschine,* an ensuite performance of Shakespeare's *Hamlet* and Müller's *Hamletmaschine* that he directed at the Deutsches Theater in 1990, Müller interrupted Shakespeare's dramaturgy by inserting his own *Hamletmaschine*—which he calls "a shrunken head version of *Hamlet*"—after act 4.[56] Whereas Wangenheim tried to *appropriate* Shakespeare's *Hamlet* to mobilize his audience for a better democratic and socialist future, Müller tried to *deconstruct* the play to demonstrate that hope for any kind of a future for humanity was a chimera for which, like Hamlet, time had simply run out.

In the course of the eighties, the Weimar symposia increasingly became a forum for coming to grips with post-1968 critical approaches to Shake-speare: American new historicism, British cultural materialism, feminism, and deconstruction. This development was preceded by Robert Weimann's 1981 address to the World Shakespeare Congress in Stratford-upon-Avon, "'Representation and Authority' in Shakespeare's Theater,"[57] and developed further in his address to the plenary session of the Weimar Shakespeare Society in 1983, the "Luther Year."[58] The question of authority and its legiti-mation hit at the core of the official GDR Shakespeare ideology. The high point in this development was at the 1987 Weimar meeting organized around the theme of "Gender, Power and Humanity in Shakespeare." East German writer Waldtraut Lewin gave the Shakespeare lecture and partici-pants Stephen Greenblatt, John Drakakis, Graham Holderness, and Kiernan Ryan made up one of the liveliest symposia ever. Even Armin-Gerd Kuckhoff, longtime editor and theater reviewer for the *Jahrbuch*, suggested in his 1987 keynote address that it was finally time to rethink many basic precepts of the traditional interpretation of Shakespeare. He was especially concerned with the idea of continuity between Shakespeare and the socialist utopia in the light of contemporary GDR social reality.[59] Günther Klotz tried to bring the history of East German Shakespeare adaptations into a relationship with the specific historical situation of their genesis.[60] Thomas Sorge took this one step further in 1989 and placed the East German Shakespeare tradition in relationship to the historical development of an East German cultural ideology tradition in his lecture "Our Shakespeares: Reflections on a Com-panion."[61] By 1991 things had developed to a point that Günter Walch's keynote address on "Reason and Chaos in Shakespeare"[62] could be under-stood as a long overdue reckoning up with any notion of using Shakespeare to demonstrate the ordered continuity between the Renaissance and social-ism. At the same time Müller's *Hamlet/Maschine,* the story of the modernist Hamlet caught in a postmodern world, was playing to packed houses at Berlin's Deutsches Theater.

VI
Post-Wende (1989 to the present)

The decisive changes that have transformed the face of eastern Germany since 1989 have also had their effect on Shakespeare reception. When asked what had changed, Johanna Schall, granddaughter of Bertolt Brecht and daughter of leading Berliner Ensemble actor Ekkehard Schall, immediately replied: "The audience. They smell different."[63] The makeup of and on the spectators is new, both literally and figuratively. It reflects a drastic rise in ticket prices and the accessibility of the East German stage. Whereas the most expensive tickets used to be twelve marks, they now range over fifty.[64] The audience is wealthier, and in many cases it is older and more settled in its ways. This, in turn, has also resulted in a tendency toward lighter fare and fewer critical productions. This new audience is less interested in a political Shakespeare, even though there is still plenty to criticize and subvert.[65] When asked the same question as Johanna Schall, Ursula Karusseit replied: "Everything! Not only who goes to the theater but what is performed and how it is performed. Anything goes."[66] In eastern Germany it is now possible to say on stage anything about anyone without the threat of reprisal, but surprisingly this is not always beneficial for Shakespeare performance. Especially heavily subsidized theaters in what was the "West"—West Berlin, Hamburg, Munich, and Vienna—seem to have lost touch with their audiences and too often direct their performance more at the reviewer and critic than at the spectator. Another basic change since 1990 is that more women than ever before are directing plays, including works by Shakespeare. Despite some notable exceptions (e.g., Ruth Berghaus), women were the exception when it came to directing, especially Shakespeare, in both East and West Germany.[67] Since the "Wende," women, especially younger women, have become an established item on the Shakespeare agenda: Katja Paryla reworked and directed a novel production of *Henry VI* at the Deutsches Theater (1991), Hella Müller directed *Romeo and Juliet* in Cottbus (1991), East German Katherina Thalbach staged East German poet-dramatist Thomas Brasch's rendition of *Romeo and Juliet* at the now closed Schiller Theater in the western part of Berlin (1993), Christine Friedrich directed *Macbeth* in Weimar (1994), and Karin Baier directed *Romeo and Juliet* in Düsseldorf (1994). And in a new twist on the Elizabethan all-male cast, Martin Meltke's 1991 *Twelfth Night* at the Maxim Gorki Theater on Unter den Linden had an all-female cast.

It would be unfair and irresponsible to discuss East German Shakespeare scholarship and performance solely in terms of its political dimension, that is, as a reflection of, or resistance to, an appropriative cultural policy. This would ignore the enduring critical value and aesthetic excellence of the work, which I hope has become evident. Since the end of the German Democratic Republic as a sovereign state, scholars, theaters, ensembles, and directors in the eastern part of Germany have continued to maintain a high level of achievement.[68]

In 1991 and 1992 *Theater heute* named East Berlin's Deutsches Theater (under the direction of Thomas Langhoff) the German language "theater of the year." It has virtually the same ensemble and many of the same directors as in 1989. In 1993 East Berlin's Volksbühne under Frank Castorf's leadership was chosen as "theater of the year" and Jürgen Holtz as "actor of the year"; in 1994 it was Henry Hübchen of the Volksbühne. These facts speak for themselves.

Part One
Literary Theory and History (Essays)

1

National History and Theater Performance: Shakespeare on the East German Stage, 1945–1990

ARMIN-GERD KUCKHOFF

I

THE first attempts to perform Shakespeare immediately after World War II, in the years 1945 and 1946, can hardly be termed specifically "German" or even "East German,"[1] but must be seen within the historical context of this time: the defeat of fascism, material and human devastation, the complete collapse of the intellectual as well as the material foundations of life, and the despair and helplessness of people lacking direction and purpose. These were the spectators for whom theater was performed. Theater had both to struggle for material survival and to confront the existential problems of its spectators if it was to establish its legitimacy as a social force. Consequently, plays were looked upon as "scores" for performance rather than as "texts" that demanded a particular approach, and many a production was one-sided, slanted, and made "contemporary" in ways that the playwright could have never intended.

In 1945 the "theater worlds" of the American and the Soviet sectors of Berlin were not very far apart. The dramaturgical concept behind the production of *Macbeth* directed by Karl-Heinz Martin at the Hebbel Theater in the U.S. sector, portrayed Macbeth as a power-hungry "führer" who, in his megalomanic rages, destroyed both himself and his country. The tyrant's defeat by Malcolm and Macduff was given more attention than they are in Shakespeare's play; the performance ended with the hope of a promising future.

The dramaturgical concept behind the production of *Hamlet* directed by Gustav von Wangenheim at the bombed-out Deutsches Theater in the Soviet sector centered on the necessity for Hamlet to act. The performance marshalled any theater means possible to make Hamlet's will to act visible on

61

stage. It was a performance intended to encourage the spectators to resist "the sea of troubles" besetting them.[2] In light of the political situation in Berlin in 1945, Fortinbras could not be depicted as a soldier of shady character or questionable motives. This would have positioned the outcome of the dramatic action in line with the historical pessimism of fascist ideology peopled with antihumanistic prototypes—a concept still dominant in the minds of the audience. On the contrary, Fortinbras was depicted as the hope of the future, as Hamlet's heir apparent, who would complete Hamlet's task of setting the time right. Twenty years later, a 1964 production directed by Hans-Dieter Mäde in Karl-Marx-Stadt (Chemnitz), saw the entrance of Fortinbras at the end of the play in a very different light. The appearance of Fortinbras after Hamlet's death was neither a happy ending nor a cyclical repetition of what had just occurred. It did not signal the defeat of Hamlet's humanistic ideals but only the postponement of their realization until another day.[3]

Whereas Shakespeare's conclusion leaves the perspective for the future open, Wangenheim's 1945 production took on a more concrete human form. Fortinbras was played by Heinrich Greif, an actor with tremendous stage presence, and he wore a bright, luminescent costume to emphasize his majesty and dignity. The few spotlights the Deutsches Theater possessed were all trained on Fortinbras. His monologue was spoken at the front of the stage close to the audience so that his promise of a better future, immediately after the tragic death of the protagonist, became visible and tangible for the audience sitting in an unheated auditorium without even a roof over their heads. That this production succeeded in making this utopian promise seem concrete and worthwhile for the audience was substantiated by the reactions of the spectators, especially the young ones, in Sunday morning discussions following the performance.[4]

In all four zones into which Germany had been divided in 1945 by the Potsdam Conference, people realized the necessity and the possibility of starting over again. Although the division of Germany into a "west zone" and an "east zone" was an oppressive burden, it was accepted in the beginning, especially since during the early years the flow of information—the possibility of attending theater performances in eastern or western sectors of the city—was relatively unimpeded. Furthermore, it was not readily noticeable that Germany was drifting apart. In all four zones, there was a feeling of heading off in the direction of a new, better, and more humane social order.

Hardly noticed at first, two different economic systems developed in the two "zones" that finally led to opposing domestic and foreign policies. By 1947 the tension had become apparent and had escalated into the dangerous confrontations of the cold war. Under the patronage and pressure of the Western Allies, the Federal Republic of Germany was founded on 7 September 1949 on the principles of a market economy. Likewise, the patronage and pressure of the Soviet Union led to the founding of the German Democratic Republic shortly thereafter on 7 October 1949. It was to have a planned economy and a socialist order as an alternative to capitalism, the disadvantages and dangers of which had been directly experienced by the Germans during the Weimar Republic and the Third Reich.[5]

A fresh start in the area of culture, including theater, had a vital impact on life in all areas of Germany, including the "eastern zone." Divided into four sectors, but unhindered in attending theater performances before 1947, the inhabitants of Berlin were introduced to world theater after being cut off from it for twelve years by Nazi cultural policy. In contrast to the optimistic feelings about the future, however, were the difficult realities of daily life which were even more stringent in the east than in the west. Yet, slowly but surely, economic success confirmed and strengthened a feeling of hope among the populace.[6]

The first two decades of the GDR was a period of extensive building construction and radical social reform. Historically outdated social structures that were felt to be the cause of war and exploitation in the past were replaced, especially control over the means of production (e.g., land reform and the capitalistic market economy), and the legal system was overhauled (especially labor law and health care). These concrete reforms contributed to a feeling of optimism (*Lebensgefühl*) among the people. They became more and more convinced that it was possible to avoid social chaos and war by steering the economic and political development as well as the intellectual climate of a society through a Marxist analysis of history.

The hope of a more humane future was manifested in the concept of "humanity" in the sense of the German classics—Herder, Goethe, and Kant—and in the concept of "harmony" in the sense of a dialectical unity of those contradictions at work in society. This hope was based on the conviction that the "new social order" of the present would overcome the social conflicts inherent in capitalism and thus fulfill the humanistic ideals of the past. For this reason the "romantic dream" of a better future and utopian ideas became prominent in the collective consciousness of East German society.

A central unifying factor for people in eastern Germany immediately after 1945 was the common goal of creating a society in which the individual was in harmony with himself and his social environment in contrast to the disharmony of class conflict in a capitalist society. The intellectual sources were the thoughts and ideas of the European and American Enlightenment and the German classics: Voltaire, Diderot, Emerson, Herder, Lessing, and Kant. The application of these concepts in the practical work of the theater as well as in theater criticism was known as "the appropriation of the heritage" (*Aneignung des Erbes*). It was felt that the validity of a dramatic work was not limited to a particular time in the past but was also relevant to the present, even though it was first and foremost a "reflection" (*Wider-spiegelung*) of the age of its genesis.[7] This was based on the conviction that a work from the past "anticipated" in the sense of Goethe the humanistic hope of a society based on social harmony.[8] The ideas of the playwright, a utopian vision in his time, were to be depicted as within the grasp of the contemporary spectator and encourage him or her to work for humanity and harmony in the present day.

Theater in the GDR, even some time immediately after 1945, accentuated the important role of all elements in society for the creation of a more humane social order. The emphasis on scenic details outside the general development of the dramatic action often resulted in a shift in focus but fit the needs and feelings of the audience, especially the many working class spectators in the audience who had a direct and practical view of reality. In 1956 Fritz Wisten directed a production of *King John* in Dresden that made the scene between Arthur and Hubert de Burgh (act 4, scene 1) the central episode of the performance. This was probably not Shakespeare's intention, yet the audience was particularly moved, and some even wept.

In the years between the founding of the GDR in 1949 until the end of the 1950s, theater and intellectual life were dominated by a feeling of being "on the right path." I am not suggesting, however, that there was a consensus or uniformity in dramaturgical concepts behind the productions. This can be exemplified by two very different productions of *A Midsummer Night's Dream* performed in 1956. Fritz Wisten's production at the Volksbühne in Berlin combined the playful and erotic, yet dreamily ironic sketches of the painter Max Schwimmer as stage decorations with the "romantic" music of Mendelssohn-Bartholdy. It created an appearance of romanticism, as an optimistic "anticipation" by Shakespeare of the possibility for humans to live in harmony with each other despite the seriousness of the situation. Wisten, a Jew, who had been persecuted and imprisoned by the Nazis, was especially interested in searching for solutions to contemporary problems in Shakespeare's plays. Later when the intellectual and political conflicts within the GDR became more virulent, the term "romantic" was often used to discredit Shakespeare productions that propagated the illusion of social harmony, that is, that did not distance themselves from or even negate the utopian dream of a socialist future.[9]

In the same year, Rudi Kurz staged the same play in Leipzig, but what a contrast! On a rotating stage with various tiers were three levels of action harshly set off against each other by red, brown, and green colors, and a backdrop of black curtains. Red stood for the Athenian court and the aristocracy; green stood for nature, the woods, the world of fairy tales, Oberons, Titanias, Pucks and elves; and brown stood for the world of the Athenian craftsmen. The range of portrayal by the actors was as limited and limiting as the stage decorations. The confrontation between the various levels of action was stiff and mechanical, the result of analyzing solely the historical and political aspects of the play. The craftsmen, completely infatuated by their play, were portrayed extremely sympathetically as "representatives of a rising bourgeoisie in a progressive phase of their development," an approach which went over as well with the actors as it did with the audience. The world of the craftsmen—the bourgeoisie—served as a contrast to the life of the feudal court with its lust for power (Theseus) and restrictive authoritarian structures (Egeus). This came off most sharply when the enthusiastic craftsmen performed for the blasé courtiers. The currency of the plays was supposed to be achieved by an implied association of the obsolete feudal society and feudal class of the past with the obsolete bourgeoisie of today.[10]

Today it may be easy to chuckle at these simplifying productions that reduced the rich and colorful view of life in this play to its sociological components, yet this turn to "historical truth" (*gesellschaftliche Wahrheit*) had at first very positive practical results: a solid basis for interpretation and an in-depth understanding of the many interconnections at work in the play itself. This approach provided actors and actresses with an abundance of concrete details and material from daily life which they, in turn, could use to create and motivate a character's behavior. By stressing the tension between the implied historicity of the play and the explicit actuality of the performance, the "sociological approach" insisted on a direct line of descent of humanistic hopes and ideals from classical antiquity to Shakespeare, and continuing down through the Age of Enlightenment and the emancipation of the bourgeoisie only to be finally realized today in a socialist society. While any performance of Shakespeare exists within a field of tension between past significance and present meaning, how to make this visible on stage often resulted in heated debates in critical reviews and articles, especially in the official theater journal, *Theater der Zeit.*[11]

II

The optimism about the future that characterized the frame of mind of the East German theater audiences in the fifties and well into the sixties began to be replaced by criticism and even pessimism about the situation and the future of the country. The experience of daily life and the work place led to a nagging sense of doubt about the way things were going. The source was the construction of the Berlin Wall on 13 August 1961 and the state's attempt to seal off its citizens hermetically from the West. The political and ideological leaders of the GDR and the ever smaller group around them became discredited. Their inability to change isolated them more and more from the majority of the population and increasingly caused a sense of insecurity and distance.

The seventies marked a visible shift in the intellectual currents of the country. Whereas public media and scholarship had always been under the control of the censor, the arts (especially theater) provided free space in which growing disaffection and dissatisfaction with the social and political situation could be articulated despite increasing ideological and political pressure. Public discussions about performances of contemporary plays and novels by younger playwrights, for instance, Jürgen Groß, *Match* (1978); Ulrich Plenzdorf, *Die neuen Leiden des Jungen W.* (1972); Heiner Müller, *Die Bauern* (1976), *Die Schlacht* (1975), *Der Auftrag* (1980), Volker Braun, *Die Kipper* (1972), *Großer Frieden* (1979), and *Die Übergangsgesellschaft* (1988), became more heated.

Performances of classical plays focused more on the social problems within the play and as such became an element in the unofficial public discourse. Especially Shakespeare performances, which had been a secure component of the "appropriated cultural inheritance," now questioned the contemporary relevance of the plays, the meaning of the plot, the direction of dramatic confrontation, the structure of the characters, and above all the perspectives for humanity. This process had begun already in 1964 with Adolf Dresen's *Hamlet* in Greifswald but not recognized as such at the time, because it was only a small minor theater and it was soon taken off the bill. Nevertheless, it influenced other important theater people. This production signaled a turning away from the dramatic tradition of the bourgeois Enlightenment and the linear development down to "socialist realist" performances. This "problematizing" approach began to be applied also to many classical German dramas, such as Goethe's *Faust* (Deutsches Theater, 1968) directed by Adolf Dresen and Wolfgang Heinz. Another signal was *Leben und Tod von Richard dem Dritten/(Richard III)* (Deutsches Theater, 1972), directed by Manfred Wekwerth.

This "problematizing" approach was ahead of its time, and the majority of theater people continued to follow the trend, supposedly from Shakespeare himself, of a hopeful and optimistic picture of humanity that culminated in the "socialist age." The slump in attendance in these theaters was proof, however, that the consensus between audience and theater performance that had existed during the sixties no longer existed, especially among those social groups that had been attracted to the theater after 1945. In this altered political situation, it became necessary to search for new ways of representing the dramatic action for the audience and for the actor.

In 1980 both the Deutsches Theater and the nearby Maxim Gorki Theater performed two very different versions of *A Midsummer Night's Dream* which, though uniquely different in style and theatrical means, exemplified a new consensus in their approach to the cultural heritage. The common stance was that this play is about the world in which we live, historically, geographically, or socially, and our perception of it. The world is brutal, cruel, inhuman, demonic, compulsive, and driven by its physical instincts, yet at the same time we yearn for humanity and harmony among peoples. This tension, simultaneously represented on stage and directly felt by the spectators, accounted for the intensity of the performances and their effect on the audience. Both productions began with the social situation in the GDR as it was rather than as it was supposed to be, not as a dialectical unity but as a chaotic one. In both productions, these contradictions became concrete in the relationships between the lovers, love as a yearning for existential meaning, and sexuality as a natural instinct.

Alexander Lang's production at the Deutsches Theater depicted humans as potentially rational beings caught up in a cruel nightmare world full of contradictions. It opened with the actors asleep on the stage who "awoke" to experience a "daydream" only to sink back into a deathlike sleep at the end of the play. In this dream, Demetrius and Lysander, ostensibly educated and civilized courtiers, hunted after Hermia and Helena with brutal lust and ended up as bitter rivals. Theseus brutally documented his claim to the defeated Hippolyta and brutality characterized the struggle between Oberon and Titania as well as the relationship between Oberon and Puck. Through historic costumes, which only appeared to be removed from the dramatic action, the characters and their behavior seemed archetypically timeless.

What moved the spectator, nevertheless, was the ever-present yearning for a world that was different and more humane, coupled with a feeling that humane relationships were in the end the individual responsibility of each and every one of us. One of the most moving moments in the performance was when the four confused young lovers ended their crazy chase with arms intertwined, like a group of entangled trees in the midst of the wilderness, in an attempt to rediscover themselves and each other.

The production at the Maxim Gorki Theater, directed by Thomas Langhoff, had as its starting point the poetry of the play, which exists alongside the brutality and humanity. The diverging dramaturgical concepts underlying these two productions were visible in the stage designs. In Lang's production, the stage consisted of a bare red box with a low ceiling and two small doors, more like holes, on each side in the rear for entrances and exits. It had an air of claustrophobia about it. Langhoff's stage was framed on both sides by construction scaffolds reaching to the ceiling and into the auditorium. The decorations were colorful as well, but the stage floor provided no stable foundation, and the characters swayed, bounced, and swung on a trampoline, large cushions or ropes, and swings.[12] This created a sense of floating between tender love and desire mixed with outbursts of violence towards each other and social rebellion against their oppressors: Titania against Oberon, Puck against his master, Hippolyta against Theseus. There was no romantic glossing over that which took place in the dark between people, yet this was not a cruel nightmare. It showed the audience that it was possible to transform this world into a better place.

Not only in the major theaters in Berlin but especially in theaters in smaller towns outside of Berlin, theaters that were highly sensitive to their audiences, one found performances that raised questions about the difficult relationship between persons and society. For example, a 1984 production of *Merchant of Venice* at the Meininger Theater directed by A. R. Pasch rejected any harmonious happy ending in Belmont but ended with Portia, Nerissa, and Jessica singly and thoughtfully observing their partners.[13] This was the opposite of the secure, "positive," and harmonious future that was still being propagated by the Socialist Unity Party.

Theater now tried with all possible means at its disposal to suggest a connection between the dramas of the past and the social situation of the present, for example, Mistress Overdone's brothel in *Measure for Measure* directed by Peter Schroth and Peter Kleinert (Weimar, 1983) was a business-like Eros Center with well-trained personnel. Suddenly it disappeared, and we saw at the end of a long dark tunnel Claudio, almost naked, hanging as if crucified on long ropes, a poor, pale worm, shaking with fear, the classical picture of "ecce homo."[14]

For thirty years the "legitimate approach" to the "progressive cultural heritage," ostensibly traceable back to Shakespeare's "anticipation" of a socialist society, had necessarily smoothed over contradictions and incon-sistencies in the text concerning character and plot. To disregard this was not without risk. Failures were expected and they were frequent, but when it was for the sake of breaking taboos, especially ideological taboos cloaked in the form of "aesthetic premises," theater people were willing to risk a flop. It was their declared intention to subvert such restrictions with the means of theater performance.

The new developments in the social foundation and the loss of the foun-dation on which the theaters had stood until now, resulted in a deep change in the GDR theater's ideas about itself and its effect on its audiences. It had to rethink its function in society from the ground up. It was no longer enough to simply address the audience. Now they were called upon to perform in a manner which offered their audience alternative modes of understanding and evaluating what went on stage. Now they were called upon to perform in a way which incited their audience to look for possible alternatives themselves and to question their effectiveness. It was no longer a case of provoking the audience to think things through themselves, or act out by themselves new variations of the dramatic material. This placed new demands on the spectator as well as on the actors. Both were now forced to leave their familiar and clearly structured terrain behind them, and in doing so they gained for themselves new free space, despite the restrictive old power structures that were still in effect.

Shakespeare performance in the GDR during the 1980s developed in two different directions, each of which took into account that there was a new relationship between theater and the audience and between the theater and the age.[15] On the one hand, there was a tendency to ignore, to alter, or even wilfully to destroy the recognizable dramatic structures within the play, including the order of the scenes, internal dramaturgical structures, and even the wording.[16] On the other hand, many directors attempted to place their productions within a larger aesthetic context. They experimented with new, freer, and more variable open forms of interaction between actors and audience, e.g., "happenings" and complex "spectacles," They attempted to resolve the distinction between stage and auditorium, which allowed the audience little space for itself, and create a new relationship between stage and spectator. Now not only the stage but the whole theater became a performance area—rehearsal stage, foyer, workshops, practice rooms in which all kinds of performance (e.g., sketches, readings, pantomime, cabaret, excerpts from different plays) were performed simultaneously.[17]

So-called free groups of professional and/or amateur actors came together to experiment. In 1985, "Theaterwürfel," a group of young actors and actresses from various East Berlin theaters, put on scenes from B. K. Tragelehn's translation of *Troilus and Cressida,* entitled "War, Peace, Love— A Rehearsal of Shakespeare" (*Krieg, Frieden, Liebe—Eine Probe zu Shakespeare*), in the third floor of the Volksbühne. It was a version of Shakespeare's dramatic material by and for a younger generation.[18] In this way East German theaters turned away from the restrictions of the dramatic form and structure in the playwrights' text for the sake of accentuating the contemporary relevance of the play, an approach deemed necessary by theater people and demanded by the audience. It was an attempt to unlock the material the playwright had formed in the past and to make it productive for the audience of the present, an approach to be found in Brecht and Dürrenmatt as well.

Characteristic, yet not necessarily typical, of this approach, was the work of Heiner Müller as playwright, director, and translator of Shakespeare. His radical approach to Shakespeare, not the least of which was his negation of the official Shakespeare canon, was directed at the contemporary East German audience and was a seminal influence on other East German directors. Like his master Brecht, Müller used the cultural heritage as a quarry to mine for dramatic material to confront Shakespeare's dramatic vision. Müller's idiosyncratic renditions of Shakespeare—*As You Like It, Titus Andronicus, Macbeth, Hamlet*—go beyond translation to become individual works of their own comparable to Brecht's *Coriolan.* They have less to do with Shakespeare and Elizabethan England and more to do with Müller and the GDR.[19] His *Hamlet/Maschine,* which he directed himself at the Deutsches Theater (1990), consists of his translation of *Hamlet* into which he inserted his own *Die Hamletmaschine* (1977), as a kind of interlude and philosophical-dramaturgical commentary on his own use of Shakespeare's materials as the director.[20]

The problem with the often arbitrary and questionable destruction of Shakespeare's plays by young directors was that the audience did not know what to do with the wreck. In the process there were many flops, which could have been subtitled "Shakespeare's ugly characters." An example of this trend was a production of *Twelfth Night* directed by Martin Meltke in Brandenburg (1981). Down front left was Feste's office, a boat complete with a typewriter (symbol of the artist's fear of modern technology), on which Feste kept busy writing. Down front right was a toilet bowl, frequented often by Sir Andrew Aguecheek, Maria, and Sir Toby, who enjoyed investigating the excrement of the person who used the toilet before him. What was most disturbing about this performance was less the props than that it reduced all human actions to sexual drives and primitive physical instincts paired with a lust for power and money. When one ignores the contradictions and complexity of real life as embodied in Shakespeare's characters, one likewise alienates the drama and the stage from the auditorium and denies the communication between actors and audience with which Shakespeare so richly supplies them. This is exactly what happened.

It would be misleading to claim that the experiments described above were general fare during the eighties, yet even in conservative Shakespeare performances one could always discern individual attacks on the basic conventions of theater performance and audience behavior; implicit in them was a critique on contemporary social life in the GDR. This was true of both large and small theaters.

More widespread than this trend toward destruction were the new approaches to classical drama. Examples of this were visible in Langhoff's *A Midsummer Night's Dream* (1980) discussed earlier as well as in various other theaters. At the center of this was an attempt to accentuate the dialectical unity of "continuity" and "discontinuity." By "continuity" I mean the attempt to understand and reevaluate the experience, cultural treasures, and values of the past and take them one step further within the present system of reference. "Discontinuity" in the appreciation and performance of Shakespeare comes automatically with changes in the intellectual landscape.

Alexander Lang emphasized "disunity" in his production of *A Midsummer Night's Dream.* He sacrificed the GDR tradition, which emphasized the complementary perspective of the so-called plebeian characters (*Volksgestalten*), for example, Thersites in *Troilus,* the servants in *Taming of the Shrew,* for the sake of his dramaturgical concept that Shakespeare's "Dream" is in reality a cruel "nightmare."[21] Lang's "Rude Mechanicals" were not willing but unskilled amateur actors but tired professionals while Langhoff's "Mechanicals" rode their bicycles onto the stage not as a gag but as a visible means to make these folk characters accessible to a present-day audience.

Among the directors who tried to redefine the unity between past and present, unity and discontinuity, were Klaus-Dieter Kirst (Dresden), Peter Schroth and Peter Kleinert (Weimar/Berlin), and many more. This approach was most visible in the work of Christoph Schroth in Schwerin. He was rewarded with audience appreciation and produced some of the high points of Shakespeare performance in the GDR during the 1980s, among them his "Shakespeare Project" (1986), ensuite performances of *Romeo and Juliet* and *Winter's Tale*. By pairing up such very different plays, Schroth discovered surprisingly that there was, in fact, a shared frame of reference that became visible in the contemporary political context. The effect was a new and intensive approach to older dramatic material and a revitalization of the GDR theater tradition.[22]

Schroth's point of departure was two young girls (Juliet and Perdita) on the threshold to adulthood, who are forced to confront the harsh reality of the world in which they live for the sake of love. At the center of the performance was the youthfulness of the two main characters—accentuated by the youthfulness of the actors and actresses who played these roles—and their development into uncompromising, yet mature personalities. (*Zwei Kinder (zwei Mädchen) reifen zu kompromißlosen Persönlichkeiten.*)[23] The fact that the Schwerin Theater had to perform on an interim stage added to the intensity of the performance because it could fully ignore performance conventions that would have been forced upon them if they had been performing in a courtly or bourgeois theater architecture. For *Romeo and Juliet* that meant no festive hall, no balcony, no garden for Friar Lawrence, no cemetery, and no tomb. Instead the audience sat above and looked down into a kind of circus menagerie or gladiator arena. Like spectators at a soccer match, the audience sat above and around the performance area and looked down upon a symbolic and visually suggestive dramatic arrangement, e.g., a piece of white cloth on the stage separated the feuding families. Only Mercutio and the young lovers crossed the demarcation line. The costumes of Tybalt as well as those of the servants of both houses, and even Romeo and his friends, were dominated by unrestrained wildness and aggression fitting to a society dominated by violence and selfish power struggles. It was not by chance that the costumes reminded the spectator of skinhead attire. The counterpoint to such a world is the self-fulfillment and a partnership of love.[24]

Astonishingly, the scenery for *A Winter's Tale* on the same stage was very different. The performance area in front of the audience was a wide and bright landscape which the audience again looked down upon as from upon a hill. In such a setting the unnaturalness of a feudal court, be it Sicily or Bohemia, seemed strangely foreign and doubly evil, even though ephemeral and temporary. This is not only an element of the romances; it was due to a perspective on the action relevant to the current political situation. It was the confirmation of the power of the human personality in opposition to tyranny and despotism. The current relevance of this to the final years of the GDR was obvious to many in the audience, especially in the intensity and creative power of the actresses who played Pauline (Lore Tappe) and Hermione (Cornelia Lippert) as they opposed arbitrary tyranny with uncompromising cunning and wisdom.

The productions in Schwerin testified to the fact that theaters in the GDR were able to circumvent and subvert successfully the ideological bastions of official GDR cultural policy, "holding a mirror up to nature" (*Widerspiegelungstheorie*), and the "appropriation of the cultural heritage." They prepared their audiences for a new way of looking at the world, which was a source of creative power in the disturbances which led to the "turning point" (*Wende*) in the fall of 1989.

III

With the theatrical means at its disposal, e.g., the Shakespeare performances described above, the East German theater prepared its audiences and helped motivate them to take the necessary action demanded by the political situation. From the beginning of the 1980s theaters in the GDR were in the midst of the changes in the thoughts and feelings of the people. It was not by chance but the consequence of this development that many actors, musicians, and other artists were in the front rows of demonstrations in the fall of 1989. They too demanded, "Wir sind das Volk." It was theater people, along with young Christians and many others, who with wisdom, cleverness, and peaceful energy pushed through ever larger demonstrations. The nonviolence, despite the tremendous pressure of suppressed aggression, desperation, and rage, proved to be stronger than the uniformed and armed police, tanks, and the gigantic apparatus of the dominant power. It was especially popular actors, well-known for their Shakespeare roles, who organized the huge demonstration attended by hundreds of thousand on 4 November 1989, a few days before the GDR came to an end.

With the end of the German Democratic Republic the curtain also came down on Shakespeare performance on the East German stage. It is still too early to declare which elements of Shakespeare performance were specific to the GDR and which have to be seen in relationship to developments in West Germany. The path history will take is still too unclear at the moment, and it is impossible to say what will last and what will pass by the way. Only the future can tell and will be reflected in the work of the theater.

2

From Goethe to *Gestus*: Shakespeare into German

Maik Hamburger

Ever since Germans have been translating Shakespeare—and the first attempt of literary note was *Julius Caesar* put into Alexandrines in 1741 by the Prussian envoy to London, Caspar Wilhelm Borck—Shakespeare's drama has exerted a vigorous influence on the evolution of German culture and, in particular, the German language. Modern German is in any case unthinkable without the creative thrust of seminal translations: the Luther Bible, the Voss Homer, and the Wieland, Schlegel, Tieck, and Baudissin versions of Shakespeare's plays. Thus Goethe's claim for his time: "All educated [*gebildete*] Germany owes its style to Wieland. . . . The ability to express oneself comes from Wieland through Shakespeare."[1]

By far the most renowned rendering until recently, held to be synonymous with Shakespeare, was the so-called Schlegel-Tieck translation; however, the trade name with its implication of a homogeneous oeuvre is quite misleading. Schlegel's pioneering contribution, made at the turn of the nineteenth century when German national literature was reaching a culmination point, is rightly regarded as a masterpiece of linguistic achievement and a major literary production of German Romanticism. The remaining plays translated some thirty years later by Ludwig Tieck's daughter, Dorothea, and by Wolf Graf von Baudissin, although competently rendered, lacked the inspired poetry of their predecessor.

Even Schlegel's version came in for a great deal of criticism at the time, which was one reason that he ceased work before completing the canon. Heinrich Voss, after going along with him for a while and even emulating the Schlegel manner, suddenly repudiated Schlegel's principles and set out to produce a rival translation in collaboration with his brother, Abraham, and his father, Johann Heinrich Voss, the latter already famous for his rendering of Homer. In a courageous attempt to adhere still more faithfully to the original, the Voss team stretched their native language to the utmost until it began to break down under the unusual strain. Its loss of coherence

73

due to extreme techniques of inversion and compression indicated that to try to go beyond Schlegel at that point in literary progress was to court disaster. Heine, who had praised Schlegel's early work, draws a vivid comparison between the two: "Herr Schlegel perhaps translated too smoothly, his verses are sometimes like whipped cream, and one does not know when raising them to one's mouth whether they are to be eaten or imbibed; Voss's translation, however, is as hard as stone and one must be careful not to break one's jaw when speaking his verse."[2] In his ebullient fashion, Heine was really commenting on the Scylla and Charybdis imperilling a translator of dramatic speech into nineteenth-century German: one forfeits either the mimetic terseness or the poetic harmony of the original.

Only in recent times has it been recognized that translation for the stage has its own unique requirements due to the specific quality of dramatic language. In performance the multiple functions of dramatic speech trigger complicated processes within the actor's physique and mind. This is done by virtue of a code contained in the text, a code translatable into physical action. Dramatic writing achieves its designation in a theatrical event when the art of the playwright merges with the art of a living, self-producing human being. The seeds of physical communication spring into flower through the agency of the player. These seeds are what Brecht calls the *Gestus* of a text, which takes into account the fact that in speech the whole body participates as a signifier. A wholly theatrical text is completely oriented toward dramatic presentation, and thus it is only decodable through adequate reference to its corporal message.

The term *gestus* is difficult to translate. It derives from the word *Geste*, which means "gesture" or "attitude," but it has nothing to do with gesticulation. A term devised for practical theatrical purposes, it eludes attempts at formal definition; even though formal elements such as stylistic levels, speech rhythms, phrasing, syntactic deviations, metrical structures, sound patterns, and in short, anything that may affect bodily expression, enter into it. Obviously, the term *gestus* can have both social and individual connotations.

To explain *gestus*, Brecht uses a Biblical example that can easily be transposed into English, since Tyndale happens to employ the same phrasing as Luther. Brecht writes:

> The sentence . . . 'pluck out the eye that offends thee' has an underlying *Gestus* of a command, but this is not expressed in a pure *gestic* manner, since 'that offends thee' has another *Gestus* which is not expressed, namely that of a motivation. *Gestically* expressed, the sentence reads (and Luther who 'took speech from the lips of the common people' shapes it thus): 'If thine eye offend thee, pluck it out!' One can see at a glance that this wording is gestically much richer and purer. The first part contains an assumption, whose special quality can be fully

expressed in the intonation. Then there is a short pause of perplexity and only then the surprising advice.[3]

Significantly, Brecht establishes a connection between Luther's *gestic* qualities and his custom—as expounded in his *Epistle on Interpreting*—to draw amply from the well of popular speech.[4] A theatrical text amalgamates the literary and the spoken word in a dramatic or gestic-poetic dialogue. It was exactly this synthesis that baffled German classic poets and translators. The huge gulf between literary and vernacular German proved unbridgeable; thus, theatrical texts always leaned backwards towards literature. The difficulty was rooted in German history and insurmountable by literary competence alone. Attempts to resolve the problem invariably turned out to have political implications; poets who persisted such as Lenz, Kleist, Büchner, and Hölderlin were persecuted, slandered, and driven into isolation, finally perishing through sickness, suicide, or madness. There was no point in postmedieval German history at which it might have been possible to weld all strata of language together into a medium relevant to the whole nation. Never did a social constellation come about to support a popular theater of national dimensions. Literature was cut off from everyday life and its language deprived of the elements of popular speech, the speech of that section of the population engaged in material production. The poets were condemned to a literary world without impact on social issues. The act of perlocution—of generating word energy out of social activity and transforming word energy into action—was not within the realm of a German poet's experience (as it obviously was in Shakespeare's). Goethe comments on this disparity when his Faust—the German intellectual, chafing at his secluded life—makes a pathetic attempt at emancipation by mistranslating the Bible. Instead of the original, "In the beginning was the word," he tries a number of variations and finally writes, *Am Anfang war die Tat*—"In the beginning was the deed." The deed remains imprisoned in its verbal cage.

Thus the evolution of the German language tended toward the poetical and the philosophical. Poetry closed like an oyster around each grain of sand and made it into a pearl. Indisputably, this created objects of great beauty but the snag was that elevated language was no longer able simply to talk about sand. Friedrich Engels hits the nail on the head when he comments on the "unwieldiness of the German language for everyday use and its enormous facility in the treatment of the most difficult themes."[5] The Austrian writer Karl Kraus, a profound virtuoso in linguistic matters, compresses the same thought into a single aphorism when he says: "The German language is the deepest. German speech is the shallowest."[6] Heiner Müller, the leading German playwright today, once remarked that in Germany we had the lofty pathos of Schiller and we had popular bawdy verse (*Wirtinnen-Verse*) but in between there was a large vacuum.

It has often been observed that Hegel's philosophy is rooted in the German language, and even today it is difficult for a translator to escape being sucked into the philosophic vortex of his mother tongue. Hamlet's "To be or not be" can only be translated as *Sein oder Nichtsein* (Fontane's more correct version *Sein oder nicht sein* is acoustically the same). Unavoidably, the personal problem of the character Hamlet (which in Shakespeare's metaphoric language eventually takes on existential dimensions) is transmuted into a primarily philosophical problem that happens to be posed by a character named Hamlet. When I pointed this out to the German philosopher Peter Ruben, he was horrified and insisted the translation should be *Zu sein oder nicht zu sein;* this is clumsy German, but if I were to start translating *Hamlet* again, I might consider using this phrasing, which would have been unthinkable in 1964. It is more precise, and it gets rid of a worn-out phrase—a foreigner's advantage the English cannot share. However, the construction being so unusual, it could obtrude itself as a mannerism—which would make things worse. The final test would have to be the stage.

It may be inferred from this brief historical excursion that translating Shakespeare today is not just a matter of modernizing some antiquated language. The translator must try to recapture the *theatrical* dimension of Shakespeare's dramatic speech—its physical component—and to find adequate forms for this in German. This has been made possible by the linguistic developments beginning in the 1920s and advanced chiefly through the work of Bertolt Brecht. It is no coincidence that the first successful breakthrough in overcoming the philosophic-poetical bureaucratic fabric of *Hochdeutsch* should be by a playwright. To gauge Brecht's achievement, one has to realize that he was forced to bypass the classical era of German literature and to return to the Luther Bible as the historical referent for his language. Brecht created a popular, albeit highly artificial, synthesis of Luther's German with his own native colloquial South German, seasoned with a generous sprinkling of anglicisms. What Brecht's epic and gestic style owes to Shakespeare and Marlowe has been investigated by several authors, for instance, by Ute Baum.[7]

A present-day German translator works under quite favorable premises for approaching Shakespeare's drama. He can, to start with, exploit the results of modern philology available in annotated English editions. He can also link up with the sensual and gestic language evolved by Brecht and developed further by contemporary German-language theater. He is assisted by the modernization of blank verse, also initiated by Brecht, who endeavored to open up the iambic pentameter to accommodate a language mainly determined by dactylic rhythms. This was grist to the mill of playwrights in the German Democratic Republic. They were always on the lookout for a formal medium to grapple with the complex network of tensions confronting them in society. Thus there exists a considerable body of GDR drama written in verse by playwrights such as Heiner Müller, Peter Hacks, Volker Braun, and Stefan Schütz. The sophisticated forms of blank verse were forged out of the material of everyday speech of working men and women. This feat was backed up by the poets' conviction at that time that despite all setbacks, the common man under socialism was subjectively making history rather than being a mere object of history: this allowed him a dignity and a sense of purpose compatible with heightened stage articulation. No matter how we may judge socialist self-awareness from a present-day point of view—and we should be careful of oversimplifications—the fact remains that the blank verse evolved in the GDR was remarkable for its force, its vividness, and its creative break with academic formality.[8] A translator was able to draw from a broad linguistic spectrum ranging from modern colloquial speech to the loftiest literary forms.

However, one cannot emulate Shakespeare merely by mixing various levels of speech. The theatrical significance of the dramatist's lines have to be observed. The physical action is the common denominator that unites a disparity of styles and renders them artistically acceptable. Bringing forth the gestic element of speech enables the playwright, as Brecht notes, to "make the antithesis between simple and elevated language compatible and makes 'simple', 'natural' speech sound noble just as it makes elevated speech sound popular."[9] In translation practice this means always making linguistic decisions with an acting situation in mind. Post-Brechtian Shakespeare translators in the GDR were all closely connected with theatrical practice: playwright and director Heiner Müller, directors Adolf Dresen and B. K. Tragelehn, dramaturg and director Maik Hamburger.

German translators are more fortunate than those of many countries in that they do have blank verse at their disposal. The iambic pentameter in use in classic German drama from Lessing onward underwent considerable modification through Shakespeare's verse. Already Schlegel had declared in a letter to Tieck: "My translation has changed the German theater. Just compare Schiller's iambs in *Wallenstein* to those in *Don Karlos* to see the extent to which he passed through my school." Although the *Wallenstein* trilogy (1798/99) certainly displays a considerably more flexible versification than the monotonously regular iambs of *Don Karlos* (1787), classic German blank verse was still different in structure from that used in Elizabethan drama. In Shakespeare's verse, each line floats freely and at the same time is bound to the overall rhythm and meaning of the passage. Each line alone communicates a piece of gestic information; in fact, this applies even more to the enjambed verse of the later plays than to the earlier end-stopped verse. A sequence of lines works both in a linear and in a cumulative mode. New information is added and new perspectives are repeatedly discovered, exposed, and made visible, repeatedly opened up, enriching the fabric of the whole speech. Thus extremely complicated arguments and subtle relationships between characters, as for instance the clash between Angelo and Isabella in *Measure for Measure,* can be built up step by step in sensorial acting and made apprehensible to a very diverse audience. Consider the following passage:

> *Angelo.* The law hath not been dead, though it hath slept:
> Those many had not dar'd to do that evil
> If the first that did th'edict infringe
> Had answer'd for his deed. Now 'tis awake,
> Takes note of what is done, and like a prophet
> Looks in a glass that shows what future evils,
> Either new, or by remissness new conceiv'd,
> And so in progress to be hatch'd and born,
> Are now to have no successive degrees,
> But ere they live, to end.
>
> *Isabella.*   Yet show some pity.
>
> *Angelo.* I show it most of all when I show justice;
> For then I pity those I do not know,
> Which a dismiss'd offence would after gall,
> And do him right that, answering one foul wrong,
> Lives not to act another. Be satisfied;
> Your brother dies tomorrow; be content.
>
> (*Measure for Measure.* 2.2.90–105)

Parts of this are extremely difficult to understand even for a sophisticated intellect, but the message as passed on through the actor is quite clear. Shorter and longer spans of tension and meaning overlap; the verse adapts itself, as it were, to the mental grasp of each spectator. If the Elizabethan audience member missed a line during a performance at the Globe, it was still possible to get the gist of the passage. Not so with German classic blank verse. Due to complicated hypotactic structures, the meaning can often only be construed in retrospect at the end of a long sentence, and the slightest acoustical misunderstanding can totally confuse the listener. Here is a random example from Goethe's *Iphigenie auf Tauris:*

> Wer hat den alten grausamen Gebrauch
> Daß am Altar Dianens jeder Fremde
> Sein Leben blutend läßt, von Jahr zu Jahr
> Mit sanfter Überlegung aufgehalten
> Und die Gefangenen vom gewissen Tod
> Ins Vaterland so oft zurückgeschickt?[10]

This passage and the previous one deal with similar fields of discourse. Its overt statement is in fact a reversal of the former one. The wording and the train of thought are much less complex. But in contrast to Angelo's lines, Iphigenia's speech provides scarcely any material for an actress to communicate sense through bodily expression. The signifier remains purely lexical. Theatrical communication here requires verbal modulation rather than physical engagement. This kind of verse with its high demands on audience concentration speaks a priori to educated spectators.

When putting Shakespeare's verse into German, it is essential to reproduce the physical autonomy of each line. This often means introducing unconventional inversions and deviating from customary syntax. Such texts are occasionally condemned as "un-German" or "un-poetic," but in fact actors can handle them to good advantage.

However, inversions in the target language should not go as far as to cover up Shakespeare's own inversions; these have often gone by unheeded because they were regarded as poetic quirks by translators unaware of their gestic significance. There is a conspicuous example of this in the beginning of *Measure for Measure*. As he often does, Shakespeare strikes the central theme of the play in its opening lines. The Duke says,

> Of Government the properties to unfold
> Would seem in me t'affect speech and discourse,
> Since I am put to know that your own science.

These lines are metrically flawed and syntacticly awkward; they articulate badly. Obviously the poet was ready to sacrifice all these considerations to get one thing absolutely right: to force the actor to put full vocal and physical stress on the noun "Government." I defy any actor to speak these lines without placing the emphasis on this key word of the play. The normal word order ("The properties of Government . . .") sounds like a political treatise and, the gestic emphasis being on both nouns, an actor would be tempted to declaim rather than to seek a concrete and meaningful rendition. This is the version we find in the standard translation of Baudissin:

> Das Wesen der Regierung zu entfalten,
> Erschien' in mir als Lust an eitler Rede.

But in fact the English passage involves a threefold inversion;[11] in normal usage the verb "to unfold" would be at the beginning of the phrase, and it can be argued that the second line should actually come before the first: "It would seem in me to affect speech and discourse to unfold the properties of Government." This is indeed what Heinrich Döring, translating in the 1870s, makes of the text:

> Redselig würd' es scheinen, wenn ich euch
> Des Herrschens Eigenschaft entfalten wollte.[12]

This actually has a much clearer *gestus* than the Baudissin version, but the stress is now plainly laid on the Duke's loquacity. The only nineteenth-century translator to perceive the point was Abraham Voss, who has (in 1818),

> Der Reichsverwaltung Pflichten durchzugehn,
> Das schien' an mir unzeit'ge Redesucht.[13]

Apart from the antiquated vocabulary, this is a true and theatrically effective rendering. To avoid the pathos of the German inverted genitive, Maik Hamburger and Adolf Dresen chose to begin their translation thus:

> Wie man regieren soll, das darzustelln,
> Säh aus an mir wie müßiges Geschwätz.[14]

Here, the two nouns are replaced by a verb and an auxiliary, and the dialogue immediately fastens upon the central concept. Possibly some element of the Duke's pompous diction is lost. This would then have to be compensated for elsewhere. Tragelehn resorts to another device, placing the operative word at line-end:

> Erklärn, was eigentlich das ist: regiern
> Schiene an mir wie Neigung zu Geschwätz.[15]

The colon construction to set off an accentuated term is characteristic for a post-Brechtian style adopted by many GDR playwrights; to become effective, it presupposes a theater versed in techniques of epic performance.

Syntactic deviation is, of course, only one of the many formal elements contributing to the gestus of a text. These formal components include speech rhythms, rhetorical techniques, its deictic connotations and so on. Of great importance is the tempo rhythm of a passage or a verbal exchange. It is difficult to achieve a correlative rhythm if speeches are significantly longer in the target language than in the original. Some languages do indeed use more words and longer words than others, yet each language also has idiomatic modes of reaching a conciseness of expression. A tendency to verboseness seems to adhere to all translations irrespective of language. The first English translation of Goethe's *Faust* (by Dr. John Anster) exceeds the German by about one-seventh. However, there's no German translator who has not groaned with frustration at the prolix nature of his mother tongue.

When the Ghost in *Hamlet* vanishes (1.1.56), Marcellus says "'Tis gone and will not answer." There's a laconic matter-of-factness in this speech, emphasized by the break in meter. The missing two feet are filled out by a little pause of bewilderment or contemplation before Bernardo turns to

Horatio: "How now Horatio? You tremble and look pale." A literal German translation would read: "'S ist gegangen und wird nicht antworten." That is ten syllables for seven. Schlegel's excellent version catches the melody of the phrase: "Fort ist's und will nicht reden." J. H. Voss has: "Schon fort; antworten will's nicht," which preserves the verb and reproduces the terseness of speech, but at the price of extreme irregularity. A more recent translation by Rudolf Schaller willfully inflates the line: "S'ist fort und will uns keine Antwort geben;" this stops up the metrical gap and levels out the rhetoric, leaving no *gestus* except for a blurred pathos quite out of place here.[16]

Recognizably, the gestic rhythm acts as a signifier in *Hamlet* (5.2.221–22) when the prince resigns to fate: "If it be now, tis not to come; if it is not to come, it will be now; if it be not now, yet it will come: the readiness is all." A rhythmic correspondence can be discerned to "Fate's knock" in the opening bars of Beethoven's Fifth Symphony. Heuristic analogies of that kind can be significant to actors and, consequently, to translators too. Once perceived, the beat is easily reproduced, e.g., "Ist es gleich jetzt, ist es nicht künftig; ist es nicht künftig, ist es gleich jetzt; ist es nicht jetzt, wird es doch kommen: bereit sein ist alles."[17]

When Hamlet chides his "too, too solid flesh", the syncopated stress on "too, too" provides a double-pounding *gestus* directed at the actor's own body. The physical quality of this line is weakened in Schlegel's literary "O schmölze doch dies allzufeste Fleisch" with its umlaut subjunctive and paraphrase superlative. Voss tries to save the syncope: "Dass doch dies zu zu derbe Fleisch zerschmölz," and similarly a recent translation by Erich Fried: "O, dass dies zu zu feste Fleisch doch schmölze." However, these translations do not get around the literary subjunctive, and the sibilant "zu zu" lacks the drive of the English. Hamburger/Dresen have a version very much committed to performance: "O daß dies sture sture Fleisch zerginge." The adjective "stur" denotes "stolid", "stubborn," and in conjunction with "Fleisch" gives a good image; for the censorious it may deviate too far from the literal, but this is a borderline case. The liberties taken may be exonerated in view of editorial uncertainty as to whether Shakespeare's word actually was "solid" or "sullied." As an absolute contrast to the fleshly pounding of this line is Hamlet's aerial exclamation upon perceiving his father's ghost: "Angels and ministers of grace defend us"—unexpected, light, and sibilant.

Until the advent of a sharpened social awareness in the GDR theater, partly due to Brecht and partly to a national ideological orientation, the German tradition had seen Shakespeare's plebeian characters as "funny folk," as stage comics without concrete social connotations. Significantly, for a century and a half, the Mechanicals' scenes in *A Midsummer Night's Dream* were known as "lout scenes" (*Rüpelszenen*) and only recently has the term *Handwerkerszenen* gained acceptance. In translation the language of the lower orders was stylistically upgraded: this meant they did not live out their own language. Displaced from their real sphere, they were in fact dramaturgically downgraded. GDR translators were the first to give these characters their own realistic speech based on present-day German vernacular. It was, however, not sufficient merely to copy everyday speech the way Gerhart Hauptmann had copied the workers' diction in *Die Weber*. In Shakespeare, the social idiom, the utterances of the Mechanicals, of Lance, Pompey, Autolycus and others is as exquisitely heightened as that of the aristocrats. A translator has to give them language that is both credible and imaginative. You have to find the "ruby on the head of the toad," as Sean O'Casey, himself a master of plebian drama, expresses it.

In the fifties and sixties, there was a marked tendency in GDR theater as well as in academic studies to overstress the role of the lower orders—sometimes even exalting them above the main characters. Curiously enough, this revaluation of Shakespeare's plebeian lore, which of course concurred with official doctrine, did not lead to official acceptance of his plebeian dialogue. The very functionaries propagating a new social perspective balked at the colloquial utterances proffered by new translations, regarding them as an outrageous profanation of the classical heritage.

Mention should be made of the work of Robert Weimann, which combines scholarly precision with a fine understanding of stagecraft. Weimann has shed light on an all-encompassing gestic dimension present in Shakespeare's drama. The playwright brings a complementary perspective to bear on the main plot, enacted upstage, by means of downstage audience-oriented commentaries expressing a plebeian, or "common sense," point of view.[18] This two-eyed dramaturgy is of paramount significance for achieving the full theatrical effectiveness of a Shakespeare play. However, it can only operate if both perspectives are given their full due in terms of linguistic and mimetic representation, and if the lowlife scenes are not treated as mere comic relief on the periphery of the main action.

Yet, even at a higher level of speech, a tendency to genteelism pervaded early translations. To make a habit of saying *Leichnam* instead of *Leiche* for "a body," *Nahrung* instead of *Essen* for "food," *töten* instead of *erschlagen* for "to slay" waters down the force of theatrical expression. There are passages of deliberate coarseness, such as Hamlet's line referring to the slain Polonius: "I'll lug the guts into the neighbour room" (3.4.219), where "guts" may be translated in the figurative sense ("Ich will den Wanst ins nächste Zimmer schleppen," Schlegel and Heiner Müller) or in the initial sense ("Ich schlepp die Kuddeln in den Nachbarraum," Hamburger/Dresen). In Horatio's farewell to dying Hamlet "Good night, sweet prince / And flights of angels sing thee to thy rest," the physical collective brings the angels down to earth and gives the phrase a vivid material image. This is lost in Schlegel's conventional "Engelscharen," the customary collective noun for angels, which approaches the transcendental "angel host." This passage contains another notable feature: the form of address 'prince' comes up for the first and only time in the tragedy. It shines like a freshly minted coin. It establishes Hamlet's royalty at the moment of his death. Its illustrious ring could never have been heard if it had not been bandied about throughout the five acts of the play; the same is of course true of this line in a translated text.

The conflict between Schlegel and Voss mentioned earlier in fact goes to the roots of translation practice. To be innovative, to activate the target language, a translation has to bring in foreign elements. Goethe observed that when translating, "one has to go up to the untranslatable: only then will one become aware of the alien nation and the alien language,"[19] while more recently Rudolf Pannwitz, a writer of the 1920s, commented: "Our translations, even the best, start out from a false principle. They want to germanize the Indian, Greek, or English instead of indianizing, or grecianizing the German. . . . The basic error of the translator is that he holds on to the accidental level of his own language instead of letting it be mightily moved by the strange language."[20] Similar views can be cited from Walter Benjamin to Peter Hacks. However, the foreign elements must be assimilated. If they become obtrusive or mannered, the translation defeats its own purpose. The balance that may be struck at any particular time is an historical category. The target language changes constantly in itself and in its relation to the original language. A translator of tomorrow may easily be able to say things that seem impossible today.

Translating Shakespeare is an unending process. His original text always emerges anew, however successful the current translation may be, and it always carries with it a new challenge. This dialectic is succinctly formulated by Fritz Kortner, the actor and director, who says: "The more a translation of today goes back to the original work, which is of course older than the existing translations, the younger it will become."[21] It is no coincidence that this quotation comes from a theater person. A theater translator is aware that the line translated today will be acted live on the stage tomorrow. This is a perpetual incentive to draw nearer and nearer to Shakespeare's language at all its levels of communication.

3

Shakespeare Contemporized: GDR Shakespeare Adaptations from Bertolt Brecht to Heiner Müller

GÜNTHER KLOTZ

CONTRARY to the widespread notion, promulgated by Kenneth Muir and others[1] that one cannot "improve" Shakespeare through revision, adaptation, or transformation, Bertolt Brecht remarked: "I think we can alter Shakespeare if we can alter him."[2] Since Brecht, a majority of theatergoers and readers have become increasingly fascinated by adaptations of theater classics that relate to their personal lives and to the contemporary state of affairs in their own society. In the case of Shakespeare, there are so many different kinds of adaptations that one must look beyond traditional textual criticism and investigate these complex phenomena within a broader historical context.

Looking back into German history, one immediately realizes that adaptations of Shakespeare have had both literary and cultural significance. Whenever cultural values and issues have been at stake, such as during the formative years of the German national theater (the "Sturm und Drang" period) in the second half of the eighteenth century, Shakespeare played a central role. He did so in the "Sickingen" debate between Marx and Engels and Lasalle (1859), in the historicizing productions of the Meininger (1866–90), in the innovations of Max Reinhardt (1904–33 in Berlin) and Leopold Jessner (1919–1933), and he was very present in the theaters of the German Democratic Republic. When the new English drama of the 1960s and 1970s struggled to establish an artistic alternative to the commercial theater, playwrights looked to their great predecessor, who, as Brecht remarked, "had shoveled so much raw material onto the stage."[3] Joan Littlewood, Bernard Kops, Tom Stoppard, Edward Bond, Arnold Wesker, Howard Brenton, and others adapted Shakespeare's plays to shape their own understanding of contemporary English life.

The history of Shakespeare adaptations in the German Democratic Re-

84

public began with those post–World War II years when the ruins in the streets of Berlin as well as the debris in the minds of the people had to be removed. Two dramatists of different generations, Bertolt Brecht and Heiner Müller, the younger the pupil of the elder, mark divergent positions in (1) the development of the GDR theater and (2) in the reception of the national and international theatrical heritage. When the GDR was still known as the Soviet Occupied Zone, Gustav von Wangenheim, director of the Deutsches Theater in Berlin, who had just produced *Hamlet* (1945), borrowed the mousetrap motif of the play within a play to prove an onlookers's guilt in his new play *Die Maus in der Falle* (*The Mouse in the Trap*, 1948). As early as 1931, he had used this motif in *Die Mausefalle*, (*The Mousetrap*), a play that exposed the lower middle-class illusion that it should be possible to remain neutral in a class conflict. His postwar play, *Die Maus in der Falle*, subtitled "a comedy," deals with young people in 1947 who want to open a theater, and with older men returning from prisoner-of-war and concentration camps. Thematically, the play deals with the conflict between individualism and the efficiency of a group and above all with antifascist resistance, with betrayal and guilt, with the difficulty of coming to terms with the past and with the reconstruction of a war-torn country. Although this "whodunnit" with surrealist elements tells a different story than Shakespeare's tragedy, part of the play's matter lends itself to the discovery of the crime: Shakespeare's playacting in the service of truth here is transformed into playacting in the service of both individual and social efforts to construct a new, democratic society. Shakespeare's dramatic device of showing how theater performance may lead us to the reality of Hamlet's Denmark, was adapted by von Wangenheim to the historical conditions of 1947, the period of GDR history we referred to as the "anti-fascist democratic order." Von Wangenheim's use of Shakespeare's *Hamlet* as raw material in the sense of what Brecht calls "material value theory" (*Materialwerttheorie*) (Heiner Müller will later introduce the term "stone quarry," *Steinbruch*), clearly sets off this play from the contemplative, psychological, and internalizing middle-class theater that had become discredited by the historical events of 1933–45.

In his notes on the 1955 Berliner Ensemble production of Johannes R. Becher's *Winterschlacht* (directed by Brecht and Manfred Wekwerth), Brecht wrote,

> Becher's play has an important function for political education in the GDR but neglected in our postwar literature, i.e., coming to grips ideologically with the Nazi period. This clearing is part of the foundation on which the new house is to be built.[4]

With *Winterschlacht* (*Winter Battle*), the theater as an institution again demonstrated that it was able to represent and form history with the help of the new theater's reference to its own dramatic heritage. Johannes Hörder, the hero of Becher's play, is a private in the German Wehrmacht during World War II and "a German Hamlet figure."[5] The play, originally called "The Battle of Moscow," was written during that battle; it was first performed in 1943 by German emigrants in Mexico, revised several times, renamed *Winterschlacht*, and staged in Prague in 1952. Max Burghardt directed the first GDR production in Leipzig in 1954.

Like Hamlet's Denmark, the Germany of this play is a country in which something is "rotten." The scene shifts between the Russian front in 1941 with private Hörder and his comrade Sergeant Nohl, and the home of Hörder's parents in Berlin where Hörder Sr. is a judge on Hitler's infamous *Volksgerichtshof* (the so-called people's court). The credulous Hörder believes in "Germany," but "Germany" for him and his parents means Hitler. Nohl recognizes the fascist crimes for what they are; his belief in Germany is directed against Hitler, so he defects to the Soviet side. When Hörder learns that his beloved brother has been shot by Germans as an antifascist, he begins to have his doubts; when he is ordered to shoot his friend Nohl, who has been taken prisoner, he disobeys and shoots himself instead. Hörder retains his humanity but sacrifices his life. Becher makes him realize that his belief has been misused for the sake of an ordinary imperialist war and that "Germany" is not identical with fascism. This important insight was the foundation for the social renewal in the GDR after 1945.

Becher's tragedy can take up Shakespearean elements only by way of modification. Hamlet's action could have a direct effect on the struggle for power and the state of affairs in Denmark. Hörder's actions cannot effect anything; rather, he is affected by the events. As to the closure of the two plays, they differ sharply. To close the plot, Shakespeare introduces Fortinbras and his troops; Fortinbras's (presumed) ascension to Denmark's throne is but another militaristic variant of the same feudalism that has existed in Denmark. In *Winterschlacht,* Germany's military adversary, the Soviet Union, represents a different social pattern that provides a concept of change with a new social content. The contrast manifests itself in antithetic values, in the moral decay of fascism on the one hand, and in the moral of national and social liberation on the other.

With its epic elements, long confessional soliloquies, and alternations between verse and prose at turning points in the action, the structure of Becher's play reminds us of Shakespeare's. However, the basic tone of *Winterschlacht* and its social function as a play of political education make it rather un-Shakespearean. Despite its epic traits, *Winterschlacht* is basically a well-made domestic tragedy. Brecht's theater, however, will go far beyond this, even when he makes use of Shakespeare.

Brecht never staged a play by Shakespeare, yet upon his return to Berlin in 1948 and with the founding of the Berliner Ensemble in 1949 a number of considerations prompted him to work on *Coriolanus*. First, in the years immediately following World War II, he thought about the role the masses have played in history and dramatized this concern in *Die Tage der Commune* (*The Days of the Commune*, 1948/49). Second, directly related to his intention to reevaluate the role of the masses in history was his concern to provide plays at the Berliner Ensemble that would sharpen the audience's critical ability to assess fascism and recent history. For this reason, he postponed the production of *Der aufhaltsame Aufstieg des Arturo Ui* (*The Resistible Rise of Arturo Ui*, finished in 1941) in favor of staging his own *Furcht und Elend des Dritten Reiches* (*Fear and Misery of the Third Reich*, 1938) and Becher's *Winterschlacht* (1952). At the same time, he decided to approach Shakespeare. He said,

> Not only in order to provide plays for the German theater, the classical repertoire of which is shrinking terribly in these cataclysmic times, but also to pave the way to Shakespeare, without whom a national theater can hardly be realized, it seemed to be expedient to go back to the origins of the classical drama which was still realistic, yet at the same time poetic. In plays like Lenz' *Der Hofmeister* we can find out how to put Shakespeare on the stage because here we have his first reverberations in Germany.[6]

Third, and finally, Brecht saw historical parallels between Germany after the destruction of the Third Reich and the early Roman Republic.

In the process of adapting Shakespeare's *Coriolanus*, which lasted from 1951 to 1955, Brecht's ideas about Shakespeare changed. The result was *Coriolan von Shakespeare (Bearbeitung)* (*Coriolanus by Shakespeare [Revised]*). Brecht died in 1956, and the play was not performed by the Berliner Ensemble until 1964 under the direction of Manfred Wekwerth and Joachim Tenschert.

In the twenties and the thirties, Brecht had claimed "that the great Shakespearean plays, the foundation of our drama, no longer work," since it was passion that kept them going.[7] According to Brecht, their purpose was the experience of the great individual and the barbarian pleasure that they yield derived from an inescapable fate; therefore, it would be best to free ourselves of the classical repertoire. This on the whole negative attitude towards Shakespeare had given way to a more discriminating view. Brecht was now determined to present Coriolanus's story in its proper historical dimension in order to rid it of bourgeois myths that had become embedded in the prevailing concepts of Shakespeare. The cultural heritage should not be used to reconcile the offensive side of life. Instead, a new "reading" ("*Lesart*" is Brecht's term) should present the contradictions and miseries of life as the result of man's own doing and therefore as surmountable. Brecht found everything necessary to achieve this in Shakespeare, and he thought only minor textual additions and changes would be necessary.

Brecht even declared that later audiences might take pleasure in the original work: "With a more vigorous development of an historical sensibility—and when the self-assurance of the masses grows—you pretty well can leave everything as it is."[8]

As late as 1949, in *Kleines Organon* (*Little Organon*), Brecht had disputed that Shakespeare had embedded the plot in its historical conditions. However, a few years later he appropriated this Shakespearean quality when working on his *Coriolan* and used it for his own purpose. Intending to bring out the primal ideals of the play, he retained the essential content of Shakespeare's tragedy. For Brecht this lay in the contradiction that "the plot demands that [the plebeians] have to win Coriolanus's war as well as the war against Coriolanus."[9] This perspective historically extends the catastrophe, which, of course, also had its bearing on the character of the hero. Brecht remarked that

> [a]s to the pleasure found in the hero and as to the tragedy, we must go beyond mere empathy with the hero Marcius (Coriolanus) to attain a richer pleasure; apart from the tragedy of Coriolan we should at least be able to experience the tragedy of Rome, too, particularly that of the plebeians.[10]

Brecht went on to say that our society was interested in another aspect that concerned it more directly: Coriolanus's belief that he was irreplaceable. Shakespeare's tragedy of pride did not have to be blunted.

Brecht's adaptation demonstrated that the people cannot be blackmailed and that one can do without a Coriolanus but not without the people. This almost amounted to a glorification of the masses, which was scarcely historically justifiable considering the limited social consciousness of the masses in ancient Rome. Brecht might be justified to a degree, however, by occurrences in England in 1608 when Shakespeare wrote his play. Peasants rose to fight against enclosures, and parliamentary opposition to the absolutist Stuarts grew, leading to the revolution a few decades later. Shakespeare might have regarded the conflict between the crown and the people as a setback from the Tudor Compromise, but Brecht regarded it as a positive step on the way to a republic. He did so in agreement with the concept of history that prevailed in the young German Democratic Republic, in which and for which his theater was working.

Whereas Shakespeare's plebeians appear to be wavering, jealous of the specialist in warfare and easy to manipulate, Brecht places the contrast between Coriolan and the plebeians in a new light from the very first scene. He sketches individual profiles among the masses and provides more minor characters with speaking roles. Some of the men are resolute, others remain undecided, and one even carries a child. Whatever the case, their views are determined by their social situation. While Shakespeare's tribunes patronize the plebeians, Brecht's are sincere leaders and true representatives of the people who become a force of counteraction. Even in the war against a foreign enemy, they do not forget the enemy at home. Before the final battle when Coriolanus and the Volscians stand before the gates of Rome, Shakespeare's tribunes suggest that the Senate send further petitions to Coriolanus; then they disappear from the play. Brecht's tribunes despise those who want to surrender and call for armed resistance. Some patricians flee, others now side with the people to save Rome, among them Volumnia, Coriolan's mother. In the end, the property is distributed among the plebeians. Brecht's Coriolan does not fail on account of his pride. He fails because he is unable to grasp the social forces at work in the historical situation and because he refused to listen to advice.

Brecht's play clearly suggested the historical situation of the GDR in 1955, especially in its portrayal of the contradictions between those in power and those not, and in the contrast between the powerful individual and the people. He narrated the story in a balladlike way and laid the hero's passion open to criticism. Coriolan's pride was too expensive for Rome. On stage, directors Wekwerth and Tenschert eventually cut back the idealization of the masses, and stressed their antihierarchical conduct and reactions in face of the slaughtering enemies and the rituals of power. Brecht's poetic/ dramatic goals squared with the political demands of the time: to invert the bourgeois concept of the great personality and to create a theater that presented the people as the dramatic hero. Brecht's dramaturgy, however, was so didactic that within a few years this adaptation lost its efficacy; the historical consciousness of his GDR audience had grown in the process of establishing a new democratic socialist republic.

The adaptations by von Wangenheim, Becher, and Brecht share some common ground: they tell a story through characters who react to a given situation that more or less resembles Shakespearean motifs and matter, or as in the case of Brecht's *Coriolan,* by newly shaping and accentuating the old play. This is also true of various ballets and musicals based on Shakespearean materials as well as of narrative adaptations such as Franz Fühmann's marvelous *Shakespeare-Märchen,*[11] which are not dealt with here.

After Cole Porter's *Kiss Me Kate* (1940), Leonard Bernstein's *West Side Story* (1957), and other shows inspired by Shakespeare, the GDR had its own musical, *Was Ihr Wollt (What You Will),* based on Shakespeare's *Twelfth Night,* with music by Klaus Fehmel and lyrics by Günther Deicke. It premiered in 1963 at a Berlin theater for young people, the Theater der Freundschaft, and later played successfully throughout the GDR for about twenty years. It did not rely on glamorous sets, a chorus line, or sensational special effects. Shakespeare's plot and characters remained the foremost attraction. Despite a shortened text, the story does not deviate from Shakespeare's. The music did not create any top hits, nor did it follow any particular fashion or trend. The songs accompany the action and allow the characters and the action the limelight. The tremendous response it met with resulted from its appeal to young people. It defended the joy of living, individual courage, and a natural behavior as opposed to the sanctimoniousness of an orthodox authoritarianism. During the early years of its run there were discussions in the GDR youth organization about whether it was feasible and practical to screen off our country from blue jeans or to discriminate against boys and girls who owned records or texts by the Beatles. In this discussion, the musical *Was Ihr Wollt* pleaded for love, tolerance, and the pursuit of happiness.

In 1981 the Komische Oper in Berlin added to its repertoire Tom Schilling's ballet adaptation *Ein neuer Sommernachtstraum* (*A New Midsummer Night's Dream*); Bernd Köllinger wrote the libretto. It adheres to the basic pattern of a romantic ballet: the tension between experienced reality and the potential envisioned in one's dreams. This antinomy is set in the historical present when antagonistic social contradictions have been eliminated and deeper human motives and conflicts can come to the fore. These forces increasingly shape the way we treat one another. This is Shakespeare contemporized. Oberon and Titania, the fairy king and queen, appear, but Theseus, Hippolyta, and the young lovers have become people of today with common names. Puck and "the rude mechanicals" have been left out altogether. However, there is a pas de deux with one, who, unnoticed by himself, is transformed into an ass. The lovers' emotional bewilderment arises from their own lives, not from any magic, and they have to sort out what has happened to them by themselves. In 1987 the same team produced a second adaptation of *A Midsummer Night's Dream* entitled *Puck*. After the war, a young man stands in front of the ruins of his theater. Puck comes to lead him into a cheerful active dream world full of Shakespearean associations. This dream is to encourage him—as well as his audience—to face destruction and danger with confidence in life, in dreams as well as in the arts.

Heiner Müller's Shakespeare adaptations are a leap into another world, into a post-Brechtian theater epoch. Apart from his translation of *Hamlet*, he has written three adaptations to date which draw upon *Macbeth*, *Hamlet*, and *Titus Andronicus*. One is tempted to conclude that Müller's *Hamletmaschine* (*Hamlet Machine*, 1977) signifies the end of all theater; Hamlet takes leave of his story and the author instructs the actor playing Hamlet to tear up the author's large photograph on stage. Has Müller's theater landed in a cul-de-sac? Not at all. In fact, Müller wrote *Wolokolamsker Chaussee* (*The Road to Wolokolamsk*) while writing his Shakespeare adaptations. In direct contrast to *Hamletmaschine*, *Wolokolamsker Chaussee* (already five parts since 1984) offers a story, or stories, and employs simpler language (in blank verse). It deals with the socialist revolution and the differing attitudes people can assume during a social conflict.

However, the relationship between Müller's adaptations and Shakespeare's plays is totally different from that of Becher's or Brecht's. While Becher and Brecht used Shakespeare's plays to create or recreate stories with a new content, Müller breaks Shakespeare's plays apart and uses their material to expose the audience to the frailty and destructibility of the world they live in. Müller's own images and situations clash with Shakespearean references subverting the meaning of those references. On Müller's stage humanity has become a theater sign, absolutely decentralized. Müller resists Brecht's homogeneous world view. With a theatrical zest for catastrophe, he criticizes the audience's expectation that if in the theater contradictions are resolved by some kind of reconciliation, then real-life contradictions might be as easily reconciled. In this process Müller has claimed that Shakespeare is of even greater importance for him than Brecht.[12]

In 1972 theaters in Brandenburg and Basel performed Müller's *Macbeth nach Shakespeare* (*Macbeth after Shakespeare*), an adaptation for an age which is writing its history in wars, genocide, and mass liquidation, as well as in the assassination of political leaders and families. Müller felt it necessary to strike out at the growing propensity to become accustomed to violence and to put up with cruelty as if it were something ordinary, something acceptable, and to be expected in the daily news media. He is concerned that violence is becoming aestheticized by the Western, by crime movies, and by other forms of mass culture. Into the tragedy of Macbeth, a story from the time when royal succession by election was being replaced by dynastic succession, Müller incorporated the distressed peasants and soldiers suffering in a cycle of violence brought about by the struggles for power among the nobility.

Ten years later, in 1982, Müller and his wife, Ginka Tscholakowa, directed their own version of *Macbeth* at the Volksbühne in Berlin. Now it became obvious that by reducing Shakespeare's complexity the present day dramatist and director could create a different kind of theater. Müller's play assumed that Shakespeare's story of the Scottish King Duncan and his murderer was already familiar to the audience; he then played with the story material to contradict the audience's expectations. This is what was really new. The most striking characteristic of the Volksbühne production was its rapid succession of overpowering images of violence and cruelty—fantastic and grotesque—as well as the behavior connected with violence, such as treason, seduction, and Lady Macbeth's power-hungry, self-destructive emancipation. In some scenes Macbeth's lines are spoken by three different actors playing other roles at the same time. Actors repeat passages chorically. Audience expectations are deconstructed: actresses play

Macbeth, **DIR. Müller/Tscholakowa, 1982. Witches kiss Macbeth 2 (Beyer), Macbeth 1 (Montag), Banquo (Mühe) kneeling. Photo: Adelheid Beyer, courtesy of the Volksbühne Berlin.**

men, the three witches appear as bald-headed ladies in evening gowns waltzing to "The Blue Danube," Lady Macduff is trapped in a telephone booth, and people to be shot are lined up against a wall while Banquo appears as Christ and Duncan as a guru. Associations run rampant, yet at the same time there is a constant disjunction of signs from the expected meanings and the conventional mode of signification is continually being called into question. The characters are but elements of metaphors, exchangeable signs in a kaleidoscope that does not imitate life but gives sensual form to the most grievous phenomena of life in a stylized and strained artificiality. For the actors it is impossible to defamiliarize these images in a Brechtian way because they are not in any way familiar. Therefore, the actors cannot expose the metaphors to any criticism. They simply expose the spectators to the images which are, in turn, as irrefutable as television commercials.

Here the practice of Brecht's material value theory (Müller's "stone-quarry") in the theater turns against the theater itself as it has been understood from Shakespeare to Brecht. Mimesis, whether Aristotelian or epic, is abandoned, and character is dissolved. When Müller speaks of reducing things to their skeleton,[13] he means dispensing with plot and character as basic elements of the European drama as its fundamental structures imparting form and meaning to a play. The end of plot and character marks the end of the enlightening imitation of nature and the end of modernity. This is what Jürgen Habermas has called an "unfinished project";[14] the end of the modern age which believed in reason, in the philosophy of history, and in the emancipation of humanity. Müller's *Macbeth* already stands on the other side of modernism, dissociating itself from the Horation and Brechtian concept of instructing through pleasing.

In *Hamletmaschine* (1977) Müller dismantles the tragedy of the responsible individual by dis-individualizing and even liquidating the dramatic character. *Hamletmaschine* lacks a plot, characters who do something, and any conflict between knowledge and behavior. The play draws its dynamics from the process of demolishing the old play. By means of new texts and new pictures, *Hamletmaschine* produces its author's views on the catastrophes of recent history and on the making of art in an apocalyptic time. In their visualization, Müller's views are refracted in the mirror of Shakespeare's ideas. The relation of *Hamletmaschine* to *Hamlet* is not that of an appropriated heritage but that of a sign to a referent from a different continuum. There are also intertextual referents in Müller's play to *Macbeth,* to *Richard III,* and to texts by Sophocles, Bonaventura, and Lautréamont as well as to other plays by Heiner Müller himself. On stage the aesthetic difference of the historic continuum is brought about by replacing the plot with a series of pictures, conflict with contrast, history with tableau, dialogue with recital and declamation. In the playbill for Robert Wilson's 1986 production at the Thalia Theater in Hamburg, the dramatis personae are called "woman in a swivel chair," and "man bent over." However, they are not identical with the names of the speakers in the text, among them "Hamlet," "actor playing Hamlet," and "Ophelia/Chorus/Hamlet."

Hamletmaschine refuses to show any sign of hope. Because of his basically pessimistic assessment of the state of affairs in the GDR and society in general, Müller was severely criticized and some of his plays were not performed in the seventies. Referring to the GDR (in 1978) Müller observed, "We live in a time of stagnation, with history marking time," and with regard to *Hamletmaschine,* he declared: "There is no more substance for a dialogue because there is no more history."[15] Four years later he said, "The European concept of history is finished" because in huge industries "many of the best brains work at the disappearance of humanity."[16]

Hamletmaschine is a short text. It packs its metaphors in textual clusters. In Robert Wilson's slow moving production, the visual and the textual performance were incongruent and independent of each other. Thus no coherent meaning evolved that could have placed the visual and the textual images in any kind of relationship to each other. In the text, there are only thematic fields of associations that refer to the removal from power, the

Hamlet/Maschine, DIR. Müller, 1990. Lady in the Wheel Chair from *Die Hamletmaschine*. Photo: Wolfhard Theile.

legitimation of murder by murder, the search for a way of behaving that breaks the vicious circle of violence and injustice, and the raising of doubts about the prevailing function of art. There is Stalin's death, the 1956 Hungarian uprising, and the self-destruction of the arts in order to escape guilt through complicity with power. At the play's end, the voice of Ophelia/ Elektra recants the world to which she had given birth. The "machine" in the play's title may suggest inevitability, the sorcerer's apprentice syndrome, or the perfection of violence. It may also suggest the reduction of the human being to a state immunizing him against pain as well as against ideas. Robert Wilson's production, with its mechanical movements and recitation, precisely repeated the four acts to be seen from four different sides, suggested that the machine might also be the freedom to observe and to think while moving in routines. In this play, Hamlet walks out of his story, and the author as an essential ingredient of the arts is destroyed in effigy. Asking, as we are still accustomed to, what this could possibly mean, the closest we can come is to take it as a call for the theater to renounce institutionalized art serving the ruling discourse.

At first glance it seems as if Müller has only combined the negation of development from the theater of the absurd with the cruelty of the theater of cruelty. However, with this Shakespeare adaptation—if we agree to stretch the term so far as to include *Hamletmaschine*—Müller has established a theater language of its own. The visual happenings composed by figures, movements, gestures, makeup, setting properties, and lighting work together with the sound almost independent of the respective text. While they attract a more intense attention, these stage images also appear as theatrical entities in their own right, and not as parts of a well-constructed unfolding of a closed system of ideas and values. Their referentiality relinquishes the representation of universalities, the representation of something behind the text or behind the pictures. It eventually drops the aesthetic of the modern theater, which has been valid since the Renaissance in its epic, classical, romantic, realistic, or modernistic variants, imbued with a hope for improvement, progress, and perfection. However, deeper than the horrors evoked by the text or the stage images is the horror evoked by the destruction of *Hamlet*, Shakespeare's most famous tragedy. "We have not arrived at ourselves so long as Shakespeare still writes our plays."[17] If this scene of devastation is meant to beget a utopian impetus, the audience should certainly bring it along with them when they come to the theater.

Anatomie Titus Fall of Rome ein Shakespearekommentar (*Anatomy Titus Fall of Rome a Shakespeare Commentary*, hereafter *Titus*) is an adaptation of a different kind. It originated in Müller's translation of Shakespeare's *Titus Andronicus* for the Schauspielhaus Bochum. It was first performed in Bochum in 1985, then in Dresden in 1987. From the second scene of the second act onward, *Titus* follows the Shakespearean original with some minor changes and additions that comment on the events and introduce the author's (Müller's) actual being in his time. The comments are spoken by single actors or by a number of actors in chorus. The first act and the first scene of the second act are condensed and interspersed with Müller's own comments.

We can call *Titus* a new play for two reasons. The first is that Müller's language stands in even sharper contrast to Baudissin's nineteenth-century romantic translation and pre-Brechtian theater practice than his *Macbeth nach Shakespeare*. In the tradition of Mayakovsky and Brecht, Müller has reappropriated popular speech for the theater and liberated it from the conversational style and poeticized passions in order to bring it closer to Shakespeare's realism. The second is the specific intention manifest in Müller's comments in the second appendix:

> The *Titus* commentary shoots craps with accidental material, the playing field is provisional, the coordinates are anxiety and geometry. . . . [T]he crab-like gait of life in capitalism or in coexistence with it, together on this shared . . . planet, . . . breaks the bonds of the actor with (his) private property: no longer does he play a role. . . . The body a compass needle: the gesture measuring his functions (blood pressure, temperature) in the unknown landscape that might be a landscape beyond death or a place on the threshold, . . . death as a task, . . . training for the resurrection, . . . the theater as archeology's midwife: the actuality of the arts is tomorrow.[18]

Müller's metacommentary seems to imply that only the spectator's own will to endure and survive can be set against this play, which is richer than any other tragedy of world literature in physical and mental mutilations. Thus, the expropriated and liberated actor and author may enter into a dialogue with the audience—a communication not alienated from the disastrous reality by blind hopes or authoritative institutions. The content of such a dialogue in the language of the theater would be a twofold warning: first, of the global threats of the present epoch, and second, of the illusion that the contradictions determining the course of history might disappear by themselves.

Allusions to the Third World are embedded in Shakespeare's view in *Titus Andronicus* that the nomadic Goths and even the potentially good black Aaron are as cruel as imperial urban Rome. The Goths, too, fall victim to the hubris of power wherever they can exert it. Thus, the old subject matter of the story functions as a gate to a timeless knowledge. It is as if history had stood still and as if any revolutionary movement must end in a stalemate. This is the crucial point on which audiences of Müller's Shakespeare adaptations are split. Some, still confident in their humanist convictions, simply wish away the looming catastrophe, while others believe that only the most ruthless truth will allow us to become humane. Thus, Müller's

Shakespeare adaptations serve as nightmarish counterparts to his original non-Shakespearean plays which deal with historical change.

By and large the long road travelled by GDR Shakespeare adaptations from von Wangenheim, Becher, and Brecht to Müller mirrored the changes and developments in GDR theater. With the help of the new visual theater and its radical approach to truth, a number of young directors such as Wolfgang Engel, Frank Castorf, and Leander Haussmann turned against mass-cultural banalizations as well as against the optimistic conventions of the more traditional theater. Curiously enough, they realized their ideas more frequently in the productions of old plays than in the staging of new ones. Obviously, because of their richness in subject matter, Shakespeare's plays rank large among them. In some cases, as with Müller, it is difficult to distinguish between a particular production of a Shakespearean play, an adaptation, and a new work itself. Be that as it may, adapting Shakespeare was never a playful end in itself in the GDR, but it always had something to do with personal life experience during a particular phase of our history.

4

The Sixties: Hamlet's Utopia Come True?

THOMAS SORGE

In the exciting days of November 1989 people were storming box offices to watch a movie that had been produced a quarter of a century ago: Frank Beyer's *The Trace of Bricks* (*Spur der Steine*), based on Erik Neutsch's novel of the same title. The few showings the film had in summer 1966 were disturbed by hired party hecklers. Allegedly misrepresenting the GDR working class, the film was soon prohibited, thus sharing the fate of a number of other films of the time. Dramatic art was also affected in the sixties, seeing a virtual disappearance from the stage of plays dealing with acute present-day problems. Heiner Müller's dramatization of *The Trace of Bricks*, for example, in his *The Construction* (*Der Bau*, 1964) came under attack by the party leadership, who stopped rehearsals at the Deutsches Theater.

By contrast, the political-cultural objectives of the decade increasingly advocated the reception of classical Greek and modern drama and strongly stressed the classical even in plays of topical interest. This concept of a "socialist classical period" influenced, among others, the widely acclaimed former Brecht pupil Peter Hacks, and even Heiner Müller changed step and chose to represent current issues in terms of the themes and subject matter of classical Greek drama.

Shakespeare's works occupied an outstanding position within this re-evaluation of classic drama. In 1964, the year of the Shakespeare Quarter-centennial, the traditional Weimar Shakespeare festival was extended from three days to eight, and a Shakespeare committee headed up by Deputy Prime Minister Alexander Abusch was established especially for the occasion. Abusch's keynote address in the presence of party leader Walter Ulbricht was televised live to the nation. Ulbricht remained a whole day in Weimar before traveling on to Bitterfeld to attend the most important political-cultural conference of the sixties. The official theatrical journal, *Theater der Zeit*, commented that this conference did "not accidentally take place subsequent to the German celebration of Shakespeare."[1]

This remark also suggests that the Shakespeare productions of the ongoing season, during which almost every one of the approximately fifty GDR theaters staged at least one Shakespeare play, were by no means merely paying homage to the quatercentenary. The emphasis of Shakespeare's typical representation and greatness fits well into the officially promulgated cultural policy of the time. Thus, the elevation of Shakespeare to the position of a "classic" playwright and the increased attention given to his plays can be seen as a move toward the creation of a certain subject position for both the audience and the reading public. The reception of Shakespeare therefore helps us to analyze a characteristic contemporary ideological pattern. The creation of a "humanistic" *Weltanschauung* as advanced by classical playwrights like Shakespeare and Goethe exercised a lasting influence especially on a generation born about the time the GDR was founded (1949). It had an impact even on those who would normally reject ideological maxims. It makes itself felt even now when individuals believe themselves emancipated from those maxims. Thus, my concern here is also with those contradictions that many of the sixties generation have dragged into the eighties and nineties.

Statements from large-circulation newspapers and journals as well as from conference reports illustrate the general political-cultural climate that resulted in a very specific reading of Shakespeare. My point of departure will be two diametrically opposed Shakespeare productions from the year 1964: Adolf Dresen's *Hamlet* in Greifswald, and Hans-Dieter Mäde's *Hamlet* in Karl-Marx-Stadt. The latter was canonized; the former was pilloried and had to be taken off the stage almost immediately after its premiere in spring 1964. The incident was blown out of all proportion and even the official national (and only) satiric journal, *Der Eulenspiegel*, contributed its one-page share of scolding:

As a Shakespearean tragedy is not a shoe, it has no sole. Nor has it a heel which can be nailed to the tip of the sole. What was to be done? This is a question that confronted the young stage revolutionaries at the Greifswald theater when they decided to knock off a production of *Hamlet,* the fame of which might become acknowledged only by the dazzled posterity. Preliminary work began with the observation that the usual German translations of Shakespeare were out of date. . . . Michael Hamburger and Adolf Dresen, both free of the scholarly scruples that arise from proper English studies, took Old William's tragic story of Hamlet, Prince of Denmark, to task and translated it into our mother tongue in their very own fashion. If a little damage was done to the text during this transaction, one should give credit to the fact that a new speed record was set by devoting just a good month's time to it. By comparison, sluggish Professor Rudolph Schaller needed ten months of intense work because his whole translation had to be so scholarly and, moreover, even poetic. Besides, the Greifswald Two have the edge on him—they employed the so-called *gestus,* i.e. the 'attitude of the speaker pointing towards his social position, his individual characteristics and reactions to the given situation.' . . . All things considered, the Hamburger/

Dresen version does just as much away with the prejudice that Shakespeare wrote very poetically as with the delusion of a Hamlet located in Denmark. . . . According to the director's concept, Herr Jürgen Holtz acts Hamlet as a kind of cynical, unsavory rake having so much fun with playing the madman that he cannot stop it anymore. His bleating laughter will remain a lasting memory with the audience. . . . Now the theater's principal director . . . is . . . both very much dismayed at this *Hamlet* farce and angry with its initiators. And rightly so.[2]

This lackluster satiric review clearly postulates an interdependence of the scholarly and the poetic. It articulates the incompatibility of poetic language with a theatrical-gestural appropriation of the text. It proceeds from the assumption that a play is a closed illusionist dramatic fiction and turns against a representation of Hamlet in which the character himself is submitted to a critique. At first glance, we might conclude that nineteenth-century critical values had lived on in the reviewer, who does not seem to have encountered Brecht's dramaturgy. However, we are dealing not simply with the survival of outdated aesthetic values but with their function within a new political-cultural context that stressed the artistic quality of classic playwrights as the normative standard. Thus, in one of its 1964 April editions, *Der Eulenspiegel* copiously castigated the inclination of contemporary dramatists to use conflicts in classic characters as foils to their own plays. A modernization of the *Hamlet* subject serves as a striking example to satirize this preference: Hamlet as a keen engineer striving to put technological innovations into practice and consequently fighting pitched battles against the ossified, insensitive, and narrow-minded management of the People's Enterprise for which he works. The reviewer's predictable conclusion: such dramatic efforts do not achieve the depth of Shakespeare and other classics.[3]

In another April edition, the satiric journal quite unsatirically dispenses praise. Fortunately, it concludes, the works of classical writers are still fairly frequently bought and read. However, the journal finds fault with a group of amateur players, who, for all their acting, no longer find sufficient time for reading:

They do read, but not enough. Their play instinct weakens another fundamental need: their hunger for mental food. Most of them have not yet understood those words that were written on culture: Acquire it in order to have it—only then can you pass it on.

There follows an acid critique of contemporary dramatists, particularly the amateur playwrights published by Henschel Verlag, who "harden us pretty much against our love of literature."[4] Shakespeare is especially offered as an example of classical perfection. Dieter Hoffmeier's article in *Theater der*

Zeit with the didactic title, "Teacher Across Four Centuries. Shakespeare and Other Playwrights," registers this:

> But by appropriating [Shakespeare's] work, our new audience also develops their aesthetic demands vis-à-vis contemporary plays. Very rarely, however, do [these plays] fulfill such expectations. . . . In this connection we would like to ask whether the literary-aesthetic and the directly literary reception has not been somewhat neglected compared to the directly theatrical, dramaturgic-practical one during this Shakespeare memorial anniversary. We do not need to . . . return to the classical period in order to realize how much a nascent national theater can rise to the level it did by providing a literary-aesthetic reception of Shakespeare.[5]

Here, the privileging of the reading experience over theatrical play is shaped into a concept of national theater notable for its "literariness." Just as the extent and the quality of the individual act of reading provided the litmus test for a cultured way of life, so "literariness" represented the ultimate reference point for the theatrical preoccupation with classical dramatists.

This kind of orientation implies, for example, the idea of a "valid" production based on an equally "valid" interpretation. The primary task of the director and the dramaturg, therefore, is to apply the analytical tools of literary criticism to stage an "adequate" production. Accordingly, the audience was expected to make the "valid" interpretation of the play their own. Any concrete personal interests he or she might have were disregarded. The audience profited from the performance to the degree to which they acquired an insight into the philosophical and literary values manifest in the production. A teacher-pupil relationship between the Shakespeare production and the audience was posited in which the pragmatic interest of the audience was prescribed. By participating in the insights of classical masters such as Shakespeare, the audience could best learn to master contemporary social progress. Apart from the strongly affective nature of the intended audience response, there is an almost complete overlap between the artistic and the philosophical reception. In fact, the artistic essentially functions as an instrument of the philosophical. Here we are again reminded of the *Eulenspiegel* critique of the Greifswald *Hamlet,* which expressed the importance of a scholarly and poetic translation. The gesturally informed translation by Hamburger and Dresen, its foregrounding of the colloquial dimension of Hamlet's language, and the representation of a partially deranged protagonist scandalously violated a supposedly "valid" reading of the play.

The reasons for the remarkable reevaluation of a classic like Shakespeare are in the final analysis to be found in the forced realization of a specific, Stalinist-administrative model of socialism initiated by the GDR's leading party in the 1960s. At the end of the 1950s, labeled as the "transitional period to socialism," party leader Walter Ulbricht demanded that the "cultural needs of the masses be satisfied on a higher level, so that entertainment and culture become reunited and be placed at the service of establishing a socialist consciousness."[6] Thus, art was assigned a specific educative, political, and ideological function, an idea grafted onto the classical paradigm of German national culture, exemplified in Schiller's concept of the theater as the moral institution of the nation. (*Die Schaubühne als moralische Anstalt*).

Ulbricht's aim was twofold: First, the state and the economy needed well-educated, skilled workers whose professional competence enabled them to move within the framework of a specific socialist ideology. Second, the various phenomena of a mass culture that were felt to be hostile to such an ideology (e.g., rock and roll, jazz, Mersey Beat) were to be shut out. Even before the 1964 Shakespearean celebrations, an article entitled "Shakespeare Contra Portable Radio" appeared in *Der Eulenspiegel*.[7] On the one hand, a new mass culture was to be developed while at the same time the people were to "storm the heights of culture and take possession of them."[8] Thus, a cultured way of life became synonymous with a *socialist* way of life, and the massively propagated concept of "the educated nation" (*die gebildete Nation*) was to stand for "the socialist nation."

The integrative effect of this political-cultural offensive on parts of the intelligentsia, on traditionally social-democratic groups, and on upwardly mobile individuals leaving the working class, cannot be denied. Particularly in the wake of the First Bitterfeld Conference, April 1959, many new efforts in mass culture (e.g., amateur writers, amateur theater groups) were visible. However, the subordination of mass culture to works of art thought to belong on the "heights of culture" was questionable. According to Alfred Kurella, mass culture was to be merely a "link in our policy of culture . . . connecting the cultivation of the cultural heritage of the past with the promotion and development of a new socialist art."[9] Mass-cultural activities were regarded as little more than exercises to make sophisticated art more easily accessible. Seen in this light, the masters of socialist art are closer to the classical masters of bourgeois culture than to the existing mass culture in their own country—an official view fostered by the assumption that the new socialist art is but a linear continuation "of everything that is great and beautiful" in the arts of the world.[10]

In the long run, mass culture did not have its own basis; ideally it was to be absorbed by a socialist art of supreme standards. But even in a state in which all art has the "required" qualities, a few works of art of a directive nature remain. This was made clear at the 1960 Berlin conference on culture:

This society in which everybody makes music, draws, paints, writes, dances, acts, becomes the substratum for the creativity of those ingenious individuals in whom the general artistic skills rise to exceptional heights, [the substratum for] the great "masters" who master the artistic reflection and the recording of reality with the highest perfection. It is they who create the great individual works which we call ingenious and which find their place in public life where they are both examples and paragons for everybody's artistic activity.[11]

Thus, even a developed socialist national culture retains the educative function of the "classic." If we substitute "produce" for "makes music, etc." and "political" for "artistic," this statement can be read like the claim to the leading role in society by the Stalinist administrative faction; in the same way that the "classic" Shakespeare was recommended as a landmark for mass culture so, too, the Socialist Unity Party defined its relationship to the people. The reference to "classics" like Shakespeare has the advantage of tacitly insinuating the necessity of a political force able to educate the nation.

Of course, this briefly outlined relationship between mass culture and the "heights of culture," between amateur artists and the masters, harbored certain risks. Both mass culture and theater productions frequently drew attention to the acute social contradictions in the country without offering reconciliations. The powerful political-cultural initiative of the 1950s and 1960s helped to create an atmosphere in which a polyphony of emancipation could express itself. It was not accidental, for example, that already in 1960 Alfred Kurella, head of the Commission for Cultural Affairs with the politburo of the Socialist Unity Party's central committee, ominously stated that because "the individual great artist as well as the scientist has power in public life," the commission ought to concentrate its attention on the ideological content of "high" art considerably more than it used to.[12]

It was of decisive importance that Kurella's call for a masterly and accomplished "reflection and recording of reality" proved to be of a specific cast. In a turn against members of the Academy of Arts, Kurella clarifies his idea of what inopportune art was and what the right trim of seasonable great art ought to be:

Perhaps . . . a common link for many members of the Academy [is] the common experience of the '20s, [is] perhaps . . . that thesis according to which the major progress of new art is manifest in the discovery that the world can be changed. . . . To adhere to this thesis today . . . means falling prey to a new academicism. . . . Today, we have to learn that what matters most is to understand our world as already changed, and to realize the quality, the nature and the sense of this change with all the necessary consequences. This implies the recognition and the appreciation of those to whom we are indebted for having . . . brought about . . . the socialist change of the society.[13]

As everybody then knew, the main force of socialist change was claimed by the Socialist Unity Party as the organized vanguard of the working class.

Artists could prove their gratefulness to the party by embracing the task of representing the new "socialist" conditions of society and by giving prominence to their exemplary character. They were not supposed to display the contradictions of these new conditions but their inevitability and superiority. Dramatic art was to fill the audience with enthusiasm for the new. To achieve this, Hans-Rainer John, chief dramaturg of the Deutsches Theater Berlin, recommended dramatizing "exciting stories with exemplary people."[14] Such thinking also led to a normative reevaluation of the fervent, resolute hero conscious of his cause. The intellectual horizon of the hero, considered to be one of the many univocal heralds of the time to come, "largely determined the quality of dramatic works." The choice of the hero became the "central aesthetic issue of contemporary socialist drama."[15]

From this critical perspective, the concept of the Greifswald *Hamlet* was incomprehensible, or at least, inappropriate. For example, Armin-Gerd Kuckhoff observes,

> In view of the specificity of the audience among whom staff and students from the university were prominent, the theater aimed to show the danger of an abstract idealism detached from reality. Thus, proportions shifted. At the beginning, Claudius appeared to be a legitimate opponent fitting in with the needs of the moment.[16]

The dubious nature of such an interpretation of *Hamlet* seemed already noticeable in their theoretical approach. The Hamburger/Dresen critical view of the protagonist was supported by the sociological tradition in literary criticism. This theory, which was promoted by, among others, Plekhanov, Mehring, and the Lunatscharski in the twenties, primarily looks for the class basis of the author, the plays, or the individual characters. The sociological approach understands Claudius as a politically expedient but historically necessary ruler, a progressive in the transitional period from feudalism to capitalism. Furthermore, it supports a view of Hamlet as both a feudal prince and a representative of bourgeois-humanist ideals (considered illusionary because of their *bourgeois* nature).

The theater reviewer Alexander Weigel took this theoretical stand to ward off the almost monolithic attacks by his colleagues against the Hamburger and Dresen production. Rejecting the notion of a "positive hero," Weigel emphasized the "discrepancy between theory and practice in a hero" and compared the Greifswald *Hamlet* with the contemporaneous Potsdam production that also proceeded from the "contradiction between the humanist ideals of Hamlet and the 'capitalist' practice of the king."[17] The basic effect the Greifswald production aimed to produce was a vitalization of this sociological reading. The foregrounding of the dangerousness of an attempt to carry through ideals irrespective of the real historical circumstances implied a provocation of the audience. This production did not allow any affective identification with the ideality of the main character. Thus it contained an ambiguity adverse to the political-cultural climate of the day. On the one hand, it aimed at parts of an audience who, from the lofty vantage point of abstract ideals, disregarded several democratic achievements. On the other hand, the production could just as well be interpreted as a critical commentary on the hypertrophic orientation towards "socialist-humanist" ideals behind which the strongly contradictory reality of the sixties disappeared.

It is no wonder then that the Greifswald production was pitted against a "valid" *Hamlet,* Hans-Dieter Mäde's production in Karl-Marx-Stadt. But before discussing Mäde's concept, it will be helpful to sketch what contemporary theory had to say about the specificity of the classical hero and of the classical heritage itself.

The dictum that the existence of socialist conditions in the GDR excluded the existence of sharp contradictions in principle had considerable repercussions for the reception of tragic heroes of the past. These heroes are usually dramatic devices reflecting antagonistic social forces. But party leader Ulbricht had concluded that contradictions per se were of no interest for the time being:

> What is interesting and exciting is the *solution* of contradictions by means of the conscious, organized work of the party, the government, and the masses. . . . Today, people are not at the mercy of contradictions; instead, they master and solve them better and better, and this is what matters.[18]

But how could the fall of a tragic hero like Hamlet be of any significance, asked Ulbricht, if the new art saw "its ideals in the victory over contradictions and conflicts as a triumph of humanity?"[19] The dramatic heritage was linked with contemporary issues by combining a gnoseological (reflectionist) view of literature with a hypertrophic interest in the writer as a category of production aesthetics. An ideological category was brought in, of artistic anticipation, favored by a linear idea of social progress towards socialism. Thus, those plays proved especially useful that were best qualified to reflect the course of the history of man from a lower to a higher level. Shakespeare, as Rolf Rohmer observes, seemed exceptionally well suited for this:

> The writer William Shakespeare had the opportunity but even more so the faculty to discern, represent and pass on to a worldwide audience general laws of the development of mankind and the role of human action in history.[20]

According to this understanding of history, the playwright necessarily occupied a central position in the interpretation of history. Like a scientist, he analyzed objective processes, forecast developments, and assessed the commitment of human subjects in historical conflicts. The incorporation of these dimensions into the dramatic text was the principal condition for his educative effect on the audience. Thus, the playwright was, as it were, master of his historical situation; he was no prisoner of a partial contemporary perspective but, instead, provided a vantage point over and above the turmoil of his time. Centuries earlier, the playwright Shakespeare was able to fulfill a task which the Second Bitterfield Conference on Culture (1964) demanded of every citizen of the GDR: To develop the capacity "to perceive and shape our reality from the point of view of the planner and leader, not only from that of an empirical observer."[21] Consequently, attention was directed not only to a specific image of humanity (*Menschenbild*) *in* Shakespeare's plays but to William Shakespeare himself *as* an image of humankind worth striving for. Shakespeare was seen as a champion of social progress, who convincingly envisioned a truly humanist society in the future. Shakespeare, the "ingenious shaper of man," was to exercise influence not only through his plays but also through his outstanding personal example, which the millions of builders of the socialist society were encouraged to emulate. In a condensed form, Shakespeare's work becomes a microcosmic metamorphosis of his individual personality. As the minister of culture, Alexander Abusch, wrote in *Neues Deutschland* (24 April 1964), the official party newspaper,

> The vast plenitude of his characters proves nothing else but the entire dissolution of the creator in his work, in which every line, every sub-plot, every character, every feeling and every thought emanates his unmistakable personality. Shakespeare might have drawn not only from life but also from unprinted plays for the theater of his time. . . . This, however, was nothing else but the legitimate poetic treatment of raw material the plot and characters of which received by him only its ideational quality and which was thus elevated to the level of great dramatic poetry (p. 4).

Here again we find the image of Shakespeare breathing life into things profane as a kind of administrative vanguard of the GDR brand of socialism, determining and shaping social life down to the minutest detail.

The dramatic heritage was used to substantiate the claim that all social conflicts had been resolved and all past humanist endeavors had been realized in the socialist reality of the 1960s. Thus, classical drama, especially Shakespeare, assumed a legitimizing function within the framework of the dominant ideologic and political system. Shakespeare was not used to foreground or accentuate contemporary conflicts but to strengthen the official ideology. Social contradictions were supposed to be represented on stage as both severe and surmountable. This inevitably led to the psychologizing of dramatic conflicts. Thus, for the individuals of the sixties, a socialist society was shown to be available and accessible, in fact, only waiting to be taken over. Conflicts could only result from insufficient readiness to meet this challenge. Theater critic Dieter Hoffmeier refers to contemporary conflicts that were as acute as those in Shakespeare's plays yet could be "unravelled non-tragically." As a consequence,

> the weight of the conflicts has to be excitingly brought home to the audience. Not only the social necessity of a decision is to be visibly and convincingly represented but also all that which a hero fights out in his emotional life in the course of those conflicts. Here we can learn from Shakespeare.[22]

The audience is led to knowledge through emotional identification with the dramatic hero. This kind of audience response is more necessary the more received the conflicts of the past appear to be. If the humanist aspirations of the Renaissance were supposed to have found their material realization and perfection in the socialist reality of the sixties, then the re-production of Renaissance plays was possible only as a cathartic reexperiencing of the conflicts of the past. Therefore it was necessary to develop an aesthetic sense of tradition which, as Erika Stephan observes,

> does not merely take cognizance of the materialistically explicable historical fact in the artistic image. In it, there are also active recognizable forces which pass the relay baton of human longing and human will to work on to a spectator who— seeing himself fastened [sic] to the end of this fine chain—receives strength and responsibility by this in order to tackle and master the tasks of his time with at least as much commitment. As far as opportunities for recognition and action are concerned, we have almost every advantage over a poor man like Hamlet. But do we always bestow the same amount of passion and desire for knowledge, of depth of feeling and readiness for action like him?[23]

Stephan is referring to a discussion of the Karl-Marx-Stadt *Hamlet* directed by Mäde, which was in line with the cultural policy sketched out above. Mäde, who stated his theoretical positions in the lecture "Hamlet and the Problem of the Ideal,"[24] assumed that the humanist ideals of the past had already "entered the realm of reality" and that "the continuous closing of the gap between ideal and reality belongs to the essence of our historical development and to the center of our historical actions." Assuming that Hamlet's humanist ideals were equivalent with those of Shakespeare's, Mäde tried to create a unity of poetic intention, a projection of humanistic ideals and a normative dramatic image of humankind. In order to portray the realization of the Renaissance humanist ideal in the everyday life of the GDR in the sixties, Mäde divided the stage action into two areas: the corrupt court world and the protagonist's sharply detached area of contemplation. Hamlet's often less-than-ideal actions—the killing of Polonius, the bloody duel at the end—took place in the area representing the feudal or absolutist past inimical to ideals. Hamlet's ideals, supposedly manifest mainly in the soliloquies and his address to the Players, were not delivered in the court area but from the front stage area close to the auditorium. "The point is to eliminate any distance from the onlooker to [Hamlet's ideal] actions."[25] Access to the play was primarily by sympathetic identification with the hero, which was implemented by the actor's use of Stanislavsky's method[26] and an approach based on a contemplative audience frame of mind. While the affective impact was to be achieved by representing Hamlet's desire for humanist change as intensively as possible, the onlooker was at the same time confronted with a "totality of the artistic image"[27] of the cruel historical conditions of the Renaissance within which Hamlet had to act. By reviewing this dramatic microcosm of the Renaissance period, the onlooker was supposed to become conscious of the tragic contradiction between the ideal and reality (i.e., the formerly *utopian* character of ideals) on the one hand, and by means of identifying with the hero he was to be urged to contribute actively to making all those ideals now within his grasp come true. Shakespeare's ideals have become Hamlet's ideals. Hamlet as the bearer of humanistic ideals is "our contemporary," but "our contemporary" is someone who, mind you, is essentially the builder of the Stalinist version of centrally administered socialism.

Although most critics showered warm praise on Mäde's production, there were some more reserved voices. Alexander Weigel, for example, while recognizing the representation of Hamlet as "a man of great talents and high moral qualities," insisted on the shortcomings of the production:

> On the other hand, the perceptive relating of Hamlet's endeavors to our socialist ideals instead of to the [historical] conditions of the play and to his own real— and bloody—deeds, the impression of a displacement of the conflict out of the play arises. Hamlet himself [assumes] a kind of loneliness due to his oversized mental capacities, which is, however, only an equivalent of a loneliness due to incapacity. Ergo, a devaluation instead of the intended . . . restoration of Hamlet as a hero. . . . The killing of Polonius and Hamlet's unscrupulousness afterwards appeared nothing but gruesome due to a dramaturgical conception bent on showing a Hamlet exclusively and always governed by reason.[28]

On the whole, however, this production apostrophized, as a reflection of political-cultural principles, had only a limited effect on GDR theater practice. The normative contrasting of "classics" and contemporary drama may have contributed to a severe reduction of contemporary plays of critical content in later years, yet by the second half of the sixties, productions of classical plays were attracting a great deal of the critical potential that could not be articulated elsewhere. The staging of "classics" thus became occasions for discussing acute contemporary issues or publicly venting general sentiments ignored by the official media.

In the field of literary criticism, the subversion of the prescribed reading of the classics, revolving around the official category of the image of the humanist, was also quick to follow. For Shakespeare criticism, this development was ushered in by Robert Weimann's *Shakespeare and the Popular Tradition* (1967). Without explicitly attacking the edifice of socialist realism, he analyzed the dramaturgical specificity of the Shakespearean stage to demolish any notion of Shakespeare's "classicity." Weimann, at first glance, seemed to be in line with the dominant political-cultural ideology by stressing the synthesis of Renaissance humanism and popular culture, i.e., of "high" art and mass culture. But he also proved that the Shakespearean theater was not a moral institution for the education of the groundlings but a place of exuberant play, a forum for discussing social issues, and a public laboratory in which the mingling of ideologically, politically, and aesthetically disparate discourses of the time transformed their official meanings. Weimann stressed this theater's potential for artistic alienation, which in many ways contradicted an aesthetics of identification with specific fictional characters. On the basis of his theoretical premises it was possible to vindicate a Hamlet who stood out because of his antic behavior and his colloquial language. Weimann reconfirmed both the once much maligned Hamburger/Dresen translation and the oddly peculiar representation of the Greifswald *Hamlet*.

Finally, for the younger generation who had been besieged by the ideals of the "classics" during literature classes in schools and who had grown up thinking that the interpretation of the classics "happens under circumstances in which Hamlet's dreams and ideals are being fulfilled,"[29] the growing discrepancy between ideal and reality in the seventies and eighties proved particularly disconcerting. They did not belong to the somewhat older generation who were more able to identify with the officially propagated idea of a "socialist community of man" in which all ideals have become a reality. Nor did they belong to the younger generation whose consciousness was to be shaped in the course of the seventies, during which official propaganda thought good conduct guaranteed by providing individual material well-being rather than by claiming the materialization of humanistic ideals. This generation, almost as old as the republic itself, never completely managed to find satisfaction by withdrawing from the issues of public life to the seemingly protected spaces of family, house, and garden. Many individuals of this generation, like Hamlet, have had to pay for occasionally enjoying the once decried products of mass culture "with pricks of conscience" because the overpowering orientation toward the "classics," like Shakespeare, during their formative years still exercises a subconscious censorship. The very constraint to live up to the great paragons of humanist enlightenment has diminished this generation's capacity to develop its own unmistakable identity. Now that a Stalinist brand of socialism has led the GDR into its final crisis, this generation sees itself again confronted with the "classics" and must ask itself whether those inscribed utopias can ever be more than a painful residue of a bygone past?

5

Dramatic Text and Body Language: GDR Theater in Existential Crisis

ANNA NAUMANN

An existential crisis within the GDR at the end of the seventies is reflected in three Shakespearean productions, especially in the portrayal of Shakespeare's women and in the relationship between the plays' dramatic language and the nonverbal language used by the actresses. These three productions in Berlin were Benno Besson's *Hamlet* (1977) at the Volksbühne and two 1980 productions of *A Midsummer Night's Dream*, the first directed by Alexander Lang at the Deutsches Theater and the second by Thomas Langhoff at the Maxim Gorki Theater. Together all three are emblematic of how the theater in the GDR was often a vehicle for social and political criticism as well as a harbinger of social upheaval that became reality in November 1989 with the fall of the Berlin Wall and the subsequent demise of the GDR.

This essay, which is a pastiche from my research completed just two months before the fall of the Berlin Wall,[1] affirms through hindsight the appropriateness of my conclusions. My argument is that the increasingly unsynchronized performances by actresses, visible in the relationship between linguistic and physical communication, reflected an existential crisis in the GDR by which official ideology and social reality had become increasingly out of touch with each other.

This phenomenon was an attempt by the theater to rid itself of a sociohistorical mission that had developed into a curious and troublesome heritage. By concentrating on the connotative qualities of text and performance, it was possible to combine both the structure of the texts and their representations, both historical description and semiotic analysis. Nevertheless, we still lack an adequate analytic language to designate connotative meaning of iconic configuration during performance.

II

A clear break with the GDR theater's social mission and heritage was made in Besson's *Hamlet*.[2] Besson put Hamlet in opposition to the world of his father, an act that questioned whether a father had the right or the authority to shape his son according to his dictates or to ruin families and communities. Reference to a "socialist community" was obvious, even if not explicitly stated in the language of the play. Ideology and praxis increasingly contradicted each other. The "mission" had to be rejected, otherwise the whole community would go to rack and ruin. The overlapping framework for all of Besson's theatrical representations, in fact, are embedded in his critique of the overall patriarchal system. The way he put it to me in an interview was to say that he didn't have a bad relationship with his father. "That's not the problem," he continued. "I only think that 2,000 years of patriarchal domination are outdated now. This form of society is fundamentally exhausted and worn out. . . . It has to be criticized; there seems to be no other way possible."[3] When questioned further about the consequences of his thoughts on the relationship between language and the bodily communication of actors in his representations, Besson remarked, "The text is the top of the iceberg, . . . a concrete matter that is moving. . . . Emotions and thoughts face each other. The text is the concrete thing. Good theater doesn't express the objective matter but suggests it. Bodily communication tells a different story. It supplements the language."

How this is implemented in performance is suggested by Heide Kipp's understanding of how she played Ophelia in Besson's production. She reveals how the body of the actress can tell another story than do the words that come out of her mouth. Under Besson's direction, Ophelia/Kipp verbally carried out the order of her father, but her body communicated that she had been forced to do so. But Hamlet misunderstands Ophelia's body language. A brief excerpt from my conversation with Kipp illustrates how this was accomplished:

Naumann: How would you describe the relationship between Hamlet and Ophelia?

Kipp: I think Ophelia loves Hamlet, but she lets her father misuse her to spy on him. In a sense, she gives her love away. Hamlet loves Ophelia, too, but he puts his supposed mission above his private life.

Naumann: Think about the scene between Hamlet and Ophelia after his soliloquy "To be or not to be." Which story did the body of your Ophelia tell and which story did her language tell? Was there any tension between the two forms of expression?

Kipp: Yes. I played Ophelia as tripping along from the very beginning of the play. The dress helped me to do so. It was a gown which tied up my breasts and didn't allow me much freedom of movement. In one hand Ophelia held a book and in the other a box. In this gown, and with these things in her hands, it was very difficult for her to embrace Hamlet. She was tied in. Her body couldn't say much, so she had to use language alone to make herself understood. But this handicap tells us a lot about her distress. She knew that she was doing something wrong because she couldn't let her father misuse her to spy upon Hamlet if she loved him so much. But yet she did; she was following her father's directions. This contradiction expressed itself in the contradiction between bodily communication and the language of her play. Her bodily communication was hesitant, but her language was straightforward, clever and quick. The language fulfilled the orders of her father, but her body told a different story when she was forced to return Hamlet's gifts.

Naumann: Do you remember some images from the scene?

Kipp: Hamlet (Manfred Karge) recited the monologue "To be or not to be" while doing push-ups over a sword. Then he noticed Ophelia watching him a little way off. He called to her and she became frightened. She felt trapped: "How does your honour for this many a day?" She really wanted to know. She was not pretending. Hamlet, temporizing, gave his answer, in a reserved manner. She moved a step towards him: "My lord." Then she carried out her father's orders quick and sure. They faced each other. She unmistakably showed that she was fulfilling an order. Her bodily communication showed that she really did not want to return the gifts. He reacts curiously: "No, not I, I never gave you aught." She was astonished. She was almost screaming. She spoke to him in a tearful voice about their love, about their common pastimes. Hamlet only looked at her inquisitively. She was frustrated. She held the gift out to him, thinking: "I can go now. At last I got through it." But he didn't take it back.

Naumann: In her disappointment she switches from blank verse to prose: "There, My lord." After this Hamlet also speaks in prose: "Ha, ha, are you honest?"

Kipp: Yes. She was shocked. Without language she panicked. She was greatly confused because her expectations had not been fulfilled. But a moment later she had herself under control: "My lord!" She pronounced it very self-consciously. (How dare you!)

Naumann: Prose surely allows a more direct intercourse between the players than verse.

Kipp: Yes. Conventions were broken. Ophelia turned away and Hamlet followed her, tracking her with his speech. Ophelia continued to express uncertainty with her body and to simulate certainty with speech.

Naumann: In this way the connotative quality of the text took on a quality of vitality. Ophelia uses blank verse again at the end of the scene. Her education carries her through.

Kipp: She is sorry for Hamlet, only because his career is going to waste.

There is a detectable connection between Hamlet/Karge playing in the tradition of the medieval Vice, a character who subversively undermined dominant authority, and Ophelia, who unconsciously rejected patriarchal structures. This expressed itself in a break between the dramatic language and the bodily communication of Ophelia/Kipp. The experience of the individual and the social reality were in contradiction. Ophelia fulfilled the order of her father contrary to her own intuitive knowledge, and Hamlet did the same. The break with outdated social norms did not take place. Hamlet and Ophelia did not listen to their inner voices but let themselves be determined by others. Body and language became increasingly unsynchronized. The consequence was a split personality and an early death for both. "Hamlet is heritage, a heavy heritage, a bloody heritage, a heritage with great consequences," Besson remarked in conversation. He continued at some length:

> Customs that are, as Hamlet says, "more honour'd in the breach than the observance." What Shakespeare discovered—rottenness in the state of Denmark—continues to rot over the whole world. Phantoms of "great" soldiers appear again and again. The poison of self destruction of families and communities is creeping through the world. Mothers are silent about the fathers to their children. And again sons are changing girls into whores or nuns like their fathers had done some years before. If a girl doesn't want to become one or the other she goes crazy and one lets her affectionately be drowned. Hamlet wants to break this law. But he can't. The father has caught him again; the son breaks up. The break with the past doesn't take place. That's the tragedy.[4]

A society with private property and authority only in the hands of men is to be questioned. That is one message Besson gives us with his fascinating form of theater which shows us a close correlation between the bodily communication and language of the actors—in a psychologically precise studied relationship between the individual and social intercourse.

III

In 1980 two unique productions of *A Midsummer Night's Dream* in Berlin, both indebted to Peter Brook's 1970 production, became focal points of heated public discussion. In *The Empty Space* (1968), Brook describes the text as the end product (not the starting point) for activity "which begins as an impulse, stimulated by attitude and behavior, which dictates the need for expression." In Germany, this expression involved two different translations that were the basis for the scripts in each production. Alexander Lang at the Deutsches Theater used Eschenburg's translation, while Thomas Langhoff at the Maxim Gorki Theater used Schlegel's.

The different translations resulted in a shift in points of emphasis. Eschenburg alternates between blank verse and prose. As a consequence some possible performance gestures were lost. Eschenburg's translation is also more bitter and his blank verse more irregular than Shakespeare's. This allowed a performance style that opened the text up more to modern feeling. By comparison, Schlegel's translation harmonizes with the original. "I think this play is a difficult one," observes Alexander Lang. "The wintertime (discordance, compulsion) has to be overcome by people and their circumstances. The winter turns into summer (into harmony, into fruitfulness). I will try to transform *A Midsummer Night's Dream* into his basic model. I hope soon so that we are able to find a very fresh and impulsive performance style."[5] Lang's production was an unorthodox view of the play. The director and his team returned to pre-Elizabethan myths and traditions; by leaving behind conventional structures they discovered new possibilities to portray passion in a hard and realistic way.

Lang's production contained numerous images which suggested that true relationships between men and women were destined to be destroyed in a patriarchally structured world and that even nature was determined by these structures. For Lang the play was not a triumph of nature over civilization. "The forest doesn't liberate people," observed the director. "The *homo naturalis* is changed into a *homo christianus.* Natural power turns into civil channels. These civil channels with their order and silence make it possible to concentrate on fertility, so to say: prosperity by productivity."

Katja Paryla, who played Titania, gave an interesting answer to my question about the correlation between language and bodily communication in performing Shakespeare: "I try to deal with the text in a very direct manner. After all I don't want to sing the text. I try to find moments where I can insert breaks, strew sand into the text, so to speak. I have to find resistances. This is why I like Shakespeare—he changes the verse—you cannot find even one regular verse in Shakespeare's texts. That allows for a living relationship with the text—much more than what happens during rehearsals of Goethe's *Iphegenie.*" Titania describes the end of the world which she sees as a result of their foolish quarrel during her first dialogue with Oberon. Paryla associates this with modern dangers—pollution of the environment, the peril of nuclear weapons—and is thus able to combine her feelings and thoughts with the text of the play:

> . . . hast disturb'd our sport.
> Therefore the winds, piping to us in vain,
> As in revenge, have suck'd up from the sea
> Contagious fogs; which, falling in the land
> Have every pelting river made so proud
> That they have overborne their continents.
>
> (2.1.87–92)

The connotative quality of the language allowed Titania/Paryla and the other actors to combine contemporary experience with the historical text. The disconnected relationships between men and women, between humanity and nature, became visible with the help of a simple, yet beastly marriage row. When Titania/Paryla reproached Oberon for the consequences of their marital strife, she used the regal gestures of a queen to push back the borders of their private quarrel and to illuminate its public dimension and effect on the natural environment. Oberon only reacted as a man, that is, he went through the motions of agreeing with her only for the purpose of bringing her to heel. After Titania's humiliation he went to bed with her thinking all things were now well.

Titania/Paryla awoke already during Bottom's song. She took off the Marilyn Monroe–like wig (a symbol for a male-determined female standard) and submitted to her new feelings of passion. Oberon tried to ridicule her, but it backfired. Titania's ardent desire for love was so strong and honest that she was able to elevate the donkey to a higher level. Paryla had researched her part well and understood the importance of text and gesture; she expressed to me quite eloquently her understanding of the dramatic situation (in an interview, December 1987):

> During the research for the proper movement, I took Marilyn Monroe in *Some Like It Hot* as my starting point. In addition, the dramatic text provided impulses for other elements of bodily speech, and the rhythm of the verse for individual motions. Alexander Lang attached great importance to developing the bodily action in conjunction with the spoken text—never with the help of substitute texts. The actors rehearsed under his direction several variations of a scenic situation. So the concrete representation consisted of a rich empirical spectrum. A very important motion of my Titania was when she cast off her wig. Without the wig she was much more touchy—it was a chance for a new and honest way of dealing with herself.
>
> Another important point was that she took off her shoes with the high heels. During the dialogue with Oberon she was running around with them as if they were boots. But in the love scene with Bottom these shoes disturbed her—she stumbled now. Suddenly the heels of the shoes were as slender as they were in reality—a feeling like walking on glass. Bottom was afraid of her. He felt creepy all over. Nevertheless, he was very proud that Titania wooed him. The comedy of the situation was not that she was in love with a rowdy; it lay in his ignorance of the situation. Both of them spoke a different form of language: he spoke in prose, she in verse. The different individuals remained different, even though they loved each other. Titania fondled the donkey Bottom even when he was asleep. Puck and Oberon had to pull Titania away by force when both woke up. Oberon's calculation was a failure. Titania was not horrified to see that she had made love with a donkey. She really was in love with him. Her marriage with Oberon was not a very happy one. Oberon only wanted to govern her, but Titania was a woman who had enormous power. She didn't want to be governed. She had no chance to live a life of her own in a patriarchally structured world.

Paryla's performance and her method of work suggests that the connotative quality of Shakespeare's text serves as the impulse for scenic activity. Clearly a performance can take place in which old structures are supplied with modern life. The suppression of female alternatives also expresses the situation of a subject living in an authoritarian society which denies her alternatives to the existing social order. That was exactly the situation of

A Midsummer Night's Dream, **DIR. Lang, 1980. 3.1: Bottom (Körner) and Titania (Paryla), who has cast off Marilyn Monroe garb. Photo: Pepita Engel, courtesy of the Deutsches Theater.**

the individual in socialist society. Therefore the subversive intellectuals in East Berlin loved the performance since it expressed their very own feelings and thinking.

IV

Thomas Langhoff said his production of *Dream* at the Maxim Gorki Theater was not "a brutal play." "Of course," he continued, "it is bad the way the youngsters are forced together—besides Demetrius stays bewitched—but the play is about hope, about a deeply felt longing of humanity: to live and understand more and more about the phenomena of life."[6] The performance used the bodily activity of the actors as a motor in this process: impulses from the circus and musical or dance theater vitalized the play. In Shakespeare's text the women (and Puck) are the active characters who break the textual norms (by shifting from verse into prose, or even by changing the verse) much more than the male characters do. Women provoke a change in the situation, but in the end they are silenced. The dreamplay in the forest ends the activity of the women, and in the end they are integrated into the patriarchal system. The silence of the women during the

A *Midsummer Night's Dream*, DIR. T. Langhoff, 1980. 4.2: "Come, sit down upon this flowery bed." Photo: Wolfram Schmidt.

last scene in Langhoff's production showed how they had been integrated into the male world. They had lost their very own tongues.

Titania (Monika Lennartz) noticed the singing Bottom and suddenly fell in love with him. First she tried to fight this feeling, but in the end she could not resist. Titania used her followers to make Bottom ready for love. While he did whatever she wanted, he really was much more interested in eating than in Titania. She was frightened about having loved an animal when Oberon freed her from the magic spell. Now she was glad to go with Oberon who had attained his goal and tamed her. Langhoff was very conscious of what he was doing here: "Maybe my effort for women is an experiment to break into the world of men. Their authority is very old. They are tired and exhausted and are losing their ability to perceive love and happiness. Women suffer from this situation (often unconsciously). Women are the ones who are suppressed and handicapped by this situation. Yet this is also their strength. They are forced to have fresh ideas and a more staying power. Their problems and demands are the those of the future."

V

The representation of a dramatic subject on stage always consists of language *and* bodily communication. The speech-act is connected with signs of language but bodily communication is able to function without them. In German Shakespeare productions during the seventeenth and eighteenth centuries, there was a close connection between bodily communication and language. In the nineteenth century, however, a process began that repressed bodily communication for the benefit of the distinctive speech act. The reason for this phenomenon is found in the development of the bourgeoisie and its rationalization of human interrelationships. A necessary consequence of this process was a loss of sensuous theater signs—a loss of variety in bodily communication. Foucault describes this phenomenon as the domination of discipline over bodily expression: "The vital impulses of the human body were broken by perfect measures of drill and taming. They were forced into a habitual system and disciplined this way. The bodily disciplines . . . form the basis of modern practices of authority."[7]

The result was a disastrous consequence for representation of females on stage. The female subject was represented more and more only in relationship to male dominant authority. In this way the cultivation of speech on stage was an expression for a development of the male bourgeois subject until a crisis developed about the turn of the century. But the lamentable degeneracy of speech culture on the modern stage was not only a reciprocal act. Spoken discourse was submerged more and more under a cloud to manipulate the individual and thus lost its power of representing reality. Bodily communication came into the spotlight because it seemed to express the original enunciative power of the human subject and was less useful for expressing ideology than language was. The "speechlessness" of GDR theater representations in the eighties seemed to result from a suspicion of the medium of language as a means of expression. The asynchrony of bodily communication and language was discovered as a discursive activity to question the legitimacy of the ruling socialist authority.

I see in this crisis in the representation of the dramatic subject a reflection of the beginnings of a social upheaval that strives to give much more responsibility to the individual. The anticipation by some theater people (and not only them) in the GDR was realized in the fall of 1989 when we got rid of a system that had had its day. The overdue collapse of the socialist order in Eastern Europe changed the situation in all of Europe dramatically. Society can not afford to do without the alternative of female thinking. As a consequence these productions of *Hamlet* and *A Midsummer Night's Dream* remain of topical interest even today.

6

Shakespeare Redefined:
A Personal Retrospect

ROBERT WEIMANN

FIVE years after the collapse of *real existierender Sozialismus* is a short time to look back upon the reception of Shakespeare in East Germany. This is especially the case when that reception is viewed as a cultural practice in which profound intellectual and political contradictions of the time were intercepted, assimilated or displaced. Although, of course, insignificant in terms of the larger political issues of the cold war period, the criticism and theatrical production of Shakespeare in the former German Democratic Republic deserves to be revisited. Here, as perhaps nowhere else in the cultural landscape of East European Socialism, was a unique space for the reception and (re)production of potentially the greatest cultural text of modern Western civilization. Here was a site on which its appropriation constituted a self-challenging, conflicting point of intersection of highly diverse discourses implicating contradictory modes of authorization and representation.

In terms of official cultural politics the reception of Shakespeare was to provide a textbook case of cultural appropriation, serving to exemplify the strength of the links between the Renaissance past and its Marxist-Leninist reinvention in the present. In its institutionalized form, this space was consistently used with dedication as well as cunning for diverse aims and strategies that could either affirm, defy, or simply ignore the dominant discourse of official *Kulturpolitik.* What resulted was to a considerable extent unforeseen: a resilient, at least partially nonconformist paradigm of assimilation.

When a Western cultural authority of the first order encountered a firmly entrenched version of Soviet-endorsed Marxism-Leninism, there were bound to be protracted areas of friction and discontinuity that had to be renegotiated in regard to at least two further discourses: in reference to a German intellectual tradition associated with the names of Lessing, Herder, Schiller, Goethe, Heine, and Hegel and, at a later stage, in response to the rebellious energies of post-1968 theories such as poststructuralism, neo-Marxism, and feminism. The site of this encounter was Weimar, the institution was the Deutsche Shakespeare-Gesellschaft, and the occasion was its annual conference and theater festival. Sponsored and supported by the Ministry of Culture, the East German Shakespeare Society provided a platform which, even while designed to legitimize the regime, rendered singular homage to a West European cultural tradition. For almost thirty years a significant selection of the country's most debatable and most talked about Shakespeare productions were performed and/or discussed; there were public conferences, panel debates, student colloquia, and teacher conferences. According to a personal rough estimate, some 120 productions were shown, about 300 scholarly or critical papers were read, and more than 50 lectures and discussions were held. Each year between a thousand and fifteen hundred members and friends participated in the Weimar events. Over the years the format of the Shakespeare festival changed, but the support of the public never waned.

The paradox was that, although East German *Kulturpolitik* was centrally prescribed, it was possible to neutralize its more aggressive and dogmatic applications. Marx and Engels had loved Shakespeare; they knew whole scenes of his plays by heart. German drama from Lessing to Brecht was profoundly indebted to, and indeed unthinkable without Shakespeare. There was in the GDR, in reaction to the barbarous aberrations of the Nazi past, a sense of renewed indebtedness, as well as genuine commitment vis-à-vis this twofold heritage. This was not a purely academic stance; in the postwar period there was a shared desire to use and identify with a cultural past that was not discredited. At the same time, it was entirely possible to reappropriate the ideology and/or the idealism of these discourses, or, for a good many members and visitors in Weimar, simply to ignore them. In any case, personal motivation for attendance varied considerably. Some came for the theater productions, some for the conferences and lectures, some for socializing, while others came because they loved Weimar. After all, the *genius loci* offered an escape from humdrum economic production and all too familiar politics and a readily accessible niche for contact with Western culture and the English language.

The intellectual fare, the standards of the proceedings, and the quality of the performances cannot be described summarily; they varied greatly, from the dullest to the finest, from the most traditional artistically as well as critically to the experimental and avant-garde in later years. This was due in part at least to a wide range of international contributions: from Shakespeare productions from Russia, Armenia, England, and Japan to the intellectual debates promulgated by distinguished scholars and critics such as Stephen Greenblatt, Wolfgang Iser, Hans Robert Jauss, Murray Krieger, George Steiner, and German writers such as Heiner Müller and Volker Braun.

But although their contributions were warmly welcomed (in fact, they cannot be rated highly enough), the most noteworthy and, potentially, the most productive aspect of the Weimar Shakespeare festival lay elsewhere. It had, more than anything, to do with the attempt to approach the Shakespearean text as a performed event and, in doing so, to combine a sense of Renaissance sociocultural history with an awareness of the most pressing issues and contradictions of our own time, especially as these were informing our own cultural and theoretical practices.

Today the conjuncture of differing levels of historicity has widely come to be accepted as a matter of course in contemporary criticism. But what needs to be remembered is that the Weimar attempt to work out a conjunctural sense of history in our approach to Shakespeare's plays for a good many years preceded both the advent of poststructuralism and the recent reorientation in Anglo-American versions of historicism. And although the East German attempt was beset with contradictions and inconsistencies (easily recognizable in the light of subsequent experience and theory), yet even today both its characteristic points of departure and its latter-day mutations appear far from despicable. On the contrary, the question may be asked to what extent it is possible to speak of an achievement of a sort, both in what was said and done and in what was not said and done under the circumstances.

Since there was no unified position among those who thought, debated, and wrote about Shakespeare in Weimar, the history of Shakespeare's reception in the former German Democratic Republic should ideally be written from variegated points of view. Although there are, on the part of West German Scholars, one well-documented book-length study and at least one incisive survey of the reception of one particular play,[1] East German scholars and critics, with few exceptions, have been slow to meet the challenge. Nor should this be surprising; for while it was possible in the old days to present at least the show of a unified perspective, latent differences and contradictions have now, since the unification of the country, become more obvious and, no doubt, troublesome. This is why, from an insider's point of view, it seems prohibitive to aim at anything like a comprehensive or, even, a representative perspective. As other essays in this volume suggest, there were differing personal perspectives by a variety of scholars, critics, and theater people directly involved in Shakespeare study and performance in the GDR.[2] Thus, a personal perspective that surrenders the collective plural to the first person pronoun is called for. In this context it seems impossible not to fall back on my own contributions, especially as these actually cover a time span from the earliest reinauguration conference in 1964 to the last independent public statement made on behalf of the Deutsche Shakespeare-Gesellschaft, Weimar, hours before the act of unification with the Deutsche Shakespeare-Gesellschaft West, Bochum.[3]

Positive Heritage vs. Conjunctural Appropriation

This is not the place to document the early history of East German Shakespeare studies and productions, but in order to realize the extent to which they positively and deliberately identified with the dominant *Kulturpolitik*, a few points of reference are needed. The 1964 reinauguration ceremony celebrating the resumption of Shakespeare Society activities, coinciding as it did with the quatercentenary, was marked by an official high-ranking government pronouncement. In his *Festvortrag* Alexander Abusch, deputy chairman of the Council of Ministers, proposed that the appropriation of Shakespeare in the GDR was part of, and helped to consummate, a tradition reaching back to eighteenth-century German receptions of Shakespeare that anticipated the heritage of humanism and realism in present socialist culture. Shakespeare's abiding greatness, it was thought, derived from a view of man which transcended the boundaries of class society and actually helped affirm and define "socialist humanism."[4]

From the more practical vantage point of the contemporary producer and director of Shakespeare's plays this appeared to involve an interpretation projected into the temporal distance between then and now, as this distance constituted a progressively meaningful space for both affirmation and anticipation. In other words, there was encouragement as well as pressure to use historical distance teleologically as a master key of fruition by which the seeds of social revolution in the Elizabethan transition from feudalism to early modern (bourgeois) society helped to prepare for and to legitimate the ultimate process of liberation and emancipation through Socialism. In the light of such ideological underpinnings, cultural workers in the theater were expected to read and direct a Shakespearean tragic hero such as Hamlet as the embodiment of the truly utopian socialist-humanist conscience.[5] Among other things, this amounted to a qualified reconfirmation of the Romantic reading of Shakespeare's hero as a "noble soul," which was designed to foreground common ground between sixteenth- and twentieth-century versions of a revolutionary image of man. As some kind of intermediate space between then and now, late-eighteenth- and early-nineteenth-century readings with their prestige (particularly viable at Weimar) were marshalled to help authorize whatever social fulfillment appeared to be promised in the present. But while the arrogance behind this claim might have been considered as little more than preposterous by academic communities in countries such as Poland or Czechoslovakia, this was not so in the East German context. There it was possible as late as 1984 for Anselm Schlösser, influential Nestor of East German Shakespeare studies and editor of the *Jahrbuch* from 1964 to 1983, to attack the "revisionist jungle of pluralistic arbitrariness of interpretation" and to call for a "guiding compass," based on a "working class standpoint," presumably to safeguard what

Schlösser elsewhere referred to as "the concept of a positive heritage" (*positives Erbe*).[6]

The point here is not to ridicule the simplicity in what was an officially endorsed concept of tradition, but to look at its more complex presuppositions with a view to tracing, out of the controversial nature of such responses, the space for a peculiar canonization of the uses of Shakespeare's text. For although the language which Mäde and Schlösser employed may today be discredited, they had in mind a concept of tradition which cannot be reduced to an opportunistic rehearsal of party politics. Rather, what the idea of "a positive heritage" stood for was the elimination of (un)necessary friction and the obliteration of any (un)bridgeable rupture between Renaissance values and Marxist-Leninist evaluations. Seeking to emphasize areas of identity, or at least of concurrence between now and then, these positions attempted, without ever saying so, to construct tradition as a principle of both orientation and control. This, as a matter of fact, was not so far removed from T. S. Eliot's sense of tradition which, in an altogether different political connection, had disparaged, if not "pluralistic arbitrariness," at least the liberal principle or, rather, "whiggery" as the unprincipled promptings of "the Inner Voice"—what Eliot conveniently referred to as "doing as one likes."[7] For these critics and theater directors, the party provided what T. S. Eliot had recommended for the writer as "the existence of an unquestioned spiritual authority outside himself, to which he has attempted to *conform.*"[8]

If this appears as too generous a comparison (it may sound less so when we substitute "ideological" for "spiritual"), it does help to explain the surprising extent to which it was accepted. Under these circumstances, for an East German academic to reject the concomitant notion of "tradition" as "an idea of order" would have been near to impossible, especially when the distance between then and now, between Renaissance culture and its contemporary cultural uses, was at least partially bridged by the splendid mediations of Lessing, Herder, Goethe, Heine, and the Schlegels. There was no doubt that, after the Nazi years of horror and pathos, these names could easily be used to privilege a sense of enlightenment, order (and control) in the reception of the classics involving both idealization and obliteration.

It is of course true that, with the possible exception of Heine, these German writers and poets could not be made to authorize a principle of historical progress that culminated in the master code of a struggle for emancipation that finally reached the working class. As Renaissance ideas of "harmony" were foregrounded through socialist idealizations (as anticipations of a classless society), their remoteness from the ordinary realities of life in East Germany became over the years more and more crippling. At this point, theater people (a director like Adolf Dresen and a translator and dramaturg like Maik Hamburger) took the lead in questioning the cultural

uses of such a heritage.[9] The Greifswald *Hamlet* (1964) refused to acknowledge unambiguous areas of identity between Renaissance ideas and contemporary "ideals" and, instead, disputed continuity between then and now.
Shockingly, the Prince of Denmark in this production appeared to undermine the ideological construct of a premature tragic humanism that anticipated a future space for harmony in the relationship between society and
the individual conscience.

It was more than coincidence when, at about the same time, Shakespeare
criticism and scholarship began to probe into current assumptions of both
continuity and historicity in theatrical as well as critical interpretations.
What, on a theoretical plane, appeared as an urgent desideratum was first
of all to confront the tension (and make distinctions) between the two levels
of historicity associated with sixteenth-century productions and twentieth-
century receptions of the Shakespearean text. In order to point at both the
gaps and the links between the two, I proposed a terminology which attempted to distinguish between "past significance and present meaning."[10]
The idea was to define historicity in the uses of the Shakespearean text
more closely and, if possible, conjuncturally, so that textual criticism became quite indistinguishable from the critical sense of the historian. To be
sure, such definition of the object of the Shakespearean scholar as critic
was, at the time, proposed within the traditional demarcations of Shakespeare studies and could not hope to address what in today's critical language would be notions of theatrical text as part of a given discursive
practice. Even so, the attempt was to cope with and make relative the notion
of continuity (teleological or otherwise) between now and then without
allowing for any diametrically opposed concept of radical discontinuity
or rupture.

Accordingly, if the object of the Shakespearean critic as historian was
neither the four-hundred-year-old text in the hands of Elizabethan actors
nor the late-twentieth-century context of its contemporary reception and
interpretation, it seemed necessary to sound the gaps as well as the links
between now and then. Neither the postulates of *Kulturpolitik* (emphasizing
"present meaning" and function) nor the standards of positivistic scholarship (emphasizing "past significance" and genesis) appeared acceptable.
On the contrary, the space for both concurrence and contradiction called
for a more complex notion of (dis)continuity between the past world of the
Shakespearean text and the present world of its reception. Once it seemed
possible to show that the pastness of the text and its theatrical context
cannot and must not be separated from Shakespeare as an experience in
the present, the task of the historian needed to be contained in the work
of the critic, and vice versa. It was not possible to isolate these two necessary aspects: merely to talk about the pastness of the text would lead into
some kind of antiquarianism while merely to regard Shakespeare as our

contemporary would prove equally unacceptable because it failed to address the conjunctural purpose of historical criticism (or theater production) as something both vitally alive in, and distant from, the present. Thus,
the very notion of (dis)continuity between then and now (although not then
spelled out in this more recent language) was one way to respond to, even
perhaps to contain, cruder notions of critical teleology. It is true that these
methodological counterproposals as developed in the late sixties and early
seventies continued to entertain a good many illusions about dialectic concepts of contingency and validity in the "historical process." But the idea
was to bring together a more complex view of this process by correlating
the text as a product of the past and the text as constituting insight into
and experience of the present. To stress the interrelationships of these
two dimensions of Shakespearean drama was to argue for more than just
expediency in the sense that an awareness of history might prevent us
from crude anachronisms in interpretation. The point was that these two
dimensions appeared inherent in the uses of the classical text itself, once
historicity was situated on the levels of both representation and reception,
between the mimesis in, and the function of, the text itself.

In order to distinguish between these two basic dimensions of Shakespearean drama further, it seemed to me to be possible (although the over-
simplification was obvious) to suggest that the Shakespearean (or any other
effective cultural) text must be conceived as not merely a product of the
past but also as a "producer" of the future. In other words, the cultural text
was seen as rooted in a capacity for "production" that can transcend the
very time and age that are the object of the mimesis. Hence, the "mimetic"
and the actualizing functions necessarily interact: the literary historian as
critic approaches an object in which *Zeitlichkeit* and *Überzeitlichkeit*, discontinuity and continuity, can be made to relate to and even to interrogate
one another.[11]

Thus, the suggestion was that in our approach to Shakespeare two cate-
gorically distinct locations of discourse, each articulating diverse temporal
interests, would collide with or react upon one another. But the resulting
contradiction was not an academic one; for the more one thought of it in
terms of the practical interpretation of Shakespeare on the modern stage,
the clearer the theoretical implications emerged. It is just as impossible to
think of Shakespeare in the theater without an interpretation as it is to have
an interpretation without Shakespeare's text. We can proceed from neither
a genuine Elizabethan production (which in itself implies an interpretation
of the text) nor from one that makes us believe that, say, *Hamlet* is a modern
(or a socialist) play. Therefore, any Shakespeare interpretation has to come
to terms with the tension between historically used signs and a later code
of their appropriation and resignification. But to be aware of this contradiction is not necessarily frustrating; for the manner in which this contradiction

is resolved constitutes the most far-reaching decisions for both historical criticism and serious theatrical interpretation.

Therefore, once it was established that such conjunctural reading would involve mutual interrogations, and even contestations, of radically different discourses, there was little room left for concepts of reception which sought to reaffirm classical notions of harmony, continuity, and closure. For both the literary critic and the theater director, the question was not whether to accept both discourses in their different worlds as points of reference, but rather how to relate them in order to obtain their maximum interaction. To put it like this may appear provocatively superficial, but to confront the contradiction one cannot minimize the conflicting elements when each is— in its different world—so inevitable and necessary. The "maximum interaction," then, could mean no more and no less than this: to transmute as much of the historical inscription and as much of the contemporary reading as possible into a new and mutually engaging articulation.

This emphasis on gaps as well as links proved stimulating at the time for both critical and theatrical interpretations of the Shakespearean text. Remarkably, such theoretical emphasis on (dis)continuity between then and now appeared in a good many productions of Shakespeare, at least well into the seventies. However, from a certain point onwards, theater practice began to challenge and upset the relative balance between the historicity of the Shakespearean text and the awareness of directions in its contemporary interpretation. Theater people began to respond to changes in the mood of their audiences, and areas of concurrence between "past significance" and "present meaning" shrank rather than expanded.

This process, however, was gradual, as indicated by Manfred Wekwerth's *Richard III* (at the Deutsches Theater, 1972), and Benno Besson's *Hamlet* (at the East Berlin Volksbühne, 1977). As opposed to the recent advent of a new generation of East German directors, such as Frank Castorf and Leander Haussmann,[12] the Wekwerth and Besson productions continued to project a sense that what was most modern (and experimental) in their readings of Shakespeare had a correlative to be explored inside the language and structure of the Shakespearean text. Wekwerth foregrounded the element of grotesque showmanship and farcical evil in Richard Gloucester, treating him as a descendent of the morality Vice, whereas Besson privileged the actors against the Danish Prince who was depicted as a half naked subversive force (physically as well as intellectually) defying major conventions of representation, closure, and decorum.

To a certain extent, both of these prominent and influential productions (for which I was privileged to serve as consultant) appeared to confirm a conjunctural approach to the plays in which bifold locations of authority and historicity appeared to be mutually stimulating. True enough, there was no minimizing the ever-larger area of discrepancy between Shakespeare's world and ours, but, as Arnold Kettle had noted, "The best way to emphasize the value of Shakespeare in our changing world is to see him in his, recognizing that the two worlds, though very different, are at the same time a unity."[13] This "unity," I then suggested, created the need for our interpretations of *Shakespeare;* the contradiction accounted for the need for our *interpretations* of Shakespeare. But in fact each was contained in the other, and the interpretation as a whole would only succeed when these two aspects were inextricably brought together.

As can easily be perceived today, such talk of the "unity" between then and now presupposed a belief in what Jürgen Habermas has called the *unvollendete* ("unfinished"/"unconsummated") "project of modernity."[14] There was as yet no sense of the modern period as having exhausted a measure of controlled balance and proportion in its project of expansion and appropriation. On the contrary, the conditions of possibility under which Shakespeare's language could be read side by side with Bacon's philosophical discourse appeared to be confirmed despite a growing awareness of its premodern components. This project, surely, was not a mean one when it presented us with a conceptual framework that allowed for representing the past neither in its identity with, nor in its isolation from, the present. If this continued to entertain an innocent concept of what, conjuncturally, was meaningful, such "meaning" precluded its location in either the shallow waters of topical propaganda or in the erudite memory of the museum. "Meaning" in Shakespeare, or so I thought, could best be discovered through this past present, or that part of it which—although past—is still present and consequently understood within a contemporary frame of reference. Theoretically, a conjunctural relationship was projected by which the temporal and the functional difference between two discourses constituted a space for mutual interrogation that could illuminate the past text as against its present reception as well as its contemporary reading against the historicity of its making.

A Heritage Redefined: Popular Voice in Renaissance Discourse

While some such theoretical groundwork for the reception of Shakespeare in East Germany was done in the sixties and early seventies, it seemed to be possible, as I suggested in *Shakespeare and the Popular Tradition in the Theater* (1967), for a premodern, precapitalist culture profoundly to enrich and be mingled with a late English version of Renaissance humanism. At this point, the emphasis on a (transitional) balance of sociopolitical forces in Elizabethan England was, at least by implication, in response to a rigid dogmatism in accordance with which class consciousness was emphatically defined as the consciousness of one particular class (as opposed to an ensemble of class relationships). Along these lines, prominent Marxist historians had tended to identify the Elizabethan Renaissance with the culture of one class alone (for Jürgen Kuczynski, for example, it was that of the bourgeoisie, while for Christopher Hill elements of a late feudal and courtly society appeared to be dominant).[15] Although my early emphasis on the "mingle-mangle" or "hodge-podge" quality of sixteenth-century English culture was designed to serve as an antidote to a more doctrinaire reading of class hegemony,[16] there were, as the years went by, a growing number of problems with this emphasis. In the given context of the German Shakespeare Society at Weimar, this approach, even while resisting dogmatism, tended to minimize social, cultural, and linguistic tensions actually inscribed in Elizabethan cultural practices. It may well be that on this basis it was impossible, at least very difficult, effectively to address the precariousness of the level on which contemporary productions of Shakespeare (notably those of Fritz Bennewitz, in the Weimar Nationaltheater) aimed at visions of social harmony and illusions of cultural perfectibility. Whatever innocence and/or complicity were involved in these productions (entangled no doubt with hopes for a socialist conscience with "a human face"), they could not be critically challenged as long as Shakespeare's reception in East Germany was dominated by modifications (along the lines of *Kulturpolitik*) of the classical-romantic paradigm. These modifications were marked by a naturalization and idealization of the Shakespearean text that, through the mediation of Enlightenment poetics, was translated into the cultural politics of a threefold demand for humanism, realism, and *Volkstümlichkeit* (in the sense of an association with the cause and the culture of the people).

In the circumstances, these positions, championed as they were in all spheres of cultural and artistic activity, constituted a rigidly circumscribed context in which classical German poetics was effectively combined with a late-nineteenth-century Russian and later Soviet cultural platform. In particular, the concept of *Volkstümlichkeit* was directly indebted to the Russian convention of *narodnosti*, originally a nineteenth-century term invoked by prerevolutionary intellectuals seeking to serve the people. But this highly undifferentiated category was, as in the Soviet criticism of Lev Tolstoy or Ivan Turgenev, indissolubly linked with an unsophisticated notion of "realism" that combined the epistemology of "reflection" ("art reflecting reality") with formal criteria of lifelike representations that privileged a poetics of empathy and naturalization.

At the time, Soviet Shakespeare criticism did not seem to have too many difficulties applying these concepts to Shakespearean drama. But in Germany, thanks to Brecht and Expressionist drama, the reception of his plays in the theater had long since discarded the traditional practice of pathos-loaded lifelike stylization. On almost every level such a platform appeared to preclude a viable awareness of contemporaneity by which contemporary criticism could honestly and unconstrainedly confront a modern sensibility in the theater.

This gap between the dogma of cultural politics and the pursuit of critical intellectuals was especially frustrating when a concept of popular culture came to be identified with a nineteenth-century notion of "realism." But the obvious area of incongruity could prove at least negatively stimulating as soon as the traces of popular culture began to be studied more closely in the context of the Elizabethan theater. In this context, it was easy to perceive the limits of both representational standards as, broadly, *imitatio vitae*, and the concomitant modern preoccupation with a theater of illusion and verisimilitude. Both positions were incompatible with Shakespeare's own reception of a potentially subversive popular culture that privileged nonrepresentational forms of clowning, "madness," disguise, and topsy-turvydom. In the circumstances to foreground the latter appeared to be a desideratum of the first order, especially when it seemed to me to be possible to do so without altogether minimizing the links between anthropology and history, between archaic form and its early modern appropriation through a social awareness of its cultural uses. Thus, in my *Shakespeare and the Popular Tradition* the idea was to study the process of assimilation and appropriation by which premodern uses of popular discourse and custom came to be adapted to the early modern "mingle-mangle" culture of the English Renaissance.

Again, theater people were the first to perceive that this was *Volkstümlichkeit* with a difference. Such redefinition of the popular tradition was, of course, deeply indebted to Anglo-American scholars like C. R. Baskerville, S. L. Bethell, C. L. Barber, and others. In the event it effectively helped unhinge the neoclassical and Romantic prefiguration (and predetermination) of the reception of Shakespeare in East Germany. The emerging gulf between Enlightenment or Romantic appropriations of Shakespeare and the historicizing approach through sixteenth-century uses of popular culture henceforth helped to redefine the reception of the classic as a cultural practice potentially divisive rather than univocal. As opposed to the representative invocation of a progressive canon (administered as part of a pragmatic master key rather than as a Marxist approach to cultural history), there was, to say the least, an immense complication in the coordinates of cultural history running counter to the overwhelming concern with the establishment of continuity between the classic text in its time and our uses of it in ours.

This redefinition of a usable tradition coincided with significant changes and experiments in the East German theater. Whereas the irreverent voices in Dresen's and Hamburger's 1964 *Hamlet* were easily muted, the theater in the seventies unabashedly set out to address contradictions in the current ideological language of harmony and closure. In particular, Benno Besson's

Hamlet (1977) presented a deep rift between neoclassical order in the humanist poetics of the Prince of Denmark and the sheer expertise, competence, and experience of the players. Rather than neutralizing these tensions in the language of the play, his production surrendered any univocal assertion of meaning in favor of a more complex projection of a divided space for sociocultural tension and conflict.

Besson's production, which was performed and discussed in Weimar,[17] provided a welcome piece of unorthodoxy. Challenging the neoclassical-Romantic appropriation of Shakespeare's text as an adequate contemporary reading, Besson redefined the role of the Prince as that of a "muddy-mettled rascal," a "John-a-dreams," who deliberately could refer to himself as "a rogue and peasant slave." The idea was not to obliterate the popular tradition but to redefine it as opposed to the dominant assumption that it was linear and univocal. Besson—the most talented and internationally influential of Brecht's disciples—contributed a striking rereading of Hamlet's advice to the players. Challenging the authority of the Renaissance Prince, the First Player, slightly bored by mere theory, appeared to know more about mimesis than any disquisition could teach him. Here we had the humanist as an all-too-obtrusive Maecenas providing learned citations; his mere verbiage was to bolster up the courtier's, soldier's, scholar's image threatened by madness and "ecstasy." The production had a sensational impact in the East German cultural scene. Hamlet, the presumed representative of both humanism and the people, was effectively (and without much fuss) dislodged from his former preeminence as premature harbinger of a revolutionary or utopian future.

Here, indeed, a tradition was questioned in terms of both what (as Shakespeare's text) was represented and what (in the contemporary theater) was doing the representing and performing. If the basic presuppositions of authority and validity, governing selection and control over a given canon, had ceased to be operative, then how does one redefine a "living heritage"? From now on, it seemed possible to think about using works of the past as beyond both the function of a metaphysical construct (as, in T. S. Eliot's phrase, some "ideal order") and the politics of canonization through which the alleged certainties of a masterful past were designed to cope with and to contain whatever uncertainty the future held.

The question, then, needed to be confronted whether "tradition" per se was usable. Was it at all possible to make some more stringently historical counterproposal according to which "tradition" would not have to be regarded as an illusory project by which some ideological consciousness (or reason, in its presumed autonomy) hoped to extend its sense of sovereignty and continuity to the events and figures of the past? In other words, could "tradition" be reconstructed, not as some version of the void on which the false plenitude of history was grafted, but in a discursive space in which the issue of textual origins was suspended in a series of cultural and textual encounters, in a process of both incessant appropriation and forgetfulness?

Poststructuralism in Weimar

As this language seeks to suggest, the more recent history of Shakespeare reception in East Germany is unthinkable without a growing awareness of poststructuralism in theory and postmodernism in culture. In the early eighties, the new paradigm, looming ever larger in Western theory and criticism, could no longer be ignored in the humanities in East Germany.[18] From the point of view of the proceedings of the German Shakespeare Society, it was difficult to think of a more forcefully challenging body of discourses than the emerging alliance, as yet scarcely differentiated, between poststructuralism, neo-Marxism, and feminism. For those who were prepared to look (and refused to follow Professor Erich Hahn, chairman of the council of GDR philosophers, in his call for putting the whole postmodernism issue on the index of the Central Committee) the challenge was formidable: it comprised basic issues of epistemology, historiography, and semiology and was unsettling especially to those positions that had gone into the orthodox uses of Shakespeare as "heritage." Not only was preferential reference to any exemplary kind of past culture (whether or not described as "heritage") put into question; henceforth the ground was prepared for what another world citizen of Weimar, Friedrich Nietzsche, had conceived as the combined uses of both memory and forgetfulness. Together, they would serve as constituents of something larger (and more problematic) than canonicity. In this connection, the concept of "repression" itself was a reminder of what Gayatri Spivak in her preface to Jacques Derrida's *Of Grammatology* called "the complexity of the act of choosing forgetfulness."[19] Thus, the *oubliance* of the critic and/or the institution would have to be acknowledged as part of an active faculty relating to the not so innocent play of knowledge and ignorance in the process of cultural appropriation itself.

At the same time, certain uses of "forgetfulness" in Weimar, so close to the horrors of Buchenwald, had an unacceptable ring. And there were other circumstances that stood in the way of an uncritical acceptance of the new paradigm, including that central part of it commonly referred to as deconstructionist. Even so, the forceful urgency of poststructuralist theory was such that elementary notions of representation and subjectivity had to be renegotiated. The ensuing discussions were contradictory and often enough unsatisfying; but for all that their direction cannot very well be understood simply in terms of an "impact" (or "influence") of the critical upheaval in Western Europe and North America. What appears no less noteworthy is the extent to which, simultaneously, the East German encounter with postmodernism in the theater and poststructuralism in critical theory was in response to indigenous needs and problems. True enough, these needs in their turn were linked to political, cultural, and technological changes on an international plane. In the circumstances, it seems fair to say that the new paradigm (here comprising new historicism and cultural materialism) immensely helped to stimulate ways and means by which the full extent of a precariously concealed indigenous crisis could be exposed and grappled with.

To illustrate these developments, it seems best in conclusion to recall at least some of the annual Weimar proceedings, especially as these gradually came to take up the postmodernist challenge. Perhaps the 1982 conference with its theme, "Theatrical Practice and Shakespeare Scholarship," was the first to suggest the beginnings of a new kind of orientation. Again, theater people were in the forefront of political and cultural change. The main attraction of these "Shakespeare Days" (as they used to be called) was a performance of Alexander Lang's radically experimental, in many ways postmodern production of *A Midsummer Night's Dream*. As its dramaturg, Alexander Weigel, seemed to imply in his conference paper, this show had to be viewed in conjunction with important cultural "changes in the relations of directing and acting." To all intents and purposes, performers had brought a "new, more sovereign and active approach to rehearsals," in connection with which the production could not be "considered as the realization of a [preconceived] concept." Signaling the sense of a "crisis" in the traditional *Regietheater,* Weigel projected the theatrical process itself as the source of ultimate authority—which authority culminated in "what was unexpected, what was not preconceived"[20] in performance.

While on this occasion literary critics and cultural historians were slow to take up this important point of departure, there was, by implication, a more adequate response to these unresolved problems when, in 1986, the theme of the conference was "Shakespeare: History and Utopia," or when, a year later, the recent upheaval in the humanities was directly faced. Although, again, in 1987 the usual run of four or five theater productions was shown and discussed, the conference, whose theme was "Gender, Power, and Humanity [*Humanität*]," remained at the center of attention. Here was a somewhat delayed occasion for the oldest literary society in Europe to come to terms with feminist criticism of Shakespeare in a context marked by the need for redefining the relations of power and discourse. This agenda, especially as it absorbed the poststructuralist and new historicist concern with relations of language and power, was, to that date, unheard of in the German Democratic Republic. It was one thing to propose to discuss epistemological questions such as might pertain to dramatic representation; it was quite another thing to open up a public platform in Weimar for such highly controversial issues as Western feminism and (non)Marxist theories and politics of power. It is true that public access to the proceedings was to a certain extent limited: the conference was bilingual and part of the discussion was in English. But even that was a *novum,* even perhaps an achievement of a sort, one that was sure to be frowned upon by doctrinaire participants. Although the whole undertaking remained a precarious one to the last moment, circumstances were fortunate for us. Among panelists and speakers we were privileged to have some of the most distinguished names in contemporary international Shakespeare studies;[21] we had the support of at least one courageous and far-sighted representative of the Ministry of Culture;[22] and, of course, we had in our project the emphatic association with Shakespeare in whose sheltered space ideological postulates could at least partially be neutralized.

However, it would be wrong to overemphasize the cunning and cooperation that, under these circumstances, were necessary to make these and similar occasions possible. The irony was that the borderline between nonconformity and "complicity" could not be sharply demarcated; and, what is more, the resulting ambivalence was certainly not of an opportunistic order. On the one hand, there was no impenetrable barrier between new historicism/cultural materialism and the less dogmatic versions of an indigenous historical materialism: the area of potential assimilation, even mutual give and take, was not inconsiderable. On the other hand, disagreements were not slurred over. For instance, the concept of *Humanität* was used in reference to the notion, exemplified in Marx's *Grundrisse,* that standards and premises of humanism cannot be abstracted from material and intellectual appropriations of the world, especially those processed through socializing forms of physical or mental labor. This position, far from being a concession to anyone, was not a departure at all from what by and large innumerable discussions in the GDR had established. Further, to develop this position served to vindicate cultural agency and event as against their textualization or fictionalization. In this respect, East German participants in the debate, like Hanna Behrend, Friederike Hajek, Brunhild de la Motte, Sabine Nathan, Ursula Püschel, Thomas Sorge, Günter Walch, and myself, did not have to go out of their way to chart common ground with feminist criticism of Shakespeare, wherever this criticism itself affirmed the need, as Lisa Jardine phrased it, "to retrieve agency for the female subject in history."[23]

Still, while important positions in the feminist project could be assimilated without too much difficulty, the question of power, especially when dissociated from gender struggle, was a more highly sensitive issue in Weimar. At least part of the reason for that was a specifically national one. After the disastrous defeat in 1933 of what arguably was the strongest European working-class movement, the German Communist Party had pursued a popular front type of policy canvassing, in particular, artists and intellectuals who would be prepared to join an antifascist alliance as fellow travelers against Hitler. Among the vanguard of distinguished names like Brecht, Becher, Seghers, Feuchtwanger, Heartfield, Piscator, Eisler, Dessau, and others, it was Heinrich Mann who, at the Paris congress of antifascist writers (1935), had formulated the need for a close bond, even "unity" (*Einheit*), between *Macht* and *Geist*, power and intellect. After 1945, when many of these exiled artists and intellectuals decided to return to the eastern part of Germany, this "unity" was reaffirmed as part of a policy of alliance and cooperation.

However, as the years went by, there developed the perception of an increasing gap between the declared principles of this policy and the actual relations of *pouvoir* and *savoir* in the country. The contradiction came to a head when, upon the forced exile of dissident poet and singer Wolf Biermann (1976), a leading group of writers, including Christa Wolf and Heiner Müller, submitted a petition to the Politbureau protesting the measure. The subsequent series of severe reprisals on those who had signed the petition tended to shatter what cautious hopes had been nourished by Erich Honecker's policy of "no taboo" in the arts. As Franz Fühmann said in an interview in 1978, writers now were thrown back upon themselves and forced "to think again about questions such as the relations of literature and power."[24]

In the circumstances, it seemed impossible to ignore the need for looking into the crisis-ridden relations of discourse and power more closely and to do so in a broadly historical perspective. No doubt there was a prehistory to these troublesome relations first culminating in early modern social, religious, and technological constellations through which a sixteenth-century crisis of authority emerged in Western and central Europe. In this period, unprecedented proliferations of discursive practices were connected with inevitable divisions between *auctoritas* and *potestas;* it was a situation when certain language uses could for the first time be considered as in opposition to or "tongue-tied by authority." Shakespeare's interest in the issue of authority could easily be established:[25] he used the term about sixty times in his writings. But was there not, in the sixteenth century, a wider context in which a passionate concern with and challenge of authority was, as it were, institutionalized? The answer was the European Reformation in which a powerfully held authority was questioned on behalf of a different type of authority which largely drew on discursive practices such as the reading, interpreting, and translation of Scripture. The Luther anniversary in Weimar (1983) was a fitting occasion for me to trace the resulting crisis of authority, one that culminated in a conflict between the dominant signs of authority (as ecclesiastical and imperial *potestas*) and that newly potent authority (*auctoritas*) in the uses of signs.[26]

From here, it was only one step further to explore conflicting uses of authority in sixteenth-century England where, in a crucial midcentury situation, the issue emerged in its full ramifications. The conservative Bishop Gardiner attacked "Certain printers, players, and preachers" for behaving "as though we know not yet how to be justified" and for seeking "to slip the anchor-hold of authority, and come to a loose disputation."[27] Shakespeare, being of course himself a player and presumably in touch with printers, was confronted with, and involved in, some such groundswell of change and crisis in the locations of authority. As the Elizabethan gaps between the fixed exercise of power and the "loose" authorization of written and spoken language grew wider, a new paradigm of authority began to loom on the horizon of modern culture. No longer available through given locations of power and meaning, authority now constituted itself not so much in a prediscursive situation or at the beginning of discourse (where given sources used to be cited as valid) but rather in the production and perception of meaning, truth, conviction, and belief as process.

In Shakespeare's time, then, important constellations in early modern culture and politics appeared to constitute a bifold court of appeal juxtaposing (as my 1987 essay phrased it) "the authority of signs versus the signs of authority."[28] The Elizabethan theater was remarkably well equipped to assimilate this division in authority to its own specific mode of representation. The platform stage harbored the traditional difference between, on the one hand, the verisimilitude of the *locus* as a closed site of representation and, on the other hand, a *platea*-like opening for what Joseph Hall called the performer's "self-resembled show." Hence, there was no unitary concept of theatrical space that by itself would have compelled a unifying mode in coming to terms with either textualized or performative locations of authority.

Under these conditions, the Elizabethan stage in its *platea*-like dimension could privilege the authority of what and who was performing; at the same time, the symbolizing and localizing potential of this same stage could foreground the authority of what and who was represented. The difference between performance and text is not, of course, identical with this (here very much oversimplified) division in the uses of theatrical space. Even so, the swift, socially and semiotically charged interplay between performance-oriented actor and text-oriented role is crucially important. This interplay inspires the interaction between existential and playful parameters of theatricality, the mutual engagements between them, as these are institutionalized in the cultural occasion called theater.

But was this "bifold authority" (*Troilus and Cressida*, 5.2.147) in Shakespeare's theater anywhere consistently contiguous with the early modern dissociation between signs of authority and the authority of signs? This question, rich in political implications for the East German reception of the bard, did not permit either a yes or a no. Enough is said here when I say that the antagonism between external power and intellectual authority, although on the Elizabethan horizon, was fully to be developed by the continental Enlightenment where it became a cogent source of the perception of the sovereignty of self-authorizing cultural practices. In Weimar in the eighties, it was tempting to resurrect this scenario if only to reassure one's own response to the deepening legitimation gap in the dominant language of ideology. But it was one thing to be tempted, in Habermas' phrase, by a *herrschaftsfreier Raum*, an unconstrained site of independent communicative practices; it was quite another matter to subscribe to the binary scenario of an opposition between material and intellectual locations of authority.

When I decided strictly to qualify rather than to reconfirm this scenario, the reason was both theoretical and political. Theoretically, my project was such that it sought to reassociate the issue of authority with the early modern stimuli and technologies of authorship as well as with the conditions of authorization. In this direction, I had become wary of an uncontaminated flow of *Geist*. More recently, any concept of the self-sufficiency of knowledge and meaning seemed especially problematic after Derrida in *Writing and Difference* had exposed unsuspected areas of complicity between force and signification, violence and metaphysics. Similarly, an innocent view of purely virtuous uses of language appeared untenable after Foucault, in *The Order of Discourse*, had conceived of discourse as by itself powerful, as a cultural practice that can forcefully intervene in, violate, and reorder the world of objects.

The confrontation with these relentless readings of the uses of language and culture was brought to a head by the political events of 1989. It is true that when the Wall came down in November of that year the oppositional relation between discursive and powerful locations of authority appeared for one long hour to be triumphantly confirmed. But after the moment of celebration was over, too many things happened that began to contradict the premises on which the critical intellect sought to overcome the bastions of petrified power. Dissident writers in particular were soon disillusioned; but then for intellectuals to have defied the regime of authoritarian power was, through a strange process of inversion, to participate in the circulation of awards and prestige resulting from, paradoxically, both the existence and the negation of the same established authoritarian power. This, precisely, was the uncanny threshold between unorthodoxy and complicity: the intellectual power of nonconformity itself thrived upon, in fact presupposed, the external enforcement of conformity. Hence, on several levels doubts appeared justified whether it was possible, then as well as now, to grasp relations between the authority of external power and the power of an internal or discursive authority in terms of a dichotomy or opposition pure and simple.

Most important, this dichotomy could not provide a satisfying pattern for the uses of authority in Shakespearean representations. To take only the *locus classicus* in question: Hamlet's thick advice on the need for harmony in the relations of "word" and "action" must not be read as an entirely impartial or disinterested emanation of theatrical authority. There is more than conjectural ground to assume that in the Elizabethan theater relations between textual authority and performative agency were not altogether free from some underlying friction. This friction cannot be understood simply as an opposition between textual and material locations of authority. To all intents and purposes there was an unsuspected area of both openness and dissension on which the imaginary construct called "Hamlet," like the Prologue to *Troilus and Cressida,* was positioned "not in confidence/Of author's pen or actor's voice" (23–24). In Marlowe's and Ben Jonson's case the dividing line of authority in representation was between "pen" and "voice," adumbrating a division at least partially marked by prolonged uneasiness in the social relations of literacy and orality. But Shakespeare was too intimately involved in the two registers of representation not to have mitigated a costly division between the authority of the playwright and "the self-resembled show" of those performers who "speak . . . more than is set down for them" (*Hamlet,* 3.2.39). But conflict there was all the same, and it does not take Will Kempe's otherwise inexplicably sudden departure from the Globe project to suggest as much.

The final point, here, in qualifying the dichotomy in authorization on Shakespeare's stage is to suggest that, whatever discontinuity there was indeed between the sociocultural institution and the "imaginary puissance" in poetic responses, this discontinuity cannot be constructed along the lines of external vs. internal locations of power. Rather, whatever friction there was must have derived, as in Marlowe's case (if we can trust his printer Richard Jones), from how the textualized "matter of worthiness" coped with a performative practice that drew on such "fond and frivolous jestures" as were greatly gaped at by audiences.

If this conclusion finally sounds like a lame stanza to replace the more dramatic scenario of the intellect triumphing to the steps of a subversive kind of grand récit, the reason is not far to seek. The price of nonconformity is dumped when the external enforcement of orthodoxy becomes utterly discredited. But this does not mean that the political events that turned the study of Shakespeare in the German Democratic Republic into matter for historiography have provided anything like a conclusive answer to the question of authority. Far from it; for many years to come these events, I assume, will be conducive to new perspectives on the validity of difference in Shakespeare. Nor is this likely to be the last court of appeal, once the topography of partition and realignment in the reception of the bard will again be radically altered from north to south.

Part Two
Theater Practice and Performance
(Interviews)

7

Christoph Schroth: "In Search of the Utopian Vision"

Lawrence Guntner: Would you see your work within the context of the creation of a socialist drama? If so, what role does or did classical drama, and Shakespeare in particular, play in this development?

Schroth: I was a director at the Mecklenbürgische Staatstheater in Schwerin for fifteen years [1974–89]. The starting point for our repertoire was contemporary drama, especially plays about the socialist societies of the GDR and the Soviet Union. They were the aesthetic and theatrical means by which we as a theater were able to contribute to a discussion of the conflicts and contradictions in East German society. In the course of these fifteen years, we developed a strategy of performing older plays and relating them to this nucleus of contemporary drama. First we turned to German classics: Schiller's *Don Karlos, Demetrius,* and *Wilhelm Tell,* as well as both parts of Goethe's *Faust.* Then we put on Pushkin's rarely performed play, *Boris Godunov,* which has a lot in common with Shakespeare. Pushkin writes in truly Shakespearean dimensions, about Boris who has become czar through usurpation, about Grischka the fugitive monk who would become czar, about political and moral conflicts, and about the role of the people. Thirdly, we turned to the Greek classics, four plays dealing with the Trojan Wars: Euripides' *Iphegenia among the Tauris* and *The Trojan Women,* Aeschylus's *Agamemnon,* and Aristophanes' *Peace.* They were all performed on one evening with the performance lasting five and a half hours. This was at the beginning of the eighties when the question of the deployment of rockets and the problems of peace and war were very urgent. Our strategy was first the German classics, then the ancient Greek classics, and finally Shakespeare. These were the three major stages in our development over periods of three, six, and nine years. In between, we always performed contemporary plays.

Andrew McLean: When you set out on this program, did you consciously set Shakespeare as your goal, as the culmination of this development?

Schroth: Yes. We knew that we had to end with Shakespeare, but we simply did not have enough confidence in ourselves to begin with him. Shake-speare is certainly the greatest, the most difficult, the most complex play-wright of all and a tremendous challenge in terms of both form and content.

Guntner: Why is he so difficult? Personally, I find Shakespeare more acces-sible than any other playwright.

Schroth: Is it really that easy? Everyone would like to perform Shakespeare; that's not the problem. We always juxtaposed contemporary playwrights with Shakespeare or the ancient classics. For us, they belonged together, integrated not isolated, and these projects required lengthy preparations. For example, we decided to do our Shakespeare project, which consisted of two plays, *Romeo and Juliet* and *A Winter's Tale*, after we did Volker Braun's *Dimitri* (an adaption of Schiller's *Demetrius* and a play of Shake-spearean dimensions) and before we performed Heiner Müller. We were interested in the problems of the individual within the socialist system in which many aspects of a person's development are curtailed. We decided to portray this social process in which the individual is caught up and cut back, his freedom reduced and his demands kept to a minimum. Thus, we placed the repression of the individual and the deformation of his or her capabilities in contemporary socialist society in contrast to the great de-mands Shakespearean characters placed on life. They became a measure for human endeavor, for individual development, and for great expectations. The love of Romeo and Juliet is a very demanding love affair in an age and a world, in a Verona, which was just as divided and fragmented, as torn apart, as ours is. We found it terribly exciting that two people would confess their love for each other so openly and demand absolute individual free-dom, outside the constraints of their society, and to live this love out, even if it means their own deaths. This was relevant to our GDR situation and to the boundaries and constraints we continually had to confront and cross. *A Winter's Tale* begins as a tragedy, with Leontes suddenly decreeing his wife's death, but all at once it turns into a fairy tale, into a vision of Utopia, in which a different form of society is possible. It is the world of the shep-herds and young people, and it ends in the hope that tragedy is unnecessary. The train of tragic events has been broken, and a utopia of human coopera-tion seems possible. Our point of departure was that the tragic love of Romeo and Juliet and the utopian vision of another way of life in *A Winter's Tale* belong together. We saw them as a reaction to the encrustation and disorientation in our own socialist society.

McLean: You took a very clear position with regard to society. What was the reaction of the audience as a whole and the theater critics in particular?

Schroth: People were moved by *Romeo and Juliet*, but curiously enough they were moved even more so by *A Winter's Tale* because there was hope. *Romeo and Juliet* ends tragically and depresses people. We live in a world of absolute hopelessness and depression, but in *A Winter's Tale* a world of hope and of human togetherness is created before our eyes, and this gave the young people immense strength. We had many discussions with members of the audience, and they always saw the play in the context of their own immediate environment and not as something remote from the sixteenth century.

Guntner: You have been a director since 1963. How has your regard for your own work in the theater and for Shakespeare in particular changed over these twenty-five years?

Schroth: I have often seen productions of *Romeo and Juliet* that bored me. The love story was spun out in a general and sentimental way. It had something to do with things in general, or with Verona, or with the nineteenth century, or with the sixteenth century. On the other hand, I was strongly impressed by Yury Lyubimov's famous production of *Hamlet* at Moscow's Taganka Theater [1971–80], and with Vladimir Vysotsky as Hamlet. This performance opened whole new vistas for me. Lyubimov demonstrated how one could set this play in direct relationship to the reality of 1960s Russia without making it topical in a cheap or trivial way. This Hamlet was a deeply discontented, aggressive, poetic, passionate man in a totally encrusted world. Everything in the play became related to the immediate environment of the audience so that Shakespeare was not a playwright from the past but our contemporary. It was a courageous lesson for me to see how this Hamlet confronted and dealt with the universal, general conflicts and problems still facing humanity today. Finding a relationship to the present was really the principal difficulty. Methodically, on the other hand, it was very difficult for the actor. In Shakespeare's time the actors had a different type of stage, and they had a different relationship with the audience. It was like sitting around a table.

In *Romeo and Juliet* we had a chain about a meter high that separated players and audience who were seated in two sets of bleachers on either side of the stage. The rest of the performance area, which was enclosed by metal walls and resembled a circus arena, could be entered through three doors. The young people—Mercutio and Tybalt—were always caged in by walls. That was their world. The actors laid down a white ribbon to mark off the boundary between the feuding families. When someone overstepped this line, it brought about conflict. Tybalt stepped over this line, and it came to a fight. We tried to use the Shakespearean stage in a modern context. It was an attempt to use space in another way.

In *A Winter's Tale*, on the other hand, we used a quite conventional stage set. It consisted of a slightly raised white marble floor through which ran a brook with real water. The brook cut through everything. This is where the story of Leontes took place. Then when the sheep-shearing festival took

Romeo and Juliet, **DIR. Schroth, 1986. 3.1: Mercutio and Tybalt lay slain. Photo: Roland Festersen.**

place, the shepherds brought bread and wine into the auditorium and celebrated together with the audience. There was drinking, and Florizel and Perdita danced and threw flowers into the audience. For a moment, there existed a togetherness you find in folk drama, until Polixenes broke everything up and drove the shepherds from the stage and out of the auditorium. Suddenly, he was alone. We tried to do direct folk theater. The shepherds' celebrations were really the beginning of Utopia.

Guntner: How has your approach to Shakespeare changed over the years? Who or what has influenced you?

Schroth: Lyubimov's *Hamlet* in Moscow, of course, but also productions of the German classics, most of all Dresen's and Heinz's *Faust* at the Deutsches Theater [1968]. This was one of the first East German attempts to locate a classical play in a concrete political environment, to find actual points of reference between it and this country as well as the audience. Up until then, the character of Faust had always been seen as an role model whose drive for recognition could only be emulated. That was the official cultural line. Walter Ulbricht, at that time the head of state and the party, even went so far as to claim that part three of *Faust* would be written in the GDR.

A Winter's Tale, DIR. Schroth, 1987. 4.4: sheep-shearing scene with audience participation.
Photo: Sigrid Meixner.

Dresen and Heinz were the first to dare to see Faust as an incompetent intellectual, full of contradictions, unable to cope with the world, and responsible for the murder of Gretchen. To subject this character to criticism was revolutionary. *Faust* was a holy cow who had now been slaughtered. It was revolutionary that one could laugh during a performance of *Faust.* You could laugh about petty bourgeois Gretchen, for example, without deriding her. We were shown her limitations but also her great ability to love. The production was full of contradictions, which was what made it so exciting. This performance of *Faust* also had important consequences for the performance of Shakespeare in the GDR as well.

About the same time, Weimann's study of the plebeian theater tradition, *Shakespeare and the Popular Tradition in the Theater* [1967] came out and with it the discovery of the Vice figure, the extent to which such characters originate in the popular theater tradition, and how Shakespeare had raised this tradition to a higher literary plane. We now had a more realistic perspective of the way things had developed, not the contradictions, however. In the socialist cultural policy, contradictions were repressed for the sake of harmony. In our *A Midsummer's Night's Dream* in Halle [1971], we tried to take a new look at the play. It was the first step in the direction that Alexander Lang was to take in 1980; however, he was even more rigorous than we were. Nevertheless, ours was the first serious attempt to come to grips with *A Midsummer Night's Dream* as a serious play with serious dramatic conflicts and not as a jolly little game in which a bunch of people run past each other in the woods.

For example, we arrived at the solution of casting only one actress for the parts of Hippolyta and Titania and one actor for Oberon and Theseus quite independently of Peter Brook. It seemed obvious that the court and the wood have something to do with each other, that the wood is a reflection of the court. All the conflicts of the court find a natural release in the wood. Then we found it very interesting that Oberon acts brutally. He suppresses Titania and goes so far as to poison her. Both women are suppressed: Theseus conquers Hippolyta, and Oberon conquers Titania. The episode with the donkey (Bottom-Titania) is also very interesting. For a long time, the donkey was maligned as being stupid, but on the contrary he is a symbol of vitality, strength, and sensuality.

Guntner: Were you influenced by Jan Kott in this?

Schroth: I did not read Kott until later. We worked closely with Peter Kuczynski, an English professor at the University of Halle, and together we arrived at this conclusion. For me, the real love story is that of Pyramus and Thisbe; they are the true lovers in this play. The court destroyed everything else.

Guntner: What did you do with Bottom and the "rude mechanicals"?

Schroth: We neither silenced nor ridiculed them but tried to depict them as they really are and still be poetic. For example, we tried to show that they can be terribly aggressive. Transformed into an ass, Bottom suddenly becomes terribly brutal, yet he also develops a great capacity for love. Titania and Bottom suddenly became beautiful beings. This was a new dimension for Titania as well. Our production was a polemic against the tradition that it was a light, pleasant, and unpolitical comedy. I let more tragic configurations develop and did not let the play become a merry comedy of mistaken identities. I felt a strong sense of aggression towards the German romantic idea of A Midsummer Night's Dream with the music of Mendelssohn-Bartholdy and his nice little elves. Max Reinhardt's productions were in this tradition, and they played an important role in the history of the German theater. He even made a Hollywood film of it, a vision of romance, daintiness, civility, charm, and harmony—with just a tiny trace of conflict. I think there is an awful lot of conflict and very little harmony in the play. Granted, there is an attempt to achieve harmony, but there's continually conflict with people being poisoned and chased about. These elements are much more significant than people think.

Guntner: Had this production anything to do with the political situation in the GDR at that time?

Schroth: Yes, because theater unconsciously reacts against all attempts to smooth over social conditions, to pretend to be harmonious, to idealize. This is not reality. So when you come to Shakespeare, you say this is the way things really are.

Guntner: Let's jump from 1971 to 1990. The social conditions and political situation have changed. Would you do A Midsummer Night's Dream again?

Schroth: Maybe not. I would do A Winter's Tale. I think the people in East Germany have a great longing for harmony—not for even more division, disharmony, and conflict. At the moment, they are experiencing so much of this that they can hardly see straight. I would put on The Tempest or A Winter's Tale, where Shakespeare develops a utopian vision of life not overshadowed by tragedy. This is what all of us are longing for most.

McLean: Would you see your own work in the theater, including your work with Shakespeare, as contributing to the development of a socialist society?

Schroth: "A developing socialist society" as it once was, no longer exists. We used Shakespeare's characters to present an alternative view of humanity to that of the official party line. Shakespeare's characters are great individuals, with ambitious plans, willing to enter into violent conflicts with others to achieve their goals. Our socialist society was characterized by the happy medium, in which extremes were frowned upon. The quality of life, the necessities, the expectations were kept to a minimum—all walled-in in a small, petty world. Shakespeare's world is populated by strong personalities, sharply defined conflicts, interesting stories, and ambitious plans. That in itself was the real challenge for both the actors and the audience—to realize that a world totally different than that which they were accustomed to really exists, to paraphrase Hamlet, that there are more things between heaven and earth than are dreamt of in our philosophy. A world in which you could say, "There's something rotten in the state of Denmark"—or rotten in the state of the GDR!

Guntner: A deliberate provocation of the government through Shakespeare?

Schroth: In German socialist theater, apart from Heiner Müller and Volker Braun, there was a tendency toward a kind of kitchen-sink drama. Plays about the small family with small petty conflicts, including a bit of this and a bit of that. There was something stale, small-time, and boring about it, and Shakespeare was just the opposite, the absolute antithesis of the kind of drama that described the workaday conditions in the GDR in a meaningless manner. It was all a sort of utilitarian kind of drama without depth—conventional and plain.

McLean: What Shakespeare play would you like to do say two years from now?

Schroth: I am interested in utopia at the moment. *The Tempest* or *A Winter's Tale*, I mentioned already, but I am also interested in *Lear*, a play about how a man gives away his kingdom to be able to live in freedom without power. He would not be an old man, around forty. He still wants to live, but without the responsibilities of power. I always find it unfair how the daughters, Regan and Goneril, are portrayed. I can sympathize with them very strongly. Lear marches into their castles with one hundred men, drinks, hunts, and makes a mess everywhere. Ten or twenty days later, he leaves the place looking like a garbage dump, coca cola cans and wine bottles everywhere. He always leaves chaos in his wake. I am very interested in Lear.

Guntner: How has your work with the actors and the theater—not so much theoretically, but more practically—your approach to a play, a text, changed over the past twenty to twenty-five years?

Schroth: Thirty years ago, I worked more naturalistically. I did my theater apprenticeship at the Maxim Gorki Theater in Berlin, and I was strongly influenced by Gorki and the naturalistic theater tradition. It is not possible to approach Shakespeare naturalistically, so it was very difficult for me to attain the aesthetic and formal dimensions necessary to deal even with Shakespearean verse. To perform Shakespeare, an actor must have a feeling for both the character and the text. He not only has to digest the text thoroughly but also convey it with dramatic emotion and intelligence, to provide it with a special form without becoming formalistic. This is where differences in the theatrical tradition become visible. I think that Shakespeare's plays were acted much faster at the time they were originally written because they were centered round the spoken content. Today we take much longer, because the actors invent much more action. They "enrich" Shakespeare with their own experiences by inventing actions in between the lines but not explicitly in the text.

Guntner: In what way has your attitude toward the relationship between written text and stage performance changed?

Schroth: On the three occasions when I did Shakespeare, I always tried to create space for the actors to express themselves physically and not be restricted by a naturalistic stage setting. Instead, we used a minimal stage set with no backdrops, only that which was necessary. I do not need a bed for *Romeo and Juliet*—a white sheet will suffice.

Guntner: Where will the socialist theater go from here? What will be the role of drama in eastern Germany? Of Shakespeare?

Schroth: I think that socialism as an economic or social system is dead for the moment. What is not dead for me is the vision of a utopian society, of solidarity between the common people, of the just distribution of the national income to all members of society, and of a society that is ecologically aware. The ideals that were formulated by socialist theoreticians from Robert Owen to Karl Marx to Rosa Luxemburg are not dead for me. I cannot get rid of them, and I do not want to. They are still worth living for. In my opinion, Shakespeare always wrote political drama in the broader sense. All of his plays have something to do with political events, and this will continue to be of significance in the future. Especially at this time, Shakespeare and the Greek classics will continue to play an important role because these authors deal with those all-pervading human conflicts that are just as exciting for us today as they were for Shakespeare four hundred years ago. There's something to that. Added to this there is a great poetic quality in the characters, the thrust of the language, and the plots concern us and get under our skin.

McLean: In the development of the GDR there were always conflicts, confrontations, and debates in which the theater and attitudes to the theater played a role. To what extent were you aware of these arguments at the time, not only the social debates, but also the theoretical discussions, or did you only become aware of them afterwards?

Schroth: We were always aware of the situation we were in. When the Wall was built in 1961, for example, I wasn't really opposed to it. First of all, we thought it would only be there for four or five years. Secondly, we thought the GDR would no longer be economically drained but would have the opportunity for the first time to become economically stable. Then we could try to establish socialist conditions of production independently of any capitalist influence; we could learn from our own inconsistencies and we could create an alternative model of society to that of the Federal Republic of Germany. We did have these illusions, I must confess. In that respect, we always tried to spur on the progress of socialism. The main point of difference was that I was always in favor of a socialist development comparable with that in Prague in 1968. I was a great sympathizer with the attempt to create a democratic socialism following the example of Prague. This is why many of us continued to struggle. This meant a struggle against all centrally directed and Stalinist cultural policies and practice. We were for socialism but against Stalinism.

Guntner: A democratic socialism.

Schroth: Yes, that was also the driving force for the theater. On November 4, 1989, not one person carried a banner demanding the unification of Germany. It was all for democratic socialism in the GDR. Then the Wall was opened, and then this pan-German takeover took place.

McLean: To what extent have the literary studies in this country influenced your own work and that of your colleagues? Was there cooperation between drama studies and practical work in the theater, or were they in opposition?

Schroth: They were never opposed because the work of the best theoreticians, such as Weimann, was not abstract but directly applicable to work in the theater. The empirical observations and analyses by scholars on the theater of Shakespeare's time had direct consequences for our work, too. It began with the stage, stage construction, characters, and effects and extended to myths, legends, and fairy tales, and ended with historical events. I have never rejected scholarly work; it would be stupid. I believe that the theater must be on a par with the most advanced level of scientific or scholarly discovery. In this context, the lectures held at the annual meeting of the Shakespeare Society in Weimar were also important.

Guntner: Which people have shaped your approach to the theater?

Schroth: I was strongly influenced by Piscator, Brecht, and Lyubimov. I also have great respect for Ariane Mnouschkin's experiments with Shakespeare. As far as films are concerned, I was very impressed by Zeffirelli's *Romeo and Juliet*. It strongly provoked me to do something different.

Guntner: Is there such a thing as post-Brechtian dramaturgy and drama? Do we see signs of this in the work of Robert Wilson or Frank Castorf in which there is no immediately apparent correlation between text and performance?

Schroth: I still base my work on the text. I take the literary text and put it on stage. Personally, Robert Wilson's experiments bore me to death. It is well done, as is Frank Castorf's work, but it is not for me. When I realize that this is a literary document by Shakespeare, then my job is to try to bring it to life on stage and make it relevant to my time. I do not want to work against Shakespeare. Perhaps I'm conventional in that respect.

(20 April 1990)

8

Adolf Dresen: "The Last Remains of the Public Sphere"

Lawrence Guntner: Do you agree with Brecht that *Hamlet* can be interpreted in various ways?

Adolf Dresen: Well, I'm not at all liberal when it comes to interpreting *Hamlet*. I don't think as Brecht did that you can look at *Hamlet* from twenty-eight different perspectives. I believe, there's really only one way and that's my way. In 1964, the commemorative year, the theater director at Greifswald had to put on something Shakespearean. I wanted to do *Timon of Athens*, but I had to do *Hamlet* instead, a play I didn't like, precisely because it's so well-known. It was while reading this play that I found out in the first place that you had to learn how to read and just how difficult that can be.[1]

I knew that Hamlet is a procrastinator, but things are happening all the time: corpses lying all over the place. They're sort of the by-products of his deeds, which he never gets around to doing. It's almost by accident that he actually kills somebody. When Hamlet leaves the praying Claudius, he runs to his mother, angry at himself. He had already vowed that something had to happen, so he abuses his mother until he only sees red. Then he spies something moving behind the curtain and stabs it. He asks if it is the king but that is impossible, because he'd just left him. "A rat! A rat!" he cries and Polonius falls out, dead. German productions tend to cut the text here because the directors notice that something can't be quite right here. Hamlet can't seriously believe that it's the king behind the curtain.

I had planned to do the same originally. And that's what drew me to the essential point: that whenever Hamlet thinks about what he is doing he finds all kinds of reasons for not doing it. Whenever he doesn't think he talks himself into a rage and only then is he capable of action. Action equals killing, but when it comes down to it, he comes up with the wrong corpse. That's the basic plan Shakespeare had in mind, if you ask me: Hamlet can act, whenever he doesn't think, and he cannot act, whenever he thinks. It's this constellation that has made it into the German public's favorite play. To quote Hölderlin, "poor in deeds and rich in thoughts"

151

(*tatenarm und gedankenreich*). Or as Heinrich Mann said, "The spirit is powerless and power is spiritless" (*Der Geist ist machtlos und die Macht ist geistlos*). In Greifswald, where I was at the time, we put it a bit more strongly: "Buchenwald is not far from Weimar." That was going too far in the GDR.

Guntner: What was it exactly that annoyed the party so much at the time?

Dresen: I've had long enough to puzzle over it. We used the Second Quarto, the longest version. We didn't leave out very much. The tempo of the performance was quick, and still it lasted four and a half hours. That was my longest performance and probably my best as well. It was a tremendous success; the audience loved it. There was laughing and crying throughout the performance—you couldn't have wished for more—and thundering ovations at the end. That performance could have run for ages. The whole gang from Berlin was there for the first performance: Heiner Müller and Benno Besson were both at the premiere. Wolfgang Heinz, head of the Deutsches Theater, was at the second performance. There were twelve performances altogether. Then it was banned.

Guntner: Who banned it?

Dresen: The head of the theater himself. It was always like that in the GDR. Nothing was banned, that was carried out by the head, a Mr. Georg Roth, from Stralsund. His reason, if I remember correctly, was that it was a "destruction of the classical heritage," "destruction of the humanistic view of man," "left wing radicalism," and "influences of the Absurd Theater." For him "Absurd Theater" was Dürrenmatt's *The Physicists.* That gives you an idea of the level of our conversation. I disappeared after that: I was the director of the play, the play was banned, and I was famous in the GDR.

Guntner: Why did you do a new translation? Was it commissioned?

Dresen: No, on the contrary. Everyone tried to stop us. I'd read all the translations I could get hold of, but I always found a fly in the ointment.

Guntner: What was it like working with Maik Hamburger?

Dresen: We already knew each other, and we were friends. That's important. He wasn't involved in theater at all. He was a qualified physicist.

Guntner: You used to be interested in physics yourself.

Dresen: Yes, we were both physicists, but we knew each other from student days and amateur dramatics. I'd already started working in the theater in the meantime and on that occasion, I remembered Michael knew English. So I called him and said, "Michael, you're our last resort; come immediately, we have to translate *Hamlet* within a month." Crazy, really. But we just didn't have any more time. We were young then, and nothing was impossible. Michael had organized the newest English editions of Shakespeare, an encyclopedia, the entire works. We worked in Berlin, stayed up all night, and were unavailable for a month; no telephone, nothing. The beginning was torturous, but then we found a way of working together and slowly it started to take shape. He was mainly responsible for a rough, line for line translation, with notes, for example, where the verse structure is important. I tried the German text, then the English and German; we went back and forth.

There are two key experiences that stick in my mind: one was the language of the ghost (act 1, scenes 4 and 5). This was confusing because it was antiquated English, even for Shakespeare. He obviously wanted to capture the language of an earlier period with its complicated syntax. Generally we tried to stick to the English as closely as possible. Shakespeare's blank verse is supported by the syntax; you can't let it overlap. We also tried to keep the sentences as short as possible, like the English, and it worked for the whole translation, but this proved particularly difficult in the case of the ghost's speech. The sentences went on and on, line after line. Finally I had a version that I thought was really good, with lots of alliteration, which is very important in Shakespeare in certain places. Then we read the English and the German versions outloud; it didn't sound quite right, but we couldn't put our finger on what was wrong. Then Maik said, "You have to act it out. Do it like you want it done." Then I acted it out, in English and in German, and it became obvious. If you listen to the text in English you will find that the Ghost only speaks in dark vowels. There was no way of playing the Ghost in full armor in broad daylight; you had to do it through the language, and I hadn't paid attention to that. When you act it out, the language takes on a completely new feeling, but that's quite difficult to render into German because something else always suffers. That was when I realized all the things you have to look out for when you translate Shakespeare.

However, the key passage in the play for me, in fact, is shortly before Hamlet goes off to duel with Laertes. For me, Hamlet is not a revolutionary, but a real intellectual with this dialectic of thinking and acting, and he can act. He defends the murder of Rosencrantz and Guildenstern. We didn't try to make it harmless—for us it was all murder—and the two chaps weren't spies and Polonius was just an old fool, but not a criminal. For me, all of Hamlet's actions seem pointless and that's exactly what gives meaning to the play. The scene is when Horatio says to Hamlet, "You will lose my lord," Hamlet utters these famous words: "If it be now, 'tis not to come; if it be not to come, it will be now; if it be not now, yet it will come—the readiness is all" (5.2.221–222). It's all in prose, but in Shakespeare prose isn't just prose. It's given a rhythm, a feeling, and there is a lyrical quality to it. It runs throughout his entire reply with the following beat: dum, dum, dum, dum . . . ; "If it be now, 'tis not to come . . . readiness is all." Do you recognize the rhythm? Of course. It's Beethoven's Fifth Symphony. Beethoven said that's how it sounds when Fate knocks at the door, and that's certainly an experience common to everyone.

Guntner: Peter Brook once said that the essence of Shakespeare doesn't lie in the words, but in the music underlying them.

Dresen: Yes, extremely so. Because for me, and that supports my theory all the more, that is the key passage in the play. It's not the moment when he goes into a revolutionary battle. In Moscow, Yury Lyubimov did it in exactly the same way in his legendary *Hamlet* with the poet Vladimir Vysotsky as the Prince of Denmark.[2] I felt that he goes passively into the last duel; he drifts into it. It's a fatal part, and it ends differently than he had imagined.

Guntner: I understand that the stage crew kept the scenery from the Greifswald production for over a year.

Dresen: There was a great deal of solidarity in all that happened there. I was sent off to an oil refinery in Greifswald to learn from the working class. But not for long because the Deutsches Theater was quicker. It was more difficult for the ensemble because they had shown solidarity with me. Jürgen Holtz, who played Hamlet, was given an award as an activist on the First of May. It was a great honor so he accepted it, but when he came back, the people in the ensemble said, "for crying out loud, Jürgen, have you gone mad? Dresen's in the oil refinery and you go and accept an award like that." Then he went back, put it in front of them and said: "Dirt!"—with a touch of the theatrical. That was one step too far. They acted out of a sense of solidarity with me, but it didn't help them. All of them were fired, the theater was shut down, and the theaters in Stralsund and Greifswald were merged. That was the end of the ensemble in Greifswald.[3] Holtz was signed up in Berlin straight away and a couple of others along with him, but I couldn't do anything for the rest of them. I could have gone to three theaters in Berlin: to Helene Weigel at the Berliner Ensemble, to Wolfgang Heinz at the Deutsches Theater, or to Horst Schönemann at the Maxim Gorki Theater. I went to Heinz who had seen *Hamlet*. It took a lot of courage for him to sign me on. He met with resistance from the ministry, but he just went ahead and did it. He could only manage a contract as an assistant director for me, and I was given the lowest salary that you could get at the Deutsches Theater. And with this small income, I directed *Faust* there in 1968.

Guntner: What was the negative side of East German theater?

Dresen: The negative side of the East German theater was precisely that which made it so excellent. They put the lid on us, so we knew exactly what we were up against. We were all convinced Marxists—Tragelehn, Heiner Müller—we were all friends. We wanted socialism but none of us wanted the brand that was being practiced in the GDR. It was a strange situation. We were for our country and half against it. The others seemed to know the extent of our opposition before we did, so we were cut down to size. Like me, Tragelehn was sent off to do manual labor. Heiner Müller couldn't get anything published or performed. Performances were banned, seven of mine. It was not exactly pleasant, but it was not as unpleasant as you might think. You ran around with a martyr's crown of thorns on your head, and you tended to be in everyone's good books. It really was a peculiar situation. I was with the Deutsches Theater for ten years. I didn't have any problems with the ensemble because I arrived there as an un-crowned king. The problems with the ensemble came a lot later, after Honecker came to power and a "liberalization" of the GDR set in.

Guntner: What changed in the seventies after Honecker's putsch in 1971?

Dresen: I can remember a conversation with Heiner Müller, that once Honecker was at the top, things would start looking up for us. He was right. A liberalization did take place, but unfortunately, it didn't bring the results we'd been hoping for. The lid pushing down on us was missing, and we needed to have something to push against. A common opponent had helped to weld ensembles together, and now they started to fall apart because there was nothing to work against. The political pressure had been removed but exactly that had kept us together. Now the link was broken. This "liberalization" didn't lead to a new truth or truthfulness in art but to corruption. That became clear in hindsight.

Guntner: What form did this corruption take?

Dresen: It was a matter of the climate, which is a lot more difficult to understand. I can't really give you any examples. I can only say that's why I left the Deutsches Theater. I just couldn't work there anymore. People had country homes now; they weren't the same people. While Ulbricht was still there, we were all convinced Marxists and knew that what was in the GDR wasn't really Marxism. It had to be different. We worked with conviction, and we identified completely with our country until 1968 when they marched into Czechoslovakia. This affected a lot of people, and it affected me greatly. Suddenly it was all over for me. I could no longer identify with this country or this kind of party. Then I was expelled from the party in 1976 for supporting Wolf Biermann;[4] but that was just a formality. By then I was in opposition anyway and playing my little games with the state. I tried to impute things and cheat them without them really noticing. It wasn't like that with *Faust* (1968). We really tried to put on a production against them.

Guntner: You're said to be a "Brechtian". Do you model yourself on anyone in the theater?

Dresen: I would never have entered the theater if it hadn't been for Brecht. The performances of the Berliner Ensemble were where I learned for the first time that you could have both theater and intelligence. Up until then I wasn't that interested in theater. While I was a student in Leipzig I became an amateur actor, and head of the university players. Brecht had a great fondness for amateur theater, and we performed *Furcht und Elend des Dritten Reiches* (*Fear and Misery of the Third Reich*) in front of Brecht's troupe at the Schwerin Amateur Theater Congress. I acted in it but didn't direct it. My first big experience in professional theater was in Magdeburg. Brecht came later. There are, however, a few other directors who were and still are in my opinion great directors: Giorgio Strehler, Peter Brook, and Yury Lyubimov. They were my three guiding stars. Lyubimov is not what he used to be, but you can always see very good productions by Strehler. As old as he is, I still envy him.

Guntner: What was it about Peter Brook that fascinated you?

Dresen: I've only seen one of Brook's productions, *A Midsummer Night's Dream* in Warsaw. We couldn't get out, so I had to wait until Brook came to Warsaw. It just knocked me out because he had taken Shakespeare seriously. There weren't any decorations, and everything that took place on the stage came from the actors: no twisted roots or trees, not the slightest traces of naturalism, only a white box, and then the clever idea of including Mendelssohn's *A Midsummer Night's Dream* music. I was enraptured and thought, "what a pity this play is lost to me forever; it can never be done differently." I was happy because such beauty existed and depressed because I would never be able to do the play myself.

II

Guntner: How would you explain the German fondness for director's theater [*Regietheater*]?

Dresen: First of all, the tradition of the actor was interrupted in Germany, and second it has to do with the fact that in Germany there's always someone who wants to be in charge. They love telling you what you can't get across. In the meantime directors have become necessary in England, too. Only they tend to stick to their job of helping actors keep both of their feet on the ground. This doesn't happen in Germany, where it is more the director fulfilling himself at the cost of the actors and most times at the cost of the play itself. You can do that in Germany because the theater is subsidized and because Germany is going through a crisis in values so no one gets a smack on the fingers. What does apply to Germany is, in any case, novelty. A play can only be made new and fresh by the director, not by the actors. Actors have to be fresh every evening. There's no other way. And that's how it happens. It's an evil inherited from German *Bildungstheater*. Brecht called it, "Intimidation through classicism." Nowadays, you could say, "Intimidation through modernity." Both are repressive. It's one of the evils of our German heritage, and it can't be found in any other country. You find it in both East and West, and it was the same in the GDR. I think the situation after 1945 was somehow more favorable in the GDR because the GDR paid more attention to achieving an antifascist start. All the important people in the theater who emigrated returned to the GDR, Brecht being the most important. The new beginnings in the theater seemed more promising in East Germany than in West Germany, mainly because of Brecht, but not only because of him. Right through the 1960s and well into the 1970s, in fact, East German theater was miles ahead of West German theater. I chose not to go to West Germany; the theater there did not interest me.

Guntner: Did things relax in the 1970s?

Dresen: There was a liberalization, which didn't go down well with the theater, because you would have had to tell the truth, about the GDR, and that of course was not what was meant by "liberalization." Then we had the 1968 movements in the West and in the East. The suppression of the uprising in Prague was an enormous setback for the entire East German intellectual scene and for the theater. It was different in the West. The awakening of '68 immediately spilled over into the intellectual scene and into a whole new theater generation: Stein, Peymann, Flimm. Not Zadek because he came more from the English theater tradition, and he was somewhat older. He never really got on with the others. Like me they were all products of the '68 student movement, only I was in the East. They all started out with Brecht who had been banned in the West. They had to catch up with the politicizing of their theater, something that we'd already done twenty years previously and they were through with it a lot more quickly than we were. I can still remember Stein coming to performances in the Deutsches Theater when I was directing there. They all came over at sometime or another. The Berliner Ensemble was no longer at its peak but the Deutsches Theater was very good. By the time I arrived in West Germany, the political business was over. It lasted only about eight years. It had gone on in the East for twenty five years. Six years during Brecht's lifetime and then it spread throughout the country. When I arrived in the West in 1977, it was obvious to me what had happened.

Guntner: Weren't classical writers, such as Shakespeare, simply a niche for difficult customers like Müller, Lang, and yourself?

Dresen: Yes. Of course, it's better to do a new piece, but if you can only do a bad one, then it is better to do an old one. In an old piece, you can gift wrap quite a lot and misuse the old texts. It was enough to recite the text as it stood because that was already directed against the GDR. But I didn't do that because I didn't want to direct my production against the GDR.

III

Guntner: Can you comment on your *Measure for Measure* at the Deutsches Theater in 1966?

Dresen: It was intended as a political production. We wanted to play Angelo as the deputy out to make a tabula rasa not only with prostitutes and pimps but with everyone. All the "Biermanns," all the directors, and all the art along with it, but it didn't quite work because Shakespeare luckily doesn't allow for it. I didn't twist everything around in the play to make it fit. I pushed things as far as they would go, but it wouldn't go any further. The production wasn't really successful but it still got good write-ups. The production ran for ages, but after the hundredth performance, I told the actors: "This production is chronically ill and will remain so. I'm going to rework it." The theater gave me a week. I changed the actors around. Lucio became Angelo, Angelo became the Duke, the Duke became Lucio, and I got a different Isabella. The production was fine then. We didn't have a premiere, we just carried on. There were four hundred performances after that! The politics, the polemics, were gone and there was just Angelo, a likeable fellow, a puritan, who falls in love. He is neither a swine nor a Tartuffe, nor is he a hypocrite; he just doesn't know anything about love. There's a dispute with Isabella where they both don't know what love is. They argue with the passion of inner turmoil, and when he says, "I love you," it's completely naive. He only has the choice between being an angel and a devil and he falls completely. Jürgen Holtz played Angelo in the new version; he was wonderful. It was, however, a defence of these people in the East.

Guntner: Doesn't Weimann's *Shakespeare and the Popular Tradition* question the authorized way of interpreting Shakespeare?

Dresen: Weimann opened up Shakespeare for the theater and for "the theater of the folk" (*Volkstheater*), too. I became aware for the first time that Shakespeare represented all levels of society which is what is meant by *Volkstheater*. He also made me realize that Shakespeare made concessions to his audiences; however, all these concessions were good. The audience were the coauthors of his plays so to speak. It was by writing for an excellent audience that Shakespeare ended up writing such good plays. He had the enormous advantage of knowing who he was writing for, and he could keep this in mind while writing.

Guntner: What do the terms "authority" and "legitimization" mean to you?

Dresen: The problem of "authority and legitimization" was extremely important for every East German citizen. While at school, Schiller was an important authority for me, later Bach became very important for me because I played the organ. This problem of authority remained, and despite

Measure for Measure, DIR. Dresen, 1966. 2.2: Angelo (Holtz) overwhelmed by feelings of love for Isabella (Karusseit). Photo: Gisela Brandt, courtesy of the Deutsches Theater.

my resisting the state, Marx was—personally speaking—a very strong authority for me. This was mainly due to the influence of my teachers in Leipzig, Ernst Bloch and Hans Mayer, and later the people I worked with in the Deutsches Theater, people I respected. They weren't just Marxists but people who had risked their lives for the cause and weren't hypocrites. You couldn't earn very much as a Marxist in the GDR. It was impossible to agree with all that was going on, you just couldn't. It wasn't a matter of corruption, not even within the party. I joined the party but I had to go through five party hearings and in the end they threw me out. Not because I had misread Marx, but just the contrary. Marx remained an authority for me for a long time, but after the invasion of Czechoslovakia in 1968, I realized I could no longer say that Stalinism was a distortion of Marxism. Stalinism is unfortunately a consequence of Marxism. This meant that Marx had to be read very carefully and that's just what I did for two years. I didn't have very much work, so together with a few friends I worked through *Das Kapital,* and all of Marx's writings on political economics. We chewed our way through and managed to find the mistakes. Afterwards Marx was no longer an authority for me.

Guntner: The minister of culture, Hans-Joachim Hoffmann, claimed that even he could not travel to the West in the company of his wife.

Dresen: I experienced something special with Hoffmann, something that was really to his credit. While I was directing in Frankfurt I had to get in touch with him on business. He was very friendly, but then he suddenly turned on me, "You made defamatory remarks about the GDR in the Pauls-kirche in Frankfurt!" There had been something in honor of Goethe, and in my capacity as head of drama I had to take part in a discussion. Apart from other things, I said that Goethe cannot be as uncontemporary as people here seem to think. In the Deutsches Theater they had, after all, banned my *Clavigo* (1970), and my *Faust* (1968) had touched off a heated debate. They wouldn't have done that if those plays had been a tour of a museum.[5] I told Hoffmann I hadn't made defamatory remarks about the GDR. Nevertheless, he carried on and while he was talking, he pushed a file over for me to read and I started looking through it. It was full of observation reports about me as head of drama at the theater in Frankfurt. He showed me all of it including the report on the incident in the Paulskirche. He criticized me loudly for the office bugging devices to hear and at the same time showed me these reports, "look here, and above all take a look at all these names, signed at the bottom, there you have it." I thought I wasn't seeing properly. Not one word was uttered between us. We never discussed that meeting again. He could always deny everything. It was fantastic. He was cultural minister, and it all happened in his office. That sort of thing happened, and they didn't have anything on him.

Guntner: You're a man between two generations, between Brecht and the younger generation. What did you notice when you came to the West?

Dresen: During rehearsals I noticed more eagerness, a readiness to work harder on the part of the actors. For the first time I saw what had happened in the GDR. There is a considerable amount of existential pressure on actors in the West which has to do with the entire theater system. It may indeed be subsidized but it's more the product that gets subsidized than the producers. The producers are put on the market. It wasn't really that different in the GDR, only there wasn't a market, so it didn't matter anyway. When theater in the GDR was politically motivated, it was exciting, but when things became liberal, it was destroyed by lethargy and officialdom. Those were my conclusions after ten years at the Deutsches Theater. I was fed up and wanted out.

You didn't have that in the West. The actors and actresses were incredibly keen and prepared to go along with practically anything. At first, it's rather nice. I didn't have to motivate the people; I could work freely. Later I noticed that the whole set up had an Achilles heel; it's all rooted in this awful director's theater. If you subsidize the product instead of the producer, that makes economic sense. In the theater world, it's different. In the theater, the producer is pushed to achieve because he's up for sale, in other words, a machine that keeps accelerating until it finally blows up. That's why you get this infernal novelty show in West German theater, all these capers which distinguish German theater in an unpleasant way from all the other theaters in the world. In Germany there is a mixture of competition and subsidies. It's a catastrophe, and meanwhile I can see the adverse effects it's having on the theater.

IV

Guntner: Was theater in the GDR a niche for people? A place to survive the ideological winter?

Dresen: I wouldn't exactly call it a niche. It was the last remains of the public sphere. Or perhaps it was exactly the opposite. We didn't really have anything like a public sphere any more in the GDR, apart from in the churches and to an extent in the theater. They could control radio and film and the publication of novels. However, this is to be taken with a grain of salt because there were good people everywhere who managed to squeeze things through. Neverthesss, in the theater, you still had more freedom because actors have a unique way of speaking. In 1974 I put on Heinrich Heine's *Deutschland. Ein Wintermärchen* at the Deutsches Theater. There were people in the audience with tape recorders who played back what we had said and accused us of changing Heine. But they couldn't prove a thing because every single word had originated from Heine. An actor can speak the words differently. When I did *Hamlet,* the text was totally from the original. But, that's precisely it, actors speak another language. It's not just verbal; they speak a subtext, and there's no way to control that. How are you going to register that on a tape recorder? You can't.

Guntner: What will remain of the GDR theater?

Dresen: The people will remain. In my opinion, that's the main thing.

Guntner Was there an East German approach to your work? To read a play, for example, from the sociological slant?

Dresen: Yes, as far as learning the trade was concerned, you were prepared relatively well in the GDR. The people in the GDR were urged to come to grips with texts and not to begin by destroying them in order to attract attention. The pressure of competition wasn't so great in the GDR. Perhaps that's why they were more thorough on a literary level and approached things in a more serious manner including research into source material.

That's what we were always taught and encouraged to do, beginning with Brecht. It's quite different here. They've all got their views, opinions concepts, and problems, only they don't do the play itself. Terrible.

Guntner: Would you like to direct at the Deutsches Theater again?

Dresen: Yes. Architecturally, the Deutsches Theater is the most beautiful theater I have ever been in. It is a beautiful building filled with enormous memories, but theater isn't about architecture or memories. It has to do with ensembles. I could go to the Deutsches Theater and start doing a production tomorrow, but then theater work for me is working with an ensemble and not primarily directing. There's hardly a director around who knows the ensemble. They just go anywhere to do a production. But I can't do that. That was why Brecht intentionally called his theater the Berliner Ensemble. It was like that in good theaters throughout the GDR. There was no jumping from one theater to the other. The ensembles remained where they were. They always acted together in varying constellations and with very varying demands on the individual actors. I had ten relatively happy years at the Deutsches Theater with very good directors, Benno Besson and Wolfgang Heinz. We were members of the same first-class ensemble, probably the best in Germany at that time. Different demands were made on all of them, continuously. I knew two years in advance who would play Faust and could prepare him for the role. Dieter Franke was to play Mephisto. I knew what had to be done with him, what Besson had to do with him, to prepare him for the role. There was no internal competition because we all felt that we were Marxists, working for the good of the GDR and yet, in opposition to it. Besson, Heinz, and myself were never in competition with one another. Besson sat in during my rehearsals and helped me. I went to his final rehearsals, and he'd ask me what was wrong. It was normal at that time, but it would be unheard of today. It's not like that at the Deutsches Theater anymore, either. The people there are completely different. Some of the people I knew at the Deutsches Theater are still there but not very many. The Deutsches Theater that I knew no longer exists. I'd have to start at the beginning again there, too.

(4 December 1990)

9

Alexander Lang: "Theater is a Living Process: Asserting Individuality"

Lawrence Guntner: Did Brecht influence you?

Alexander Lang: Yes, but through Benno Besson. As a young actor fresh out of acting school, I began my career at the Berliner Ensemble, then under the direction of Helene Weigel. Brecht was dead, but I was strongly influenced by Brecht's method, his questioning approach to plays, and less by what was being performed. I quickly perceived the rigidity that had set in in the Berliner Ensemble after Brecht's death. Besson was so important because he broke through all this. Theater in the GDR began with Brecht— the father of a whole new generation of directors—and Besson was a natural extension of Brecht. He went beyond Brecht in his manner of presentation and added something that would otherwise have been lacking. After all, he came from a different cultural milieu.

Guntner: You are well-known for drawing a great deal out of your actors.

Lang: That is because I was an actor myself. I made extreme demands on myself as an actor, so I know what an actor is capable of doing. I never begin with a developed dramaturgical concept for a play, for example, that this actor must stand on the right and the other on the left. For me, a performance is a form that gradually takes shape. I begin with a scene, improvise, and gradually after many variations, there comes a point where I say: "That's it."

Guntner: Is Shakespeare especially suited to this?

Lang: Shakespeare is perfectly suited to this, because he is the starting point of theater in the modern sense. Shakespeare is the first playwright to include the life of the streets in his plays. When Shakespeare wrote, the theater was very concerned with the politics of the day—much more than we know or acknowledge today.

Guntner: In 1980, Thomas Langhoff directed *A Midsummer Night's Dream* to bring his young ensemble together. Why did you do *A Midsummer Night's Dream?*

Lang: Shakespeare's play was a reaction to his own times. As a young actor,

I flew to Warsaw to see Peter Brook's production of *A Midsummer Night's Dream.* I had no passport, so it was impossible for me to see it in London, and I would not have had the money anyway. This performance blew me out of my seat; it was an unforgettable theatrical experience and made a lasting impression on me. It was absolutely wonderful. The lightness and poetry of the performance revealed to me a fresh and lively Shakespeare, far removed from the declamatory style we were familiar with. Brook showed us a light-hearted play full of action. This fascinated me. The performance was in the spirit of the times: the sixties and the student movement. However, by the time I directed *Dream,* the political climate had become more oppressive so that my main concern was to bring out the "nightmare" aspect in the play. This production was also an expression of the spirit of the times, and it worked just as well. This is what is so wonderful about Shakespeare and this play. One aspect is just as present as the other.

Shakespeare played an important role in the development of German drama. After the Thirty Years' War [1618–48], groups of so-called English comedians performed bastardized versions of Shakespeare in Germany, and then a new wave of Shakespeare appreciation came with the translations of August Schlegel and Dorothea Tieck. These translations played down the bawdy and political elements so that Shakespeare became rather "nice." *A Midsummer Night's Dream* was reduced to an inoffensive fairy tale with elves. For me, it was exciting to dig into Shakespeare's original text as well as into early translations, for example Eschenburg, who translated Shakespeare's English very directly into German. I reworked Eschenburg's translation a little because his seemed to be the liveliest. Then I discovered that the play contains darker elements, and I took great pleasure in uncovering these deeper layers of meaning. Finally I realized that this is not an innocuous love story but a play about the abuse of political power and political manipulation. Young people are treated with drugs against their will and put under pressure to completely reconsider their love for one another. This is a terrible state of affairs. It boils down to the point that family life and personal relationships are being determined by the state. Theseus keeps everybody under his thumb and dictates what's what. I am convinced that Shakespeare dealt with this issue because it was an issue of his time, that is, how to channel and civilize the anarchistic energy generated by personal relationships or by life in general.

Guntner: How important is the recitation of blank verse for you?

Lang: Personally, it's very important. This is related to my feeling for rhythm. Each Shakespeare play has its individual rhythm. Dramatic rhythm is expressed very strongly through language. When you break up the rhythm, you violate the intention of the writer and to some extent the quality of the work. In the fifties, American light drama began to catch on. This led to television drama in which the words are simply rattled off, in which the *gestus* of everyday speech comes to the forefront. You cannot do this with classical scripts because the structure of their language is different. I enjoy giving expression to the pathos in Schiller because it is an element of the dramatic content of his plays. For me, language is not an aspect of form but of content.

Guntner: How far can one alter a dramatic script?

Lang: Shakespeare is our best example, for, as far as I know, he had no inhibitions about deleting parts of the script and inserting others if he felt it was appropriate or topical. He regarded a play as working material and not as something that has been declared sacred. That came later. Or take Brecht, who constantly changed his scripts. Schiller also deleted sections of his own script if a performance was endangered. The dynamics of the theater demand that you do what you have to do. For the most part, plays are written in quiet rooms, but in the theater different rhythmical laws are in force, and it is legitimate to restructure, abbreviate, or even alter the material.

Guntner: Are there limits? You made fairly drastic cuts, for example, in *A Midsummer Night's Dream* to emphasize certain aspects.

Lang: I think that there should be no limits to what one can do in theater. Theater is a living process. German scholars regularly accuse me of not having paid due respect to certain aspects of a particular play. My only reply is that I am neither a scholar nor a literary historian, nor am I a curator of old plays. I cannot recreate a theater that existed in 1920 or even earlier. Theater has always been and always will be a contemporary medium, and this is exactly what makes it so wonderful. Theater only becomes interesting when it has something to do with the immediate, with the present. There will always be people who want to perform these plays to express their own feelings about the times in which they live, and they will always incorporate their personal point of view into them. This is what makes theater alive.

Guntner: Did you regard yourself as a socialist?

Lang: I was never a member of a party or political organization because I think that art is basically opposed to state-ordered structures. Of course, it was exciting to be for or against a social model that had declared itself to be utopia. The interesting point of friction was the contradiction between the state proclaimed utopia and its realization in daily life. Naturally, one had the desire to contribute and to help achieve this utopian ideal, but there was always a clash with the power structures of the state. The state had all the theory but was unable to put it into practice in human terms.

Guntner: Heiner Müller says that now that the political backdrop of dictatorship is gone, it will become more difficult for theater in the former GDR.

Lang: This backdrop was responsible for a consensus between the audience and those working in the theater. This consensus was the coded meaning. Theater classics were always performed in a very contemporary way so that the audience was always able to associate what happened on stage with their own personal situation. The situation has changed now, and this togetherness has come to an end. However, this point does not interest me anymore, because I had to undergo a painful separation from East Germany when I left. More basic questions became important for me. What is the meaning of theater at all? To what extent is it a medium with a future? How can theater in this new united Germany articulate itself in a fresh way? How can this unique Berlin theater culture—which is not to be found anywhere else in the world—use its creative energies to contribute new accents again in European theater or even world theater?

Guntner: How do you see this challenge? Do you want to take theater out of its national boundaries into a sort of world theater or theater without boundaries?

Lang: Every theater culture has its own national characteristics, and theater will remain interesting only if it retains its individuality. It is pointless to see the same theater from Moscow to New York. I want to see a different sort of theater in New York than I do in Moscow.

Guntner: You have worked more with the German classics on the stage than with Shakespeare.

Lang: That is because that I am strongly aware of German history. I was born in 1941, and sometime after 1945 I was taken to Weimar with the other children in my school class. First we saw Buchenwald and the crematorium. After Buchenwald, we went to see the houses of Goethe and Schiller. When I direct a German theater classic, I cannot exclude this contradiction between what German culture stands for and what was perpetrated in its name. That does not mean that I emphasize this topic every time I direct, but it has induced me to expose the contradictions to be found in these plays. The curious tendency of Germans to preach an ideal and their inability to practice it interests me. Out of my desire to come to terms with German history came a strong interest in German classical theater. I became increasingly interested in finding out exactly what influenced German literature. This led me to Racine and also to Shakespeare. Just how far German literature had an influence outside Germany, and to what extent English or French literature worked its way into Germany are questions that will interest me in the future.

Guntner: Why is Shakespeare so easy to direct on the stages of other cultures, and why are Schiller and Goethe so difficult?

Lang: Because Shakespeare is universal. He uses a few basic models. He was awfully lucky because he was the first to develop these archetypal forms that are still interesting and exciting today. It is this dramatic component, which is at the same time more cosmopolitan, that appeals to and comes to terms with different cultures. How this came about is another matter, but regardless of how you view it, Shakespeare is a founder of the modern theater. It is Shakespeare you have to confront and against whom you have to measure your own achievement. Goethe and Schiller are naturally much more German and therefore more difficult for other cultures to appreciate. Shakespeare continued a still living folk tradition in England: the fool, the clown, Punch and Judy and such puppet figures. In Germany, on the other hand, you find a deep separation between "high" literature and popular literature. The former became increasingly elevated and remote because of this.

Guntner: Are there scholarly works from the GDR that have influenced you?

Lang: No. I was more influenced by Jan Kott's *Shakespeare Our Contemporary* because it looked at Shakespeare from a completely different perspective. Even if you do not agree with everything Kott says, he gives you a lot of food for thought. Apart from that, I would much rather read around about the Renaissance and contemporary problems.

Guntner: Theater has an anarchistic element; it created alternative models in opposition to the official GDR model. Were the theater classics, particularly Shakespeare, better suited to this than contemporary plays?

Lang: It was very difficult to perform contemporary plays on topical themes in the GDR. You are familiar with the difficulties Heiner Müller and other writers faced when they tried to have their plays performed. It was incredibly difficult to have them authorized, so the classics were a way of circumventing this. This went so far that the authors dramatized classical themes in an encoded form, for example, Müller's *Philoktet,* in which I myself acted. There was a topical issue hidden in every performance of a classical play, no matter whether it was the original script or a modern adaptation. There is a long German tradition of using classical material to deal with present-day issues. Kleist did it, and Goethe did, too. Goethe sets *Iphigenia on Tauris* in ancient Greece, but he is really describing Germany in his own age.

Guntner: Shakespeare had the same problem. He set *Measure for Measure* in Vienna, and when he wanted to deal with sex, he had to travel to Italy.

Lang: And *Hamlet* is set in Denmark. Of course, we wanted to direct plays by new playwrights, and I was able to do this once in awhile. For example, I directed the first performance of Christoph Hein's *Ah Q* in 1983 at the Deutsches Theater. Strangely enough, the play is set somewhere in China, but it referred to the situation in the GDR. But to go back to the anarchistic element in theater and its opposition to the system, anarchy does not just mean doing crazy things. It also means asserting one's individuality. For example, in *A Midsummer Night's Dream* the young people have problems with the state's repressive apparatus. When this was made clear on stage, it was a real problem that the audience had experienced in their own lives.

Guntner: You had problems with the stage set.

Lang: Yes, that had a real Shakespearean dimension to it. I had a set designer named Hans Brosch who did not come back from an exhibition in Paris. I was left with a production that was almost ready, but for which there were no costumes, because he had not made them yet, and a stage set that became increasingly difficult. We had a net with leaves spread across the stage which was not acceptable to the fire department. Then there were things that came undone. It was the only time in my career when I simply did not know how to go on, so I told the cast that the opening night would have to be postponed. Then something wonderful happened. The actors said no, we have all worked so well together, and we definitely want to go ahead. So I set off in the middle of the night to a set designer named Gero Troike. We thought about what we could do, and he showed me a small photo of another set that had not materialized. It consisted of three red walls. That night we sat down and modeled these three red walls out of paper and wooden slats, a ramp in front and lighting grid above it, and that was it. We completely reblocked the whole play in one crazy, wonderful day in which everything went so incredibly fast that it was like a piece of theater itself. It was fascinating to experience how a new set gave the performance with the same actors a totally different quality, a wonderful sense of lightness and ease. It was almost like Shakespeare's stage, using the simplest means, and everything improvised and staged by the actors themselves. I really enjoyed that.

Guntner: What will be the lasting contribution of East German theater to the appreciation of Shakespeare?

Lang: It is hard to say because I do not know what the East German contribution to the theater will be in the long run.

Guntner: And in the short run?

Lang: It will be a page in the history of theater on which it will be remembered that a different kind of theater was once developed. It will still be evident to some extent in individual actors and directors, but generally speaking it will be absorbed or integrated into West German theater.

Guntner: West German theater is unthinkable without directors from the GDR.

Lang: True, but you should not overestimate this because West Germany has its own theatrical culture and tradition. The process is more one of integration—but the other way round. East German actors and directors have involved themselves with and contributed more to West German the-

A Midsummer's Night's Dream, **DIR. Lang, 1980. 1.1: Egeus "begs" his "privilege." From left to right: Demetrius (Mann), Theseus (Mellies), Hermia on floor (Zglinicki). Photo: Pepita Engel, courtesy of the Deutsches Theater.**

ater than vice versa. In all probability, the theoretical premise, the different historical perspective for analyzing and appreciating Shakespeare, will remain.

Guntner: When you left East Germany, you were very restrained in your public statements in contrast to Hilmar Thate or Wolf Biermann.

Lang: It was a psychological problem for me. I had suffered a great deal, and I did not want to constantly reopen old wounds. Apart from that, I simply had too many friends in the East who would have been put in a difficult position by my saying what had really gone on. Most importantly, I was simply unwilling to allow the people in power the triumph of being able to say, "See, he was against us all along." They immediately turned everything you said upside down, and I simply did not want to give them this pleasure. I had no intention of ever again being used by these people voluntarily or involuntarily in any way. I simply refused to let myself be hurt. This was the deeper reason.

It is something Shakespeare experienced as well. Shakespeare was not a stranger to theatrical disputes, with Ben Jonson or with whomever he had his problems, and he was always looking for a patron. Since the beginning of theater, the normal procedure has been that the party in power at the time set its followers up as the heads of theater. These people then pushed through their own interests in the name of the party. This clashed with my personal aesthetic standards for theater.

Guntner: What will happen to theater in the GDR now?

Lang: The main problem is a financial one. The territories of the former GDR are faced with extremely complicated social problems. There is no central national control anymore, which means that national funding is not automatically available as it was in the past. Now the individual communities will have to shoulder the responsibility for the survival of their theaters. Presumably a great deal will change since it will no longer be possible to have such a wide range of theater. Almost every minor city in the GDR had its own theater. This is the first crucial point. The second is that the very same people who were installed by the Socialist Unity Party still hold important posts in the theaters. As long as these people remain in power, there will not be a change in attitude. A new generation has to come into the theaters, and then we can see what new concepts and structures develop and whether or not they are interesting.

Guntner: In 1983, you wrote about "Living Theater in the Nineties." What is your formula for theater in 1990?[1]

Lang: My essay was an attempt to point out to the people in charge that theater requires long-term development and that we needed some new ideas. The more important reason behind this was that the "technical" media were on the increase, and I strongly felt that it was necessary for theater to formulate its own position clearly. Theater must remain different from film and television. The theater is the only place where immediate communication between the audience and the artist takes place, because there is no dividing wall, even though we may pretend that a "fourth wall" exists. The contact is direct. It is not a television set. I think that the social upheavals at the moment will result in theater becoming more aggressive, more expressive, and more explosive in the immediate future.

Guntner: What role will Shakespeare play in this?

Lang: He will play an enormous role. It is the issue Thomas Brasch deals with in his adaptation of *Romeo and Juliet* entitled *Love, Power, Death, or the Drama of Romeo and Juliet* that we are rehearsing at the moment. What is the true relationship between love, power, and death? What function does language have in our age?

Guntner: It is also the central dilemma of *Richard III.* The question of power—the misuse of power.

Lang: Yes, this "me first" mentality. This brings us back to what we said about anarchism. Society is becoming ever more regimented, more governed by technology, and uses more and more data, which is becoming more and more abstract. This subversive anarchism, which means creativity and humanity will become more and more important. The theater is the place where subversive anarchy, creativity, and humanity can manifest itself once again.

(31 October 1990)

10

Thomas Langhoff: "Growing Up with Shakespeare: Furthering the Tradition"

Andrew McLean: How did you first become interested in Shakespeare?

Thomas Langhoff: It was genetic. I honestly do not know of any theater that does not define itself in terms of, or in opposition to Shakespeare. Since I come from a theatrical family, I was brought up in the same way as an English or American theater kid. The fairy tales that my parents told me were simply Shakespearean stories. My childhood experiences in the theater also had something to do with it.

I can remember performances in the famous Zürich Schauspielhaus, where my father, Wolfgang Langhoff, was an actor from 1934 to 1945, during the time of his emigration from Nazi Germany. This period was one of the greatest moments for the German language theater in this century. As a result of the suppression in Germany, a wonderful theater came about in Zürich, the cornerstones of which were productions of Shakespeare. The comedies made a great impression on me, and, of course, *Romeo and Juliet.* You cannot get through adolescence without *Romeo and Juliet.* I saw my father perform in many Shakespearean roles, but I liked him best as Petruchio. I was very proud of him. My love for Shakespeare is like the love for a close relative or family member. I grew up with Shakespeare.

My father made Shakespeare come alive for us—even more than Goethe. Goethe was important, but my father was always involved with Shakespeare. Shakespeare always works well with children and young people. You can talk wonderfully to a group of school kids about a play by Shakespeare, but you cannot do this with Schiller or Goethe, Racine, or Corneille. They are too complicated. Shakespeare is not complicated.

Lawrence Guntner: A while ago in this theater, Heiner Müller told young directors: "We have discovered that the structures in Shakespeare are really simple and straightforward. It is only theater that makes them complicated."

Langhoff: Heiner is right, but presenting the complexity of Shakespeare is also an integral part of a lively confrontation with him. For me, his plays are like a beautiful vase that you have to fill with something. The ingenious clarity and simplicity of the form is what I always rediscovered. But you can, and should, enrich this form. Often this increases the complexity, but this is legitimate. On the other hand, topical questions are often so complicated that to use them to open up and enrich a Shakespearean play can be dangerous. I have seen productions of *A Midsummer Night's Dream* that have approached the play in a scientific psychological way and have made it so complicated that nobody could understand the images any more. If you return to Shakespeare's basic form, you will also discover the best theatrical interpretation, but first you must discover the simple basic structure for yourself.

Guntner: How was it in your 1980 production of *A Midsummer Night's Dream* at the Maxim Gorki Theater?

Langhoff: *A Midsummer Night's Dream* is for me the most ingenious play Shakespeare ever wrote. Shakespeare combines three plays in one. Each plot is fragmentary and incomplete. None of them is self-contained or finished, yet the play has an ingenious unity. Its structure is ingenious, and at the same time, open and unfinished. Some themes are left incomplete; some are broken off. *A Midsummer Night's Dream* is like the three Chinese boxes: you take out one, and there is another one inside, and then another one. It's that sort of construction. It's a continuous challenge to the theater. Whenever theater becomes tired and slightly ill, you should put on *A Midsummer Night's Dream,* and then it'll become healthy again. It's like a cure for a sick patient.

That was the starting point. A dramatic conceptualization always begins with a particular ensemble, and we were trying to create an ensemble at the Maxim Gorki Theater. The best aspect of GDR theater was the really good ensembles. *A Midsummer Night's Dream* was a good way to bring a stable ensemble together. We were looking for a new challenge and wanted to work on a new approach to acting. We were still very influenced by Peter Brook's theories, even though I had never seen his production of *Dream.* Nevertheless, his production was a theoretical point of departure for us. We were looking for a way to liberate the actor from the script with a view toward discovering the totality of the play. Shakespeare always demands the complete vision, not only the analysis of the text, not only the historical analysis, but the totality of the play, the total involvement of the actor, with all his body skills: singing, dancing, jumping, with everything at his disposal.

Guntner: The production was very physical. In the woods, the ground became a sort of trampoline. The elves were always being knocked down but always sprang back up again.

Langhoff: I am still quite pleased with this idea. In German there is this idiom: "To have the ground torn away from under your feet." Is it the same in English?

Guntner: We say, "The rug is pulled out from under your feet."

Langhoff: This is exactly what we were trying to illustrate. In the woods, the stable ground suddenly disappeared, and bounce, bounce, bounce, all the characters lost their contact with the ground, or rug. The whole stage became a single rubber floor, a trampoline. When the dream was over, as if by magic, the floor rose up again. It was suddenly rigid again. They had come back down to earth, back to everyday life. They had to prove themselves once again in the real world.

McLean: When you were working on a total conception for *A Midsummer Night's Dream* were you also trying to make a statement about life in the GDR?

Langhoff: It's not possible to say that in such a narrow way even though it was true to some extent. With Shakespeare you always try to incorporate the state of the society in which you live into the production. The contemporary is always reflected in Shakespeare, and no matter how hard you try, you cannot prevent this. However, topical theater—with direct topical references—is something I've never liked and never done. I've always had the reputation of not being political. Langhoff does the unpolitical things. That does not bother me. There is no theater that is not political because our age is always reflected in the theater. Naturally, when we depicted the society of Athens, how they treated strangers and how they treated young people, this was contemporary East German society. The theater public was aware of this, too. They knew that these were not Athenians, that this was their own society and that these were their own problems, for example, those of the young people. These were current problems of our society. The Athenian court scenes in acts 1 and 5, at the beginning and end of *A Midsummer Night's Dream*, were made relevant to the present. The dream world is another matter. That is universal. The woods is the domain of the imagination.

Guntner: Were you influenced in this production by Robert Weimann's work on plebeian theater?

Langhoff: What one learns from Weimann is the practical experience of Elizabethan theater. What was it like? How did they do that? How did they relate to the audience? How did the puns and jokes go down? *A Midsummer Night's Dream* is especially full of word play, witticisms, and very simple jokes. On the one hand, there is the humorous joke level, and on the other, you have Titania and Oberon. This amplitude is so unbelievable; it is what makes the play so difficult to perform. It is Shakespeare's most difficult play. More difficult than *Hamlet*.

Guntner: Why?

Langhoff: Because of this vast range. On the one hand you have the clowns, and on the other, there is opera and poetry, plus Oberon and Titania—three worlds in one play. It's incredibly difficult. I've seen the play done badly very often, just because it falls apart so easily. *Hamlet*—no problem. With *Hamlet,* you decide on a concept and a particular direction and do it. *Hamlet* is conceptually difficult, but the production itself isn't difficult; it directs itself. If you have a good Hamlet, your problems are over. If you have Laurence Olivier, then everything's all right. With *A Midsummer Night's Dream,* good actors alone are not enough. You have to find a way of integrating these three components so that the play doesn't fall apart.

McLean: How would you compare your starting point for *A Midsummer Night's Dream* with Alexander Lang's?

Langhoff: By coincidence, I heard that Alexander Lang was planning to direct *A Midsummer Night's Dream* at the Deutsches Theater. Alex and I are friends, so we decided to do parallel productions as friends and rivals. We even wanted to play "crosswise," but the directors of our theaters would not hear of it. I was supposed to play Bottom in his production, and he was supposed to play Oberon in mine, but the heads of our theaters stopped that, so we worked completely independently of each other.

The difference between the two productions is first of all that Alex tried to condense the problem, and I tried to expand it. Thus, Alex deleted a great deal. When you tackle a single issue, a lot in the text is just distracting, so you cut out a great deal. For Alex, only one theme was interesting: nothing works any more. Alex described clearly the final stages of a society in which nothing works any longer, not even comedy. The Rude Mechanicals are all over, too. They are just another part of the same declining frustrated society. That's what Alex was telling us, and he did so in a very stringent and exact manner—but at a great cost. Very much was left out. At Maxim Gorki, our conception was the totality of the work. We wanted to include as much as we could possibly carry even though you cannot carry everything from the play. There is too much, and it is too heavy. Alex's *Dream* was bitter and cruel; but ours included Puck's final speech: "Give me your hands if we be friends, / And Robin shall restore amends." Lang deleted that. But in ours, there was a reconciliation with the audience.

Guntner: In Lang's production Theseus and his train fell asleep.

Langhoff: Everybody fell asleep. First they slept with the girls, and then they fell asleep. And then everything was cleared away. This was a cruel and bitter ending. I understood it, but I felt sorry about it.

McLean: Which translation did you use for your production?

Langhoff: Our own translation. That is, we used a sort of mixture. We took Schlegel, and then I simply did an interlinear translation together with an American woman. It is a very interesting translation, but for us the translation is always the main problem when we decide to put on a Shakespeare play. Our access to Shakespeare is always through a translator. This is a terribly difficult situation. You are in a privileged position because you can read Shakespeare in the original. We can read him, too, but not with our hearts. The whole table is covered with different translations—sixteen or twenty maybe. The decision as to the underlying concept of a production is made when the translation is decided upon. For many years, the Schlegel-Tieck translations were said to be the best. Their translations may be imprecise and even incorrect, but to a German ear many of them are in a truly beautiful language. I knew all of the translations of *A Midsummer Night's Dream* by heart. I kept examining all of them, again and again, also phonetically. I listened to them, and then we chose Schlegel with interlinear translations and a critical apparatus explaining what an individual word meant, and what changes it had gone through. Then we did our own translation. I used a mixture. Puck's epilogue was my contribution.

McLean: Are your actors sensitive to the translated text? Do they have a problem with that? Or is the problem with the text your problem as a director?

Langhoff: It is my problem as a director, but in this case—*A Midsummer Night's Dream*—it was a collective problem. It was the actors' problem when I told them it was Shakespeare's intention to let the clowns improvise in their own scenes, that is, he would not mind if we made up our own jokes on the spot. That is what I mean by a collective problem. Or take the puns. They are so wonderful, like those of the Marx Brothers. This was where the actors were excellent. They always improvised, and we simply wrote down the best versions and used them. It was not only up to the director, it was a collective decision. But a speech by Titania or the dialogue from the political domain had to be memorized beforehand.

Guntner: What other Shakespeare have you directed beside *A Midsummer Night's Dream* and *The Merchant of Venice*?

Langhoff: These have been my only attempts so far. I worked as an actor in Shakespearean plays for many years. I had a late start in my career as a director.

McLean: Why *The Merchant of Venice* at that particular time [1985]?

Langhoff: *The Merchant of Venice* is a play that has given the Germans stomach cramps ever since 1945. It is performed very rarely, and then only under very difficult conditions. It was a challenge to perform it here at the Deutsches Theater, and, in my opinion, it was a very interesting production. Somebody once said that as long as there's one Jew who objects to it, you cannot put on this play in Germany. Should we then go around and ask all the Jews? It is very difficult to ask them all if we may perform it or not. I didn't like the fact that the problem was taboo for both sides. It was taboo for the Jewish community and for the so-called official side. So in those days the official side said: "No, we don't want that, we don't want to have a problem." So, I replied that Shakespeare was not a problem. When they said no, we don't want this play, I answered, yes, right now is the time to put on this play. After all, we were not performing it in 1945, but a lot of time has passed, and you must approach this wonderful play in a new and objective manner.

There was no antisemitism in the GDR, but things were suppressed. There were taboos. The children at school simply did not know what antisemitism was. It was presented all too schematically in accordance with the Marxist version of history. Communists and Jews were persecuted, so they were good, and the Nazis were evil. That's all there was to it. This was the way it was for a long time. I believed that a more sophisticated approach to this complex problem meant that we must also tackle this play again, so I kept repeating this again and again.

It is a wonderful play, but it also poses many problems. Shylock is the central problem. In our production, we tried—and Peter Zadek did the same in Vienna—to set the play in a social context. I was interested in this struggle between two men who represent two opposing systems. I know there are a hundred theories and complicated interpretations of *The Merchant of Venice,* but I have always supported the view that it explores the problem of the outsider, but not specifically a Jewish outsider. With Shakespeare, I can't believe that it was a specifically Jewish problem. And why should it be a Jewish problem? There were no Jews in London at that time, so there was not a problem. There was simply a character on stage who represents a principle, namely, how to make money. One person does it like this and another person does it like that, and consequently they come into conflict with each other.

Guntner: In your production the group around Antonio consisted of pimps, petty gangsters, and small-time Mafia—a very seamy atmosphere.

Langhoff: Yes, there was a gangster atmosphere that was visually influenced by Venice. It had something Italian and decadent about it, very beautiful, very colorful, very rich but also a bit unpleasant.

Guntner: Then there was that wonderful improvised scene with Ulrich Mühe as Launcelot Gobbo when he debates with himself in Saxonian dialect whether to leave Shylock or not. The Saxonian was a gestic reference to the political situation at the time of the performance, that is, whether to flee the GDR or not, and in a language derived from the specifically GDR language culture.

Langhoff: That was a burning political question at the time, and we wrote that into the text. Mühe carried on his three bricks and talked about "my little wall." Our conception for the play was to show the bright side of the

The Merchant of Venice, DIR. T. Langhoff, 1985. Shylock (Düren) in court. Photo: Wolfram Schmidt.

world. It was a generally cheerful production. My idea was to present Venice as a rather wonderful world so that the problems would become all the more visible.

McLean: How would you have approached the play in the seventies?

Langhoff: We can trace definite lines in our social and cultural development. For example, in the sixties we discovered that it was possible to approach Shakespeare from a new perspective using Brecht's method, to see Shakespeare through Brecht's spectacles, so to speak. Before that, Shakespeare had been viewed in terms of German Romanticism due to the Schlegel and Tieck translations. By supposedly applying Brecht's ideas about epic theater we came up with crazy, wild, and terrible productions with altered endings. This was healthy and good for the theater because it gave it new impulses. The only practical example by Brecht himself was his adaptation of *Coriolanus*. The application of Brechtian methodology to Shakespeare was the decisive critical point in the history of Shakespeare performance in the GDR. All the resources of epic theater, for example, to use masks and any other available means were used to bring about a so-called alienation effect. To see Shakespeare first from a sociopolitical perspective was a positive development You always began with Marx and Engels, and then you would inquire whether it worked with Shakespeare. If it worked with Shakespeare, it could be performed. Many of these productions were very boring. In the history plays, this worked very well because the Romantic element was cut out and because you approached the plays more rationally. I believe that from this point on, the reception of Shakespeare in the GDR, and in the Federal Republic of Germany, diverged very sharply. Perhaps you cannot even talk about a general tendency in the West German theater. There have always been very differing personalities. Zadek's Shakespeare was totally unlike Gründgen's. With us there were more general, broader tendencies. There was a time when all the productions of Shakespeare looked pretty much the same throughout the whole country. I still remember how all Brecht's young students, the so-called Brecht Boys, tried the same things, but this led to stagnation.

Guntner: When did this stagnation set in?

Langhoff: At the end of the sixties and into the beginning of the seventies. After 1968, things changed. After 1968, we all changed and began to think differently. There was a new generation, with new directors, such as Adolf Dresen and Benno Besson. We were all really students of Benno Besson. He was the one who really got things rolling here, even though in my opinion his Shakespeare experiments were not always successful. He did *The Two Gentlemen of Verona* here in this theater, but it was not so successful. He also did *Hamlet* at the Volksbühne.

Guntner: Which Shakespeare productions affected you?

Langhoff: There were two productions of *King Lear* at the Deutsches Theater that made lasting impressions on me: one was directed by my father in 1957 and the other was directed by Friedo Solter (starring Fred Düren as Lear) in 1976. *Lear* was a very important play in the GDR. The 1957 performance of *Lear* that my father directed was very impressive and very important. It was also very controversial, and the official reviews were terrible, just awful. In the 1950s, the official line on drama was based on a false understanding of realism in Soviet drama. At that time, Shakespeare was very illusional. The heath had to be a real heath, there had to be a castle and pretty scenes—nice fairy tale theater. Together with Brecht's experiments, this production of *King Lear* was something new. On the stage, there was a real, a simple Shakespearean stage and nothing else. Whereas Shakespeare had always been presented in the National Socialist and in the false Soviet realist traditions with grandiose scenery, this production of *Lear* was austere. It affected my life greatly, and I can still remember every scene of it. I must have seen it between ten and fifteen times.

Guntner: You mentioned that the first influence on your work in the theater was Brecht; how about later in your career?

Langhoff: That is connected with the development in the GDR: on the one hand, the rigid Brecht system, and on the other hand, the young people who said enough is enough. Benno Besson was the main point of departure. He said but what comes after Brecht?

Guntner: Brecht and beyond.

Langhoff: Exactly. The Brecht disciples had their first positions in the theater. Now along came a completely new generation who had big problems with Brecht. We, the "grandchildren," realized that all the so-called sons of Brecht called him "papa" and always recited what Brecht had said or written. And we were strongly opposed to it. Besson said that Shakespeare had to be the beginning of theater and not Brecht, so we all took up Shakespeare as a way to confront Brecht.

Guntner: There was a Brecht period and a period of freeing yourselves from Brecht. What effect did this have on your work in the theater?

Langhoff: Brecht's concentration on social, rational points in the play seemed too narrow to us. Theater has many possibilities at its disposal— the head, the heart, and the body—and we felt that Brecht concentrated too much on the head. Theater is the totality of the whole human body, and it has various means at its disposal—body, dance, song—which Brecht used, too, but didactically. We wanted to be more performative (*spielerisch*). We felt that Brecht's disciples no longer did that which Brecht had wanted to do. They were no longer theater people but pedantic teachers.

Guntner: Who else besides Besson could you name, and which theater productions do you think were characteristic for this new approach to performance.

Langhoff: This was the phase of experimentation at the Volksbühne under Besson's general direction. Successful and unsuccessful. For example, an *Othello* that my brother Matthias and Manfred Karge tried, did not work out. Adolf Dresen was another director who stood for this development. Another was Frido Solter and his *King Lear* and *Tempest*.

Guntner: And now we seem to have come to a postreaction to the Brecht phase. The cue is the Marx Brothers. Frank Castorf, for example, seems to be more influenced by Groucho Marx than Karl Marx.

Langhoff: I do not think that is the future. I believe in continuing the tradition. Tradition is not dead. Tradition means that a fire is burning and that you add something to it. That is the theater of the future. Castorf's approach is not the main track. It is wonderful, it is very amusing, but in three years it will be past.

Guntner: Who are your mentors? Your father, of course, but are there any other theater people who have had a decisive influence on you?

Langhoff: Peter Brook. Absolutely. Theoretically as well as practically he has had the most lasting influence on me. Giorgio Strehler also had a strong influence on me. At one point in my development I thought the German theater was terrible and discovered Strehler and Brook and realized that they were doing much better theater than we were—more full of life, actors' theater. That is what I do, theater with actors. I am who I am, and it is irrelevant who my mentors were; nevertheless, Peter Brook was decisive for my personal development. For Shakespeare, it was Fritz Kortner. I was never able to see him personally but thank heavens I was able to see him on television. Peter Stein was strongly influenced by Kortner; he was his assistant director in Munich.

Guntner: What will your performing space be like in the future?

Langhoff: At the moment it is an empty space. We have to put something in it. The task of theater is always the same. It is always subversive. That is what it was, and that is what it will always be. Only now the stress will be different. The basic direction, that theater is a humanistic element of society, that it struggles for justice and decency, will remain unchanged. And we are internationalists. The wonderful thing about theater is that it is a part of a world system, world theater, even in a period of isolation. We are a part of something greater, and that is why all of this is not such a problem for me. The isolation of the individual person, in front of his television set, in front of the electronic media, will become even greater. One of the few remaining places for communication is the theater. People need it, otherwise they become ill. Without art and something to do, all of humanity becomes ill, perhaps they are already ill, but it will become even worse.

Theater has an important role to play because we need it. My problem is that a part of our audience needs to see something different because they have different kinds of problems. In the GDR it was easy to find the problems; everybody knew what they were, so it was easy to get a laugh. Now the critique, the analysis, must become more exact, more concrete, and must be oriented toward the needs of the spectator. That is why I will continue to do theater as I have always done it. In theater you can never do something today like you did yesterday; you must always look forward and orient yourself to today. That is why a situation as we have today is not so unfavorable if theater is to remain young and fresh. We had become a little self-satisfied. We had no problems, we had a large enough audience, we had a name for ourselves, we had a good system of theaters, we earned enough money. We had no problems. Now we have problems, and that is good, very good.

And what will remain? Our experience, a well-functioning system of theaters with good training, a theater which puts the ensemble work first, that is what has to remain. That is what I would see as our contribution to a pan-German theater. It will remain because such an organism does not suddenly disappear by itself. We all know each other, and we all have a common point of reference, and that will remain for sure if we receive support. If there is hostility and we are ruined financially that would be terrible.

(26 April 1990)

11

Heiner Müller: "Like Sleeping with Shakespeare." A Conversation with Heiner Müller and Christa and B. K. Tragelehn

Andrew McLean: When did you become interested in Shakespeare?

Heiner Müller: It sounds so trite, but when you want to write plays—which I always wanted to do—Shakespeare remains a role model, a continual challenge, and a thorn in your side. When I was thirteen or fourteen, I wanted to read *Hamlet*. I had only had about a year of English, so it did not work, but I tried anyway. It was a lovely old English edition with many footnotes. My interest in Shakespeare was first of all my interest in *Hamlet*. *Hamlet* is more German than English; it is performed more often in Germany than in England.

McLean: What was your most interesting experience with Shakespeare?

Müller: My most interesting experience with Shakespeare was a translation of *As You Like It* I did for a performance Klaus Tragelehn directed with students at the Film Academy in Potsdam in 1969.[1] I tried to translate the text literally with the fewest alterations possible, even in the syntax. It was kind of like sleeping with Shakespeare. After awhile I felt as if I were in his body and could feel how he moved. In his dramaturgy, there was a strange mixture of big cat and snake movements, which I enjoyed. Later I rediscovered the same movements in *Richard II,* which has the same kind of rhythm. It was a physical experience, bisexual, masculine-feminine, very interesting. Since then I know what Shakespeare's intestines were like.

Lawrence Guntner: In your adaptation of *Macbeth,* which you directed with Ginka Tscholakowa at the Volksbühne [Berlin, 1982], Lady Macbeth was not simply a cunning witch who seduces poor Macbeth into killing Duncan but also a victim of her own machinations.[2]

Müller: I wanted to see what would happen when you change Shakespeare and the chance to direct *Macbeth* was just such an opportunity. I had started to translate the play and to change it since there were many things that I did not like. The text of the play is very corrupt, and Lady Macbeth is not

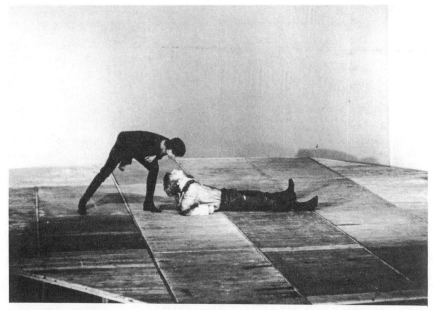

As You Like It, DIR. Tragelehn, 1969. Rosalind and Orlando. Photo: courtesy of B. K. Tragelehn.

the most successful of Shakespeare's women characters. She is sketched in very lurid tones. My rendition is not completely successful, but when I directed the play, I tried to move away from the witchlike aspect of her character. The source of this idea was the actress who played the role, Corinna Harfouch, a young actress, not long in Berlin, a real product of East Germany.

Guntner: Why did the production touch off such a scandal?

Müller: It was supposed to be taken off the program. Shakespeare was always a dangerous author in Eastern Europe. Directors were continually being banned to the provinces for directing Shakespeare. The tragedies or the histories rather than the comedies were always good for a scandal because they have something to do with power. Macbeth is Stalin, and Banquo is Trotsky, and there you have your scandal.

Guntner: Did you see the play this way?

Müller: Not so clearly at first, but as soon as someone wrote this in West Germany, this was the case, of course. At the time, I did not know that Johannes R. Becher had written a sonnet about Stalin, a poem about the feared knock on the door at four o'clock in the morning when the Soviet secret police come to arrest you. In it, Becher quotes directly from *Macbeth:*

"Macbeth murders sleep." It is a simple metaphor clearly meant to stand for Stalin in a poem written in Moscow during Becher's emigration.

McLean: It is interesting how Shakespeare is understood differently in different countries.

Müller: Yes, but only here. Shakespeare in the West is uninteresting. I think that it will become difficult to perform Shakespeare here. It will be like in the West and that will be boring. It will be extremely difficult to approach Shakespeare now, because history has come to an end for awhile, history in the European sense.

Guntner: Your dramatic work has two major poles of reference. On the one hand translations and adaptations of the theater classics, especially classical Greek drama and Shakespeare; on the other drama about recent German history, especially East German history. What do the two have to do with each other?

Müller: To begin with, Shakespeare was an opportunist. If you write for the theater, you are dependent on performances, that is, opportunities. Therefore, you go with the trend and pick up material where you can. Shakespeare did it, and Hollywood does the same today. Shakespeare created no trends; Marlowe invented more. Shakespeare invented nothing; he picked up trends that already existed and refined them. This is what makes him the prototype dramatist, an opportunist. It was opportune for me to write a play about East Germany, and when it was finished there was always trouble; then it was opportune to do an adaptation of a classic.

McLean: When we asked B. K. Tragelehn why he did translations, he answered because he did not have a job.

Müller: That is so disappointing for the reader, because he wants to hear something substantive. There is a text from Brecht in which he speaks of Shakespeare as "Willem" or "Willy," and it occurs to Brecht that Shakespeare wrote for particular voices and not for particular bodies. That means his texts were autonomous and thus they could come out of any body. The autonomy of the text is very important, especially with Shakespeare. At a very early age, I read Gustav Freitag's *Die Technik des Dramas*, a standard work for all aspiring dramatists, but I never understood it. In fact, I even began to doubt if I would ever become a dramatist at all since Freitag claimed that every character had his or her individual language—an iron rule of early naturalism, a kind of "prenaturalism." So I desperately searched for the individual language of Shakespeare's characters but heard only Shakespeare's language. It is simply not true that an individual character of his speaks differently than all the others, as if he spoke a foreign language. It is all Shakespeare's language with its tremendously varied facets, levels, and planes of meaning.

B. K. Tragelehn: This can also refer to impersonal matter such as the storm in *King Lear*. In terms of language, the storm on the heath is completely foreign, so it is ridiculous if the sound effects person has it thunder then. If thunder comes at the right place, it is stupid; it only works at the wrong place.

McLean: How would you explain to a naive American how your Shakespeare performance reflected the political reality and changes in your country?

Müller: A very difficult question—the question of the century. Here is a rather stupid example. "There is something rotten in the state of Denmark," always elicited a laugh from audiences in East Germany; I do not think that it would have interested anyone in West Germany. It did not matter if something was rotten in the state as long as the money kept coming in. That is a superficial beginning.

The other point is that the essential matters in Shakespeare's plays are simple. With Shakespeare, the subjective factors in the story/history are very concrete and vivid. In West Germany, England, or the United States things were a bit different than in Eastern Europe. Not everything depended on personalities as it did in East Germany. In Western countries, the basic factor in the balance of power was money, but this was not the case in East Germany, so people were forced to find other means of gaining power. Whatever it was, it was not money. The plays of Shakespeare were written in a pre-Puritan world in which money is not the supreme value. After the rise of the Puritans, money is the supreme value and Molière and Ben Jonson become interesting. Molière is more interesting than Shakespeare in eastern Germany at the moment.

With Shakespeare, the personality is more dominant than with any of his contemporaries, except for Marlowe. In Marlowe's plays you still find the heroic personality. Shakespeare describes the decay of the personality, and that is exactly the point of historical crisis. After Shakespeare, there are no more personalities in history for a long time, not until after the 1917 October Revolution, which was a violent, unsuccessful attempt to alter the course of history, with inadequate means, at the wrong time and the wrong place. But after 1917, Shakespeare became interesting again. That may sound a bit apocalyptic, but when have there been really Shakespearean characters in European history? I mean historical personalities we can relate to Shakespeare's protagonists. In the eighteenth century perhaps, but none in the nineteenth century; the nineteenth century was not a century for Shakespeare. Through the October Revolution, the twentieth century became a century for Shakespeare. Lenin was a Shakespearean character, Trotsky was a Shakespearean character, Stalin was a Shakespearean character. In terms of the tragedies, there were no Shakespearean personalities before them, and none after them.

Guntner: And in East Germany?

Macbeth, **DIR. Müller/Tscholakowa, 1982. Duncan (Düllmann) kneeling, behind him the three Macbeths. From left to right: Beyer, Montag, and Gwisdek. Photo: Adelheid Beyer, courtesy of the Volksbühne Berlin.**

Müller: Here we had parodies of Shakespearean characters. The background was the real characters. The German Democratic Republic never really existed; it was only a parody of the Soviet Union, a Soviet colony, or whatever you want to call it. That was the background.

Guntner: Why did Shakespeare performances evoke such strong reactions?

Müller: In the case of *Macbeth* it was the constellation Stalin-Trotsky.

Tragelehn: The stage design for Heiner's *Macbeth* in the Volksbühne was the inner court of a Berlin tenement with all three sides the same. In this way, the play was localized, and the spectator could relate what happened on stage to his own life, to the values of the social system he lived in, and to the structures of his own world.

Müller: A primitive example; a rather cheap trick on our part was that the part of Duncan was played by a woman, and she played him as an old man. That was immediately seen as the problem of the old leaders, the gerontocracy, the old men who hardly walk. When she walked on stage, to the audience she stood for Brezhnev. It was as simple as that. Everything was associated with these powerful persons. It was like a compass, and you did not have to explain a thing, which was perhaps a bit trite.

Guntner: In West Germany that would not have been obvious at all.

Müller: But this was not important in West Germany. You can let any character walk on stage with a face like Helmut Kohl's, but what is the point? It
is not interesting. The head of Helmut Kohl is completely interchangeable;
nobody is interested. In East Germany, however, this was not the case;
leaders could not be replaced so easily. Even if they were idiots, they had
tremendous power, and thus the discrepancy between the mediocrity of the
character and his scope for action was much greater. In West Germany it
is clear to everyone that the politicians do not determine government policy.
Thus they are not interesting as a point of reference for the theater. Policy
is made by industry, and industry remains invisible; you cannot put it on
stage. The movement of capital is invisible; war cannot be staged. Maybe
it was the archaic course of history here, which made it theatrical, the
archaic conditions in relationship to the those in developed capitalist countries. This archaic situation was the chance to set Shakespeare in scene, to
make Shakespeare political.

Guntner: B. K. Tragelehn, you directed Heiner Müller's adaptation of *Macbeth* in Düsseldorf. Did Müller's translation make a difference? What was
your approach? How did you localize the dramatic space, and what was
the reaction?

Müller: It was a very good production because it was very ascetic and did
not attempt to tell the audience something that it did not want to hear
anyway. It was very hermetic.

Tragelehn: For example, in act 4 when the witches return, Macbeth sat
alone in Dunsinane drinking beer. The actor who played Macbeth developed
this scene into an insane ritual walking back and forth between bottle and
glass until the witches appeared. I imagined that this was Konrad Naumann,
the party secretary in Berlin, at home. It seemed to me that if a performance
were halfway successful, and you heard the remark: "Something is rotten
in the state of Denmark," there should be some response. In West Germany
there was none. The people were so content; there was never any
discontent.

Müller: The reaction to such a statement in West Germany was one of
amusement; here it was aggressive. I thought that the drinking ritual in
Tragelehn's Düsseldorf production was terrific, but it also had another dimension for me, and that was in the stance of the actor toward a situation.
I was reminded immediately of the end of William Faulkner's *Sanctuary* in
which the killer Popeye is being convicted for a murder he did not commit,
but he is too lazy to protest the verdict. He tells his lawyer to do whatever
he likes and lays on his cot in his cell smoking cigarettes. That is what I
mean by stance, and stance is important, also in relationship to an audience. And regarding the audience in Düsseldorf, we should not forget Andy
Warhol's last significant comment on Germany. A reporter asked him: "Do

you like Germany?" and Warhol replied: "I like Düsseldorf. Everybody has ten fur coats." And this, of course, shapes an audience's response. The people who go to the theater in Düsseldorf may not have ten fur coats but perhaps eight or five. People with no fur coats do not go to the theater, and that determines how they respond to a performance.

McLean: When our students read *Hamletmaschine*, they ask what Heiner Müller's intention was. Our answer is to understand *Hamletmaschine* is to understand simultaneously particular realities: that of Hamlet, that of the twentieth century, that of East Germany, etc. What would you answer?

Müller: If it is California, I would say surf dramaturgy.

McLean: It is Wisconsin.

Müller: That is different; then I would say cows, but it is easiest to talk about how an idea came about. *Hamlet* has been an obsession for me almost since I began to read. Then I noticed parallels between the situation in *Hamlet* and what had gone on in Budapest. Imagine the son of Lazlo Rajk, the most prominent victim of the Stalinist witch-hunt trials. Rajk was a Stalinist, minister of the interior, and thus responsible for terror, so he was selected to be a scapegoat. Imagine the situation of Rajk's son in 1956, when years after the execution of his father as a spy and secret agent, the father was suddenly rehabilitated as a Communist. This was the situation of the son of a powerful father who had served a system, which the son could not accept. Suddenly there is a new system which is also suspicious, so here we had a situation similar to Hamlet's.

Tragelehn: Rajk's corpse was exhumed and officially reburied. In the midst of the gigantic demonstration, someone said: "If he were still alive, he would have turned the guns on you."

Müller: On the very people who were now for him. That is a Shakespearean situation. A man who was executed unjustly, even though he was, in fact, a killer, is exhumed and given a new funeral, which two hundred thousand people attend. Had he known that they were showing their support for him, he would have had them mowed down. That is Shakespeare. That works only as long as ideas have power and violence—so long as there is hope and expectations. And now the other side of the coin. Some time ago, I was in Münich to see a performance of *Philotekt*, and I noticed a statement on the Deutsche Bank: "ideas into markets" (*aus Ideen werden Märkte*). That is what has now happened since the downfall of socialism in Eastern Europe: no more ideas, only markets. And there is no place for Shakespeare on the stock market.

McLean: In reading your translations I get the impression that there is a poet at work here who is trying to articulate a relationship with Shakespeare, a theatrical relationship, maybe even a psychological relationship. That is not the same as someone who is just trying to translate a text. There is a sense of action and theatricality, but there is also a poet's vision at work. You simply change Shakespeare's text more than others do.

Müller: The more you change a text, the more it is the same. The text has to find another body, and it is my body, so it is a sexual relationship. You cannot translate words; you have to translate a whole context. Maybe it is a problem for philologists. When they translate, they have to translate words, but when theater people like Klaus Tragelehn translate, they translate for the theater, and they have a vision of theater.

Tragelehn: When I begin to translate and catch myself trying to achieve a particular accentuation, that is already a mistake. There have to be various possibilities for accentuation, but I cannot control this. That is up to somebody else. When I read Heiner's translation of *As You Like It*, I sense the extreme effort that went into trying to make the German as close to the English as possible. It would be much more difficult to do this today than back in the sixties. This also becomes apparent when I compare Heiner's translation of *Hamlet* with *As You Like It*. I notice it even more in my own work. I cannot put my finger on exactly what it is. I do not think *As You Like It* could be translated today as it was then, but I do not know why.

Guntner: The spectators seemed to listen more closely to every word of the text in the GDR.

Müller: We only received five television channels, two from the East and three from the West. As soon as the people can pick up twenty channels, no one will listen closely here either. The reason is that their sense of hearing will be blunted.

Tragelehn: The more television, the more language is reduced to an appendage of the visual image.

Müller: A vehicle, a message. That is the problem with *As You Like It*. It is usually the case with most of the Shakespeare productions in West Germany that the director or the dramaturg hammers together a translation out of various existing ones simply for economic reasons. They earn more if they do the translation themselves. In the case of *As You Like It*, the actors felt it was terribly complicated, even though it was not. They simply could not read it.

Guntner: You once told your actors during rehearsal that the structure of *Hamlet* is very simple and that we are the ones who tend to make it complicated. For most people, however, it is the mystery of *Hamlet* that appeals to them. What did you mean?

Müller: I noticed that the scenes shrink together to a very simple core when you rehearse them. Suddenly there it was right before my eyes. I am not able to read plays because I tend to see things as more complicated than they are. When you see the play on stage, you suddenly realize how transparent and logical everything is. The spectators as well as the players have a whole library of literature about *Hamlet* in their minds, even if they have never read the stuff themselves. They know the play is complicated, even though it is not. I was surprised to see how quickly the individual scenes shrank down to a basic core and how simple they really were. The problem was how to convince the actors that they were this simple.

McLean: If *Hamlet* can be reduced to a very simple structure or situation or contradiction, what is it?

Müller: Since I have been asked that about four hundred times already, I have an answer ready. A member of the ruling class, an intellectual, is destroyed by the fissure between two epochs. He does not like the old order—it is suspicious to him—but he does not like the new one, either.

Guntner: For Frank Castorf, Hamlet's problem is his memory. He keeps remembering what once was. He returns home from the university for his father's funeral to discover that his mother has a new husband. She tells him not to worry, but he cannot forget his father so quickly. And then the Ghost tells him what has happened. In Germany, there was a similar problem after 1945 and also after 1989.

Müller: That is very good, but I cannot talk about the play this way.

Tragelehn: It is very good because it is so simple. There is a simple core, which I can tack a lot on to. A son comes home from the university, and mom has a new husband. That happens.

Müller: I am always at a loss for words when someone asks me a question like that, so I always talk in abstractions. I am only interested in the material and not in what it means or stands for. Whatever I answer is completely arbitrary; I could just as well say something else. Whenever I say I am not interested in such questions, I always have a bad conscience, but in answering such questions I am destroying them. It is more important to keep the question alive than to kill it with an answer.

Guntner: Is it the German or European thirst for meaning? Everything has to mean something, otherwise chaos will reign.

Müller: There is a wonderful remark in the epilogue to Brecht's *Mann ist Mann:* "If you want to see something of significance, then you have to visit a pissoir." That is a very, very important sentence. Only that makes sense and nothing else. Susan Sontag tells a story about a New York taxi driver with a crucifix on his dashboard, who kept pestering her about whether she believed in UFOs or not. She was embarrassed and answered that she was not quite sure. "They exist, they do exist," he insisted. Whereupon he told her a lot stories to prove the existence of UFOs. She replied that he had a crucifix on his dashboard and asked him whether he were Catholic, and whether he went to church on Sunday. "Yes, every Sunday," he answered. "Well how do you reconcile your Catholic faith with your belief in UFOs?" she inquired. "There must be something behind God," was his answer. For Sontag, this sentence was the absolute abyss, the end of humanism. If God is not the final idea, then humanity is at its end.

Guntner: You see no true division of labor in the theater. Could we get rid of the director?

Müller: Absolutely; only not at the moment.

Tragelehn: If there is agreement concerning theater conventions, you do not need a director. Shakespeare had no director. The entrances and exits had to be organized, but plays were not "produced" in the sense that they are today. The director is necessary only if the agreements, regarding conventions, are always being changed for every performance. The director is a rather recent development who first appears at the turn of the century in Germany. The first real German director was Max Reinhardt, shortly before World War I.

Müller: That is because theater has something to do with war, and the theater director is a military profession.

Tragelehn: At the time of the Kaiser, all of the heads of theaters were ex-military people.

Müller: That is extremely important because that is the source of certain structures in the German theater. You have to confront the German audience militarily before they will accept what you are showing them. Theater in Germany is war. In England theater is entertainment, but in Germany it is war.

McLean: Between whom?

Müller: Between the actors and the director, between the actors and the audience, but that hardly works anymore because the actors are not belligerent enough anymore, and the audience neither. When Benno Besson directed his first play at the Berliner Ensemble, Brecht said "Do not worry; I will take care of the rows." At that time it was an iron law of the theater that there had to be a row at some time before any work could get done. A mechanism of suppression had to be set up and demonstrated before serious work could be accomplished. That had nothing to do with Brecht, only with his knowledge of how the German theater works.

Guntner: You once said the central question in doing *Hamlet* in East Germany was "Who is Fortinbras?"

Tragelehn: That was a clever advertising gag. Imagine the tension. The premiere was just as the German Democratic Republic was breaking up, and everyone was trying to guess who would come out at the end. But nobody understood it. Crazy. There is a remark by Carl Schmitt in the

Gabelsberger Stenographie in which he says: "Kafka is Fortinbras." I like that.

McLean: In the United States you often hear how easy it is for a theater to do whatever it wants because it has no political effect. Only a small group of intellectuals go to the theater. Now this was obviously not the case in the German Democratic Republic because Klaus spent some time in the coal mines and Heiner could not get his plays performed. What was the effect of theater performance on the spectators in the GDR?

Müller: The best way to answer that question is to tell a story about what happened after the scandal surrounding *Die Umsiedlerin* and Klaus had to go off to the coal mines. I went to see Hanns Eisler. Eisler had read the play and his first comment was: "I would have banned the play, too, because it is much too rosy." Then he said: "Müller, you ought to be grateful that you live in a country in which literature is taken so seriously." His third comment was more of a joke: "Müller, keep Schiller in mind. An Austrian tyrant is murdered in Switzerland. Those are the kinds of plays you have to write in Germany." The point was that the party functionaries had Napoleon's statement in the back of their minds: "*Figaro* is the revolution on the march." They believed in the political power of art and theater; but it no longer existed.

Guntner: But you certainly did not write the play solely as entertainment.

Müller: I wrote it to entertain myself, and Klaus directed it to entertain himself. The ideas the political functionaries had about the effect of art were always far beyond reality. The really interesting point was that power struggles were going on here continually. A balance of power between the factions within the party had to be worked out. In Western societies, people talked and still talk about money. Here money was not a power broker. Thus ideological struggles in the East were of vital significance, even though it may have appeared to be shadow boxing to the West. They were real wars. With a scandal over a theater performance, you could eliminate a rival, a functionary; that was what was at issue. For example, the film *The Trace of Bricks* (*Spur der Steine*), which is certainly not a masterpiece, opened in Halle very favorably. Everything was okay. Walter Ulbricht had given his approval and went on vacation. In Halle, the party secretary was Horst Sindermann, and Sindermann wanted to move over to Berlin. In Berlin, the party secretary, Paul Verner, did not want Sindermann in Berlin. For this reason, he waited until Ulbricht was on vacation, and when the film opened in Berlin, he made sure that the opening night was a scandal. Party members were instructed to attend the opening showing and protest. They agreed upon certain times to disturb the showing, for example, at 8:20 p.m. and then again at 8:35 p.m., even though they had never seen the film. They synchronized their watches and marched off to protest. In this way,

Sindermann's march on Berlin was delayed. Culture was used as a vehicle to carry out power struggles.

Guntner: But *The Refugee* (*Umsiedlerin*) was performed in a small studio stage in Karlshorst.[3]

Müller: And not a single farmer saw it.

Tragelehn: But you must admit that back then we still had some illusions as to what we could accomplish with theater.

Müller: Gigantic illusions. Another example is that during the rehearsals for *Umsiedlerin,* the Berlin Wall was built, and that was fine with us because now, we thought, we could discuss social problems in East Germany completely among ourselves without the West butting in. Years later I heard from Stephan Hermlin that at the same time that we had these illusions, Otto Gotsche, Walter Ulbricht's personal secretary, said to Hermlin: "Now we have the Wall, and now we will use it to squash everyone who is against us." That was the other side of the fence, but we were not aware of this at that time.

Tragelehn: In August 1961 I was working at the theater in Senftenberg, and at a party meeting almost all were of the opinion that now we would finally be able to do plays we could not have done earlier.

Müller: Now we could perform Mayakovsky because we had the Wall. What a contradiction. As an intelligent human being, you simply could not imagine stupidity of this dimension, and so we never understood what was really going on here. We were unable to think as they did; it was simply beyond the powers of our imagination.

Christa Tragelehn: The other half of your question is that culture here had exactly the opposite function that it did in West Germany. Here it had the effect as a dialectic, as the opposite side of what you just described. Since there were these limitations after 1961, theater assumed a public function that it certainly did not have in West Germany where a theater performance was only important for the director, the theater, or the media. Premieres in West Germany were and still are only for the newspapers—nothing else— and theater in general there was irrelevant. In East Germany the word was quickly spread that there was a performance you had to see, and people came to the theater who would normally never attend a theater performance.

Müller: There is the story of the farmer who died during the *Hamlet* performance in Greifswald in 1964. He was a member of the collective farm who attended a performance that was quite long for the GDR, two hours before the first intermission. In the midst of the performance, his bladder burst, but he sat in the middle and did not dare to get up and go to the toilet, so impressed was he by the performance of this great play. He died on the way to the hospital all because he did not dare to go to the toilet.

McLean: If a well-attended production of *Hamlet* is taken off the bill after only twelve performances, some kind of authority must have been challenged.

Müller: I will give you another example. Dresen's *Faust* at the Deutsches Theater [1968] was severely attacked. I happened to attend a discussion between members of the party academy—the elite school of the party—and the actors and the directors: Wolfgang Heinz was officially named as codirector and was also head of the theater. A teacher at the party academy got up and asked Herwart Grosse, who played God in the Prologue, the following question: "Although we do respect Herwart Grosse as a great actor, we are not in agreement with the satirical depiction of God the Father in the prologue in heaven." Wolfgang Heinz replied: "Comrades, we are materialists, Marxists, but we had no intention of satirizing God." Now that is characteristic. They identified with every authority figure whether it was God or the Devil or Richard the Second. Any time a leading figure in the dominant class was not presented as they wished, they smelled an attack on the party. Very primitive, but there you have it. It was so absolutely stupid and undifferentiated that you cannot even talk about it. It all came from the feeling that the party from the very beginning stood with its back to the wall, against the whole population, against the Soviet Union, against the West, against everybody. That was the situation.

(29 April 1990)

12

B. K. Tragelehn: "To Reckon with the Current Society"

Andrew McLean: How did you become interested in Shakespeare?

B. K. Tragelehn: Shakespeare has been integrated so thoroughly into German culture that I became acquainted with him at the same time I became acquainted with Goethe and Schiller. Shakespeare is a subject in school, and when one begins to go to the theater, there is always something by Shakespeare in the program of every large theater. I was born and raised in Dresden. For lower-middle-class children in Dresden, art was the easiest way out of the narrowness of life there, and that is why I started going to the theater while still in school. The first Shakespeare play I ever saw was *Romeo and Juliet* in the Staatstheater Dresden in the early 1950s. About the same time, I became interested in art and in politics. Thus, Brecht played an important role for me, but as a young boy, it was a long way from Dresden to Berlin. I saw my first Brecht play in Dresden when the Berliner Ensemble performed *Mother Courage*. I was nineteen before I arrived in Berlin, and I went to see Brecht. I was caught cheating during my chemistry final examinations (*Abitur*), so I had to repeat a whole year of school. I did not want to do that. Instead, I went to work at all kinds of jobs from warehouse worker to night watchman to mailman. Then I wrote to the Berliner Ensemble and asked if I could come and watch rehearsals. During my vacation in 1955, I went to Berlin and sat in on rehearsals when Benno Besson was rehearsing Farquhar's *The Recruiting Officer.* Hans Bunge, Besson's dramaturg, arranged an interview for me with Brecht. After talking with me for awhile, Brecht gave me a pile of photos from the *Mother Courage* production. He told me to pick out the good ones and left the room. I sorted out the best pictures; when he returned, I showed him my results. I tried to explain my choices to him, but he answered that I did not need to explain anything. He just looked at my choices and said: "Learn High German, you can't perform *Coriolanus* in Saxonian dialect—and learn English. Find an actor at the theater in Dresden to teach you High German and go to the public library and take out a book on Elizabethan drama in English—

196

and a dictionary. When you have finished the book, you can understand English. When you have written something, send it to me."

Lawrence Guntner: Was your reading on Elizabethan theater in any way decisive for your theater work?

Tragelehn: I really did not read very much on Elizabethan theater. My interview with Brecht was in February of 1955. In early summer I sent Brecht an article and visited him in Buckow. From September on, I was in Berlin. I did not really have time to think about it. My abilities in English were minimal. I had a year of school English, and then I had to switch to a school where I had to learn Latin. I started translating myself because the existing translations seemed inadequate. I simply wanted to know what the English text really said. At that time I had already met my wife, Christa, and she helped me a lot. In the beginning I had to work very hard just to find out what was in the text. In the early sixties we had hardly any lexicons or dictionaries to assist us. Today that has all changed, and it is no real problem, except for certain passages where there is room for interpretation. The difficulty is how to render it into German, how to transport as much as possible from the original English into German.

Guntner: What is your specific approach, and how has it changed in the course of the years?

Tragelehn: In Germany there is a clear division between literary language and colloquial language, which has to do with political developments. With Brecht, who borrowed much from low German dialects, this gap begins to close. With Shakespeare, a line as mundane as: "Bring me some whiskey!" will occur in blank verse and still sound very normal. Or a line may begin with very common, colloquial speech patterns, and in the next lines it develops into a tremendous chorale. This has not been possible in German until recently. In German theater there has always been a tendency toward literary language.[1] In the vernacular of the people, it was customary to place the verb after the subject as in English. This phenomenon in literary language of placing the verb at the beginning has happened only since Brecht. This has made it possible for German translators to approach the original English more closely.

Another important factor in developing a language for the theater is that verse plays were being written in East Germany. The first classical example of this is again Brecht. Writers, workers, and farmers started to write plays, and a farmer named Erwin Strittmatter wrote a scene for an amateur group that took place in the country. In cooperation with Brecht, this group developed the play known as *Katzgraben*, which marks the real beginning of East German theater. They were working together in Brecht's summer house in Buckow, and one day Strittmatter brought in a text in an unusual rhythm that Brecht diagnosed as iambic. The result was a verse play.

I met Müller in 1957, the year after Brecht died. Müller's *The Scab* (*Der Lohndrücker*), his first play, had just been printed in *Neue deutsche Literatur,* the magazine of the writers' association. I wanted to meet him, and we were introduced through a common friend. I directed his next play, on which he was working at the time, *Die Korrektur.* At that time only a fragment of the *Die Umsiedlerin* was finished. Originally it was composed in short prose sentences, like *Lohndrucker.* In the course of his work he began to write in verse, and it became a rather long play that can take up to four hours. That it became a verse play is very much due to the influence of *Katzgraben.*

Guntner: Did Müller's motivation for writing a play in verse come solely from *Katzgraben,* or did, perhaps, the tradition of Shakespearean theater play a hidden role?

Tragelehn: There is a point at which the two developments coincide. Seen historically, blank verse in German is an import. The true German verse form is so-called *Knittelvers* [four-stress rhyming couplets], sometimes called "Faust verse" by German scholars, but in the theater it was not really developed until Brecht and Müller picked it up.

Guntner: Your own Shakespeare translations often approximate English syntax. Is this an attempt to come closer to the English original or is it an attempt to make Shakespeare in German closer to an earlier vernacular form of speaking?[2]

Tragelehn: That is exactly the point at which various developments come together. To give a simple example, the position of the verb at the beginning of the sentence I mentioned before. Sometimes Schlegel will do this, too. But when a sentence is stretched over three lines, and the verb does not appear until the third line, the verse becomes sticky. Of course, this depends to some degree on the significance of the author but more so on developments in one's own national language and literature. In the Renaissance when the "English comedians" began to perform at German courts, they performed originally in English, then slowly began to repeat a few things in German, but so primitive that we cannot even speak of it as translation. At this time the German language completely lacked the worldliness, sensuality, and suppleness to express adequately the sensuality of violence as we find it in Shakespeare. It was completely impossible. Today this is different, but various developments in German literary language had to take place before it was possible to begin to approach Shakespeare's language adequately. The unique quality of translations by Heiner Müller, Maik Hamburger, and myself goes directly back to developments in East German theater and literature during the fifties and the sixties. We were reacting against the tendency in translators earlier in this century, such as Rudolf

Schaller, who only tried to improve upon Schlegel-Tieck. Heiner and I were aiming for something new, something fresh.

Guntner: Do our times demand a different verse form or a different theater language at the moment?

Tragelehn: This is most visible in translation, and I can follow this development more clearly in Müller's translations than my own. Müller's attitude in his translation of *As You Like It* from the sixties was to follow the English wording as closely as possible. The German was strained to follow the English. At that time, this sounded right. Today it is more difficult. Müller's *Hamlet* translation, which is later, is more "easy going," "milder," more "German" than his translation of *As You Like It*, which is more "English" in its German.

Guntner: How about Müller's adaptation of *Titus Andronicus*?

Tragelehn: What Müller did to *Titus* and to *Macbeth* was to interfere in the plot, to add something and cut something out, to continually alter and intervene in the play as Kleist did with Moliere when he adapted *Amphytrion* into German. It is a new play.

Guntner: How do you know if your translation is successful?

Tragelehn: Rehearsals; it works or it does not. If it does not, then you have to work at it some more. And I assume that is how Shakespeare did it, too. He probably improvised the clowning and wrote down the jokes. Shakespeare always wrote for the same actors. The clowns remained the same until one died, and another replaced him. Since Shakespeare always wrote for the same clowns, it is difficult to render the humor in a language suitable for a different actor.

McLean: Didn't Shakespeare's theater play a different role politically and culturally than the theater does today?

Tragelehn: Shakespeare's theater was centered in social reality and played a completely different role in the life of his age than our theater today. For us, theater is an aspect of culture and education. It exists in a somewhat elevated and removed cultural sphere. However, when Shakespeare began to write his plays, he already had a fully developed theater at his disposal, a whole system of agreements, for example, a certain stage form, and thus a specific dramaturgical form. This he developed even further, varied and played with the conventions. He even takes this to the extreme so that the conventions themselves become the subject matter of the drama. Young boys, for example, play the women in *As You Like It* or *Twelfth Night* in which Rosalind and Viola are boy actors who play girls who pretend to be boys. It is in the gender roles that the conventions begin to change and the differences blur. Today we do not have a theater with such binding agreements. Today you have to develop a new system for every production and put it across to your audience in the first scenes so that you can base the rest of the performance on this system of agreements and play with them. A somewhat similar situation existed in the early years of the GDR. The Berliner Ensemble set a standard in the early fifties. Up until Brecht's death in 1956 there existed a pious canon of agreements as to how you went about things in the theater. This was based on a political consensus.[3]

McLean: Did Shakespeare's theater have any such "pious canon of agreements" about how to work in the theater?

Tragelehn: What I said about Shakespeare coming upon an already developed theater and then developing it further is a bit misleading. There was a somewhat similar situation in the early years of the GDR. In the 1950s during Brecht's lifetime, the Berliner Ensemble set a standard. There was a pious canon of agreements as to how a theater was to proceed. Of course, it was based on a sociopolitical consensus. Heiner Müller and I tried to continue from there with plays like *The Scab, The Correction*, or *The Refugee*. The premiere of *Umsiedlerin* was an indescribable theater scandal. It was condemned as "counterrevolutionary, anti-Communist, and antihumanistic," and the play was banned. The scripts were collected by the secret police, and party members in attendance who did not stand up and protest during the performance were called to discipline by their party groups.

Guntner: What did the party not like?

Tragelehn: There had always been virulent opposition to new kinds of theater—even to Brecht. For example, *Katzgraben* was performed in two different versions. Müller's *The Scab* and *The Correction* were attacked as well but, in the late fifties, it was still possible to work. By 1961 it was no longer possible. The objections were incomprehensible, completely absurd. At that time, I was a party member. I was kicked out of the party and sent to work as a tipper in an open pit lignite coal mine. After a year or so, I was allowed to return to Berlin but had no work. Heiner was expelled from the Writers Association and was not able to earn any money for two years. He only survived by borrowing money. Then, in 1964, Adolf Dresen asked me to direct Ben Jonson's *Volpone* in Greifswald, but the director of the theater said no. Paul Dessau intervened for me in the Ministry of Culture, and I was allowed to do it.

Guntner: What was the reaction in Greifswald to this production?

Tragelehn: Fortunately for me there was the scandal about the Dresen/ Hamburger *Hamlet* just before, so the authorities left me in peace. Nevertheless, the program was banned. It was available for the premiere, but then it was banned. During 1967–1969, I worked as a teacher at the film academy in Babelsberg. It was an island to which some of us had withdrawn and where we could experiment internally before small groups without going public. Fritz Marquardt's production of Büchner's *Woyzeck* (Hochschule für Film und Fernsehen, 1967) was for me one of the most important performances of the entire 1960s, and it was performed only twice before fifty people in a small room. We performed *As You Like It* [1969] only three times.[4] The first two were open to the public, but the third was before a closed audience, and then we were forbidden to put it on anymore. It was supposed to be performed in Berlin and Magdeburg, but then it was rejected. The scandal involving Dresen's production of Goethe's *Faust* [1968] had been just before. The director of the film academy said that they were starting to train people for television and had no time or energy for any more theoretical debates about the classical dramatic tradition in the theater.

Guntner: What you have just said suggests that theater in the GDR provided a niche in which people who had no official access to an audience could come together. The theater might be viewed as a self-contained (and to some extent officially tolerated) world of nonconformist fantasy in which it is possible to hibernate and survive. Was Shakespeare and perhaps the whole traditional dramatic canon in the GDR also a niche, a space for the fantasy to hibernate and survive?

Tragelehn: In our work with Brecht and in our experiments with Heiner Müller, we always tried to relate older plays to contemporary reality and this work on older plays always led to conflicts.

Guntner: Conflicts with the old guys in power?

Tragelehn: That was part of it. First the cake and then the whip. When Honecker assumed power in 1971, there was a short period of liberalization, but not in the sense of a principle change or a truly Communist direction. One was able to take it easy; but, then, in the seventies things built up to a conflict. From 1972–76, I worked at the Berliner Ensemble and did three productions with Einar Schleef. First we did Erwin Strittmatter's *Katzgraben* [1972] again since *Umsiedlerin* was still banned. The second play was Frank Wedekind's *Spring Awakening* in 1974. This was the first time Wedekind had ever been performed in the GDR. We had real young people and apprentices from Berlin perform the children's roles, which was, of course, an attempt to relate the generational conflicts—the conflicts between parents and children—in the play to the exact same conflicts in contemporary GDR society. This triggered a strong reaction, but we were able to put it over. The third play was August Strindberg's *Miss Julie* in 1975. On the surface you might ask what does the sexual conflict between a Swedish baroness and her servant have to do with the GDR? But the inner core of the play concerns the relationship between master and servant, which is acted out between their legs. Again this topic was central to the political situation in the GDR. Exactly because it does not seem to have much to do with the GDR on the surface, the issues at the core of the play became immediately transparent to the audience. The party pressured Ruth Berghaus, the head, to keep the play off the bill, but again Paul Dessau intervened for us. And again there was a terrible strife; after it had played ten times, Berghaus took if off the bill.

For four years I did not have any work, even though there were many invitations from outside the GDR to work. Finally, I was allowed to accept an invitation, and I directed *Measure for Measure* in Stuttgart in 1979, the last year that Claus Peymann was there. But the problem was that I never had a visa. That was during the late seventies when the GDR simply expatriated and expelled all oppositional or critical persons. I was afraid that they would not allow me to return since I did not have a reentry visa. My wife knew the responsible bureaucrat, and she threatened a public protest on Alexanderplatz if I did not receive my visa. It worked. I was given one at the last minute. They never told you anything. They never told why you were not allowed a certain document.

McLean: Despite your experience, did and do you still see your work in the theater as a contribution to a socialist society?

Tragelehn: Of course, even when I worked in West Germany. But things have changed dramatically in West Germany. When I first came to Stuttgart in 1979, you could still notice the effects of 1968. There was still that drive. All of the people who have made a name for themselves in West German theater—Stein, Zadek, Peymann—all got started during the sixties. Before that there was only the neoconservative, noble, spectacle theater of Gustav Gründgens or Friedrich Schuh. Although the wave of 1968 had peaked years before, there was still the same thrust; the superstructure maintains certain structures long after the basis has changed and the actors were interested in learning something from someone from the GDR. This was the time of the Baader-Meinhof/Red Army Terrorist trials in Stammheim Prison near Stuttgart, and the question of the use of power by the state was very relevant. There was everything from anarchist ideas to the classical Communist model that the state assumes all the power to rid the people of power over other people, the idea that the state disappears. There were even ethnological discussions about societies with no government or about primitive societies with no form of social hierarchy. So *Measure for Measure* was very much to the point on these political issues. The theater in Stuttgart is right next to the state parliament, and armored vehicles were continually patrolling at night. In the play, when Elbow enters the court complaining, some people in the audience thought that he was a real policeman in uniform. The audience loved it. But since the "political and moral change" in West Germany and the advent of the Christian Democratic government [1982] things have changed. Everything has become more difficult. In the late seventies there was a feeling of togetherness among the actors in ensembles because everyone could relate to common political goals outside the theater. When this consensus no longer exists, when theater only relates to itself, it is like running against the wind. The result was that the ensembles broke up. Today the emphasis is on guest performances, and everyone tries to find the most attractive offer for himself. Today there is a new set of values and criteria. The emphasis is on personal success rather than achieving a common goal shared by a group of people. The directors are much more oriented toward the personal recognition they receive for their directorial concept than for taking a socially relevant point of view.

Guntner: And what about a socialist theater?

Tragelehn: When Brecht was at the Berliner Ensemble during the 1950s, he seemed to have everything he could have possibly desired: his own theater, good actors, and money. But compared to some of his experiments before 1933 or compared to his work with Charles Laughton in California on *Galileo*, he was, in fact, limited. Brecht's own comment on this situation was that a swimmer can only swim as fast as the current and his own strength allow him to. You have to reckon with the current of society, and when you want to swim against the current, it requires more effort than to swim with the current.

Guntner: Has it also become more difficult for a socialist Shakespeare?

Tragelehn: I think so.

Guntner: Are you a socialist critic of Shakespeare?

Tragelehn: That is a practical question. Take for example *Measure for Measure*. For some strange reason, it is often unsuccessful, and I think the reason is that director and actors forget that at its core is the struggle between the Duke and Angelo. People tend to overlook this because they are only together at the beginning and the end, and in between they do not confront each other. But in reality, the Duke is always present, in the underground, and fighting against Angelo. In my production in Stuttgart, I utilized this conflict as a theater metaphor.[5] We performed in the whole theater. In the middle of the audience, equidistant from the back of the stage and the back of the auditorium, we located the seat of political power. When the play began, the Duke was sitting there in the midst of the audience together with Angelo and his servant Escalus. The Duke ordered Angelo to come onto the stage and take charge of the performance, so to speak. Angelo replies that he cannot, but the Duke insisted. Then the Duke stripped off all his clothes and stood naked. Escalus carried the clothes down to Angelo on the stage, and the Duke disappeared. The power of the state has been exposed, literally, and disappears around the corner. Then Angelo took over the Duke's place, but the Duke kept sneaking back onto the stage waiting for the moment Angelo would make a mistake. We tied auditorium and stage together with a wide yellow plastic ribbon that ran around the whole stage and around the whole auditorium to define the limits of the state. In the second audience scene with Isabella [2.4], Angelo made his mistake and stumbles, and the Duke secretly began to plot his downfall, the alternative performance, so to speak. The alternative version of the performance began at the end of the play. First the curtain was pulled and an anthem was played (an old recording of the Olympic hymn from 1936, which no one remembered, but it did not matter). The curtain opened, and you saw a scene reminiscent of a political party convention: a curtain backdrop with the words "measure for measure" in velvet, a row of chairs in front of it. To the very end of the play, two approaches to government were struggling with each other, but neither is absolutely right nor wrong. For me, the Duke is not the incarnation of divine order but the peace and quiet of a cemetery. For example, this marriage with Isabella is violently forced upon her. The Duke asks Isabella twice. At first she cannot believe her ears, so she does not reply. He only mutters: "But fitter time for that." After he commands the others to marry, he asks her again. All sat in a row on their chairs, including Isabella, shocked and confused as if they were dead. The Duke came down to the front row of the auditorium, turned around to face the stage, and clapped his hands. A terrible ending. If neither approach to government is valid, then perhaps it would be better to do without any government at all.

Guntner: Didn't you have a similar problem in producing *The Tempest* in Düsseldorf in 1989?

Tragelehn: Yes, of course. *The Tempest,* traditionally called a "romance," is the story of a political ruler who has fallen from power, been expelled, and now sits embittered on his island. Suddenly his opponents show up. In my production the tempest takes place in the auditorium. The normal average criminals, the average politicians, sit in the auditorium and are brought onto the stage, onto the island. Now they go through a process of reeducation. They are driven nearly insane. In this way, the play comes closer to everyday reality. The prospect for the future, their return to Naples and Milan, is not so rosy. Have Prospero's opponents really changed? He has a bit of control over them because he knows that they have planned to assassinate the king and expropriate the crown, but he does not tell them this until the end. But the normal course of events is that the experiments on the island laboratory will be reversed.

McLean: The question of power, authority, and legitimacy became a central problem in critical work on Shakespeare in East Germany, especially in Robert Weimann's *Die Macht der Mimesis*. For Americans, it is an interesting question but not crucial. For the GDR, it seemed to be crucial.

Tragelehn: That is because of our concrete experience, the question of power, was an open question, and in the GDR, we were always confronted with it openly. This is the point at which there is a parallel to the feudal power structures as they appear in Shakespeare's plays. In West Germany, the situation was different. The movement of capital determined all questions of power, but it was invisible. How do you depict something invisible on stage? Brecht struggled with this problem even before 1933. Somewhere he remarks that a photograph of I. G. Farben says nothing about I. G. Farben.

Guntner: However, the question of authority also involves the question of correct interpretation and meaning in our time, even the authority of Shakespeare's person as a model or example for others to follow and emulate. This was a central question in the GDR in the sixties. The Dresen/Hamburger *Hamlet* [1964], Weimann's *Shakespeare and the Popular Tradition in the Theater* [1967], and yours and Heiner Müller's *As You Like It* [Potsdam, 1969] denied the legitimacy of a single authority or interpretation and suggested that meaning is determined by performance conditions and sociopolitical context among other things. The virulent attacks these theater productions elicited from official organs of the state suggest that you touched a very tender nerve in this society.

Tragelehn: Anyone who works in the theater wants to affect and move people in some way. You soon realize that performance is the key to that, and that every performance is unique. However, on the other hand, I feel that the text, the German translation, must remain unfixed. The theater performance must lead in a particular direction since it approaches the audience at a particular time and in a particular place. The dramatic text is not intended for a particular time and place, and it must remain relevant for another time and another place. I would always want the text to be independent of a particular concrete theatrical interpretation because that creates dramatic tension. A tension and contradiction between the text and the performance must always remain so that another performance is possible. For example, if I translate a particular line so that I dictate how it must be accentuated, then something is wrong. It must be translated in a way that allows it to be recited in a different way. In John Barton's *Playing Shakespeare*, Ian McKellen describes a performance of *Richard II* in Czechoslovakia in 1969, six months after the government of Alexander Dubcek had been deposed by the troops of the Warsaw Pact countries. The government wanted to cancel the tour, but contracts had already been signed, and although the government even had the posters taken down, the performances were sold out. It was a very straightforward production with Elizabethan costumes, very little scenery since they were on tour, and no intentional politics. Then came act 3, scene 2 in which Richard returns from Ireland and hears that Bolingbroke and his troops have landed in England. Richard kneels down and delivers his long monologue to the earth: "I weep for joy / To stand upon my kingdom once again. / Dear earth,

I do salute thee with my hand, / Though rebels wound thee with their horses' hoofs," and the whole audience began to weep. They saw Richard as Dubcek and Bolingbroke's troops as the invaders. The actors had never considered this as a direct political connection when they decided on the play. Shakespeare knew nothing about Communism, neither East nor West. McKellen says that he still feels cold shivers up and down his spine when he thinks about how he moved people with a single line. This is exactly what you strive for in a theater performance, to touch the hearts of the people in the audience. This is independent of time and place, and the actors have to adapt to each new situation. Schiller said: "Posterity weaves no wreaths for the actor." The performance must work at that moment. If it does not happen when the curtain opens and the lights go on, it never will. Peter Brook tells a wonderful story in *The Empty Space* about a clown in a children's theater in Hamburg after the war. To get the kids to quiet down he simply stood in the doorway and recited the names of things that nobody had after the war: sausage, cake, pudding. And suddenly, you could hear a pin drop. Or another example from Brook: He asked someone to read the list of the dead at Agincourt in *Henry V.* The person read the list woodenly like when an amateur reads a classical text out loud. Then he told the person to imagine that each of these persons had really been killed and to make a short pause after every name. World War II was not so far away, and the people could remember this. The person began to concentrate and read the names with a pause after every name and suddenly the feeling was there.

McLean: Why are you so interested in English Renaissance and Jacobean drama? Shakespeare and Jonson we can understand, but why have you also translated Chapman and Ford?

Tragelehn: I did *Volpone* in 1964, and I am convinced that *Volpone* is a great play, on a level with those of Shakespeare, and belongs to the dramatic repertoire of any theater. The other translations came about because after the scandal with *Die Umsiedlerin,* I had no employment for long stretches, so I looked for ways to earn money and still do things I enjoyed. I suggested that East German radio do a series on Shakespeare's contemporaries. The only one that was ever finished was Marlowe's *The Massacre of Paris,* which was immediately banned; nevertheless, it was finally broadcast five years later. Heiner Müller always liked the clown scene where they try to decide what to do with the corpse of the admiral, and Brecht also talked about the memory of a more fortunate period of theater history. But for me it was simply occupational therapy, so to speak, while I was looking for work at a theater. Ford's *'Tis Pity She's a Whore* is a magnificent play. I love it.[6]

Guntner: Finally, I want to ask if you were in any way influenced by Benno Besson?

Tragelehn: At the Berliner Ensemble, Besson's productions always stood out. Brecht always sat in on the rehearsals of his pupils and rehearsed with them, so the productions of Manfred Wekwerth or Peter Palitsch were similar. However, Besson brought the French tradition with him, which was completely different. The German theater tradition tends to be ponderous and heavy-handed. This was especially true in the years just after the war, in such productions as *Urfaust, Puntila,* or *Caucasian Chalk Circle* in which there was a strongly aggressive element. But the French tradition has an air of clarity, rationality, and transparency.

(29 April 1990)

13

Frank Castorf: "Shakespeare and the Marx Brothers"

Lawrence Guntner: Is theater a space where things happen that cannot happen anywhere else?

Frank Castorf: What is primary for me are people associating freely in the act of production, in this case, theater performance. How the audience reacts is not the important point. What is important is how these individual personalities organize themselves and work together in the social environment we call theater to create a product. The more extreme the form in which they bring their individual peculiarities into the two or three hours of performance, the more this personal subjectivity will be accepted by the audience as something autonomous with a quality of dignity. It is as if we create an autonomous republic of the theater. There is an urgent need for these autonomous worlds in modern society that is characterized by such incredible dependence.

I am not interested in an interacting audience that conegotiates the story, and I am not interested in Brecht. What does interest me, though, are these crazy, evil, naive, funny, deeply anthropological stories of Shakespeare's, which are still the most up to date of anyone's. Beckett and Brecht simply picked out the best parts and accentuated them. I would never say that I wanted to perform a story of Shakespeare's in its historic and concrete dimension as Manfred Wekwerth always tries to do. The Vice figure, for example, simply does not interest me. I state this as an antipode to a Marxist literary criticism, which is not really any different than bourgeois criticism as far as I am concerned. I am primarily interested in the process of creating the work of art. When I directed *Hamlet* in Cologne [1989], a lot of people said that was not Shakespeare's *Hamlet*.[1] My only reply was that when ten actors come together to perform Shakespeare's text, that is original Shakespeare for me. This is the only way I can squeeze something out of him today. And with a deeply respectful bow to Shakespeare, you see that is what has become of you today in Cologne.

Guntner: Which *Hamlet* translation did you use in Cologne?

Castorf: That was irrelevant. I could have used any translation, but since I know Heiner Müller well, and since I knew there would be no legal hassles, and since he has a great sense of humor, I decided on his translation. But I would have preferred to have performed it in the original English. When I directed *Othello* in Anklam [1982], I used the English original in the love scenes between Othello and Desdemona. It was the beginning of the eighties, and the performance was influenced by Fassbinder's film *Katzelmacher* [1969]. We had a bare stage and a bunch of young people who normally would get along well and treat each other lovingly, but when they landed on the island of Cyprus, all of sudden, all of these intrigues broke out for no reason at all. Someone always has to be the nigger, of course. In the end, everyone was gloomy, lying around or leaning against a wall, completely besides themselves. In the beginning, there was hope and togetherness on this island of young people. We tried to create an atmosphere somewhere between red and black, the feeling of a hot and sweaty Mediterranean island, a real greenhouse. For these young people from the north, it was a completely different kind of playground. They were set in motion, as when a snowball develops into an avalanche. Othello and Desdemona spoke English with each other, because that was the language they used when they were intimate. German sounds so harsh, like Charlie Chaplin in *The Great Dictator*. English flows, even for the German listener; it has another melody. Shakespeare in the original is simply beautiful. You hear accents of love. After Othello's jealousy had been aroused and he no longer wanted to be intimate with Desdemona, he could not talk to her in English anymore. When she tried to keep on speaking English with him, he insisted on replying in German. It was no longer possible for them to communicate in English. In effect, he was saying "We can no longer speak to each other in the language of our shared past." He refused and continued to speak with her in German. Again and again she tried to reclaim the past with the help of the English language. At a certain point, she sang Desdemona's aria from Verdi's *Othello* for Othello—and for the other young people who controlled the island—as a wedding gift for Othello. It was anarchic like the Marx Brothers do it in that scene in *Night at the Opera* when everyone is singing something else. Comedy, nonsense, and high seriousness exist side by side.[2]

Guntner: You have mentioned three sources of inspiration: Fassbinder's *Katzelmacher*, Chaplin's *The Great Dictator*, and the Marx Brothers' *Night at the Opera*. You were obviously influenced by Chaplin in your 1989 production of *Hamlet* in Cologne. Is film generally a source of inspiration for your work?

Castorf: Yes, a very strong influence. Especially the humor has influenced me because it is physiological or neurophysiological in the way the Marx

Brothers trigger it off in their failure to take reality seriously or their destruction of it through irony. With humor they are able to lift themselves up above their own ponderance and impotence in the face of modern society. German humor is laughing about conventions. Everybody knows what is comical. You know the conventions and when to laugh. But I like this scene with the Marx Brothers.

Guntner: As a member of the "younger" generation of theater people, did you see a difference between yourself and the older GDR theater tradition? Did you have any mentors or models?

Castorf: Oh yes, many, but not in the theater. Theater was a detour, which simply came along. I was mainly stamped by the late sixties: the radical left wing development in Europe, the "Prague Spring," the student uprisings in Warsaw, Paris, and West Berlin; and the subculture that came from England and America. Music played a strong role—Doors, Rolling Stones, Canned Heat—music in tune with breaking out and doing away with old ways of thinking and feeling, with trying to create new forms of community. There were people who tried to book a passage to India, or, like R. D. Laing, a passage into schizophrenia, but with a return trip ticket. People asked themselves, "How can I create a new harmonious community?" The Frankfurt School also pumped oxygen into my lungs. On the other hand, there was the discovery of Soviet theater in the 1920s—Mayakovsky, Bulgakov, Vakhtangov—a time when leftists tried to take part in a new social turnover and placed themselves at the disposal of this society. In the same way that Lessing had two hundred years earlier, they tried to mold that feeling into an image of humanity—something new, happier, and freer located between head, abdomen, and heart. This was interrupted by Stalinism but picked up again during the sixties. Like dadaism and surrealism, it was the antipode to this terribly dull Germanness, which included the reactionary petite bourgeois as well as that which existed in the Social Democratic and continued later in the Communist movement.

On the one hand, you had the disciplined, organized path that slowly led to the promised land and, on the other, the desire for spontaneity and the moment. This was the early Brecht and the atmosphere of the "do it now" counterculture of the sixties: the tradition of the twenties, the immediacy of life in the GDR in the sixties and seventies, and the theater development connected with names like Benno Besson at the Volksbühne: Matthias Langhoff, Fritz Marquardt, Heiner Müller. They had a strong influence on me, and I started to try things out myself. I taught myself; I did not work as anyone's assistant. I just started to work with people whenever I had the chance: Anklam, Brandenburg, and Greifswald.

When we did *Othello* in Anklam [1982], we tried to cultivate the coincidental, and the simple, and then tried to go from there. That is still the way

I work today. I have never said that I have to have this or that actor or huge stage decorations. I have always tried to work from the simple. Every street has an aesthetic dimension to it if you take a close look. You can filter it out, and that is how I try to do theater. Somehow it is made up of a whole bunch of single parts. Of course, there have been lines of development that go back to classical ancient models, to the myths and fairy tales, to the Nordic sagas, and, of course, to Shakespeare with his seeming concreteness that anticipates surrealism. *Ubu Roi* or postmodernism are simply extreme forms of Shakespeare. I am simply not interested in systematization.

Guntner: Heiner Müller tried to rework the *Hamlet* myth into a modern form by writing *Hamletmaschine*. In your Cologne production of Hamlet, you included the Cinderella myth. What were you trying to squeeze out of the Hamlet myth?

Castorf: My approach is similar to Müller's, but it is more within me. Somewhere Müller writes that he wrote *Die Hamletmaschine* to free himself from the Hamlet myth, and he came up with a radical questioning through the means of deconstruction. He freed himself, without a doubt, and now he can turn to new material. I would see that similarly as an individual psychological approach, and I would see it as a point of departure for other work. Otherwise, I do not have a particular approach.

Guntner: How did you approach *Hamlet*?

Castorf: Three women played the roles of Rosencrantz, Guildenstern, and Ophelia. Whenever I have seen the two friends they were either paper cutouts or very spylike, and I wanted to give them a certain sexual dimension. Three women and Hamlet, and then this first meeting, and somehow they had to recognize each other.

Guntner: Rosencrantz and Guildenstern are Ophelia's girl friends?

Castorf: We had four people who had been hired to perform, and we started to rehearse with act 1, scene 4, Hamlet's first monologue: "O that this too, too solid flesh would melt," and we tried to figure out which of the three women would play which role. Perhaps it was coincidence, or perhaps it was the effect of these three women together with this one man, I really do not know, but they started to play around with each other, and suddenly we had the Cinderella story with them trying on the shoe. The woman with the smallest foot actually turned out to be the woman who played Ophelia. With this game, these three women decided who was going to play Ophelia by themselves. That was not planned. I had no line of action, no game of chess in mind, in which I knew when I had to make the next move. I did have a basic idea about who communicated a certain physical presence and who should play which role.

Guntner: Do you create a certain situation and let the actors develop it by themselves, or do you tell the actors what they are supposed to bring across?

Castorf: Let me try to explain how this scene—act 1, scene 2—developed. Before that Claudius and Gertrude got Hamlet between them and said: "Look, don't be so angry. Do not go back to Wittenberg to study but stay here with us. You are our new son, Hamlet." Reluctantly he agrees and says: "Okay, I will." Afterward, he is sad because soon he notices that something is wrong with this father and mother. Hamlet does not want to forget. Everyone else says: It is zero hour, 1945 or October 1989, in the GDR. Okay, so we have some skeletons in the closet, let's just forget about them. We have to stick together, shoulder to shoulder, as before. And then someone comes along and says: "No. I can remember the past, I want to rework the past, I cannot forget so fast. I am going to ask some more questions, and think, and feel about it." He is a bit undecided whether that is positive or negative, and so he remains alone with his head in the dustbin and screams out his trials and tribulations to his divine father as opposed to this dummy Claudius. And then along come three women, like cancan girls, looking for Claudius, who is trying to play something courtly or what have you on the piano—an example of German culture for our dear spectators. What he comes up with is "Chop Sticks" [*Flohwalzer*], the "cultural heritage" [*Kulturerbe*) reduced to an absolute minimum. He is trying to play something beautiful and then these cancan girls come screaming out of the slapstick machine, the wardrobe (which served as the entrance to the stage), and they start to pull his leg. Then they realize he is not the one they are looking for so they drop him like a hot potato and decide to fish Hamlet out of the dustbin. The three of them throw him on the couch (the three together are strong), like the three witches in *Macbeth*. And then he takes up his opening lines: "Oh, if this too, too solid flesh would melt." After awhile, this sad Hamlet is caught up by the euphoria, the life force, the witch power of these three women. All three of them are on the floor and out of breath, like they are on their backs on the beach somewhere on the Baltic coast looking at the sun, and then someone starts to hum "Summertime." Everyone is content, and then the women start to cross their legs and jiggle their feet, and then the shoe starts to jiggle. One flips her shoe over—a touch of Louis Buñuel, for whom the shoe fetishism was very important. Hamlet looks and says to himself, "Well aren't those pretty shoes." And then he remembers a sonnet, in English, and goes on about these wonderful shoes: their smell, the material, and the beautiful form. He begins to fantasize, in regard to Shakespeare, how the foot and the body and the woman might be who belongs to this shoe. Then the Cinderella motif enters. One of the girls says, "That shoe fits me," but then she cannot quite walk in it. The next one has a smaller foot, but the shoe does not fit her either. Finally, the last one has the smallest foot, and she is the prettiest, too. So, of course, he falls in love with her and tells her that she is his little queen. And that is the way it goes; simple life situations combined one after the other. It is a method of the unconscious and is similar to that of the surrealists. Someone paints a picture and then turns it over, and his fantasy has to paint on from there. That is what I call method.

Guntner: "The Never-Ending Story."

Castorf: Yes, but there is still another story that corresponds to it, a covering, which is always present and under which a lot of life including that of the actors, goes on. The covering is Shakespeare, the story of Hamlet is on the top of all this, and, of course, it brings it all around in the end. At any rate, it is the attempt to do that. Sometimes you are closer, and sometimes you are not. But it is a point of reference.

Guntner: One problem in any contemporary performance of *Hamlet* is what do you do with the Ghost. In Cologne, you put the scene with the Ghost at the beginning of the play and packed him in a blue plastic bag. He even falls off the stage and lands in the first row of the audience. What was your source for this idea?

Castorf: There is always the question of how to begin a story, and we had various versions, which again had to do with that we could not perform in the Cologne theater because it was contaminated with asbestos. So we had to perform in a mobile theater which resembled a circus tent. A circus tent has the authenticity of the street; the chairs are harder, and there is a completely different approach than in a German civic theater. In this re-spect, we had to rethink our original dramaturgical conception, if you could call it that, to take the tent into consideration and our approach to the story of *Hamlet* as well. The stage flooring and the backdrop were covered with white paper. In the beginning, everything looked very clean, the immaculate conception. On May 9, 1945, the first day of freedom, everyone said Hitler was responsible and, we did not do anything. Today, it is just the same. On November 9, 1989, or after the fall of Honecker, everyone said that they did not do anything. Only two people were responsible for the catastrophes in this country: Ulbricht and Honecker. It is always the same. So everything was in white like the page of a German book. German printing has a tradi-tion. And white paper tears like human skin tears when it is very dry and no longer full of life. That was the starting point, and then someone threw in a blue plastic bag that the garbage collectors use. The Ghost, which someone had perhaps buried alive in the plastic bag, starts to whimper in a high-pitched voice like a bat. Hamlet comes along, hears him, and lets him out of the bag. He is the first one to hear anything and do something about it. Hamlet liberates this being, neither living nor dead, someone who has been buried alive. Then we had these slapstick numbers, like the Marx

Brothers, or the Vice figure if you will. The Ghost shoots Hamlet in the
behind and wounds him. Hamlet is in terrible pain and screams, but the
Ghost says: "Whats the matter? Look I shoot myself in the arm, and there's
no hole." Of course, a corpse feels no pain anymore. The old man gets
into such a fit that he accidentally falls off the stage and lands in the first
row. And because we are polite, and because the Cologne spectators had
paid a lot of money for admission, he personally greets and shakes hands
with everyone in the first row. Finally Hamlet has had enough and says:
"Papa, behave yourself. You are a king. Stop this nonsense." That is the
nonsense interlude after the realistic beginning with the plastic garbage
bag. It is like the spirit in the bottle, who has been freed, and suddenly
both actors develop this into a slapstick routine. Then he jumps up on the
refrigerator and through this shock, also in his mind, he starts to remember
and begins to recite the story of his murder.

Guntner: You rearranged the order of the scenes.

Castorf: Yes, during this scene on the refrigerator the poetry of the drama
converges on his personal experience, almost a Stanislavsky scene, and he
keeps asking himself, What happened? Your uncle? And Hamlet really lands
in this trap. The Ghost says more and more, and Hamlet wants to hear
more. He wants to know what really happened, and he believes that it
was murder. He screams out at the audience: "Murder! Murder! Murder!
Something is rotten in the state of Denmark!" All of a sudden the wardrobe
door opens and the whole court, including even the cook, are laughing,
like the scene in the cabin with the Marx Brothers. They laugh and laugh
at the silly son Hamlet who is stupid enough to believe that people could
be killed here. He is confused and hides in the anonymity of the masses.
He steps into the wardrobe and laughs along with the rest of them. Of
course, he is thinking: "How can we be responsible for the deaths of six
million Jews, complete nonsense." So he laughs along with the rest of them
and says that he was only dreaming. And then the actor who plays Claudius
says "Let's act this out and pretend there was a murder." So Hamlet reacts
as if there had been one, but all of the rest of them say "You are wrong. It
was a misunderstanding, our conscience is clean." Still Hamlet believes it
was a murder. But Hamlet is not of a disposition to remain undisturbed.
This desire for peace and quiet and continuity is not for him, and he has
to keep asking questions. From the beginning he notices how things are
covered up by the court and says: "This cannot be true." This first explosion
by Hamlet confuses everyone. That was our attempt to approach the story
from this vantage point.

(16 November 1989)

14

Alexander Weigel: "Theater Was Always Taken Seriously"

Andrew McLean: Why did Heiner Müller locate *Hamlet* in the Ice Age for his production of *Hamletmaschine?*

Alexander Weigel: The idea to stage *Hamlet* from the Ice Age to doomsday came from Heiner, but it was also an idea that the dramaturgy came up with to give the play a certain temporal structure. If you want to do justice to Shakespeare in this day and age, you have to approach him in a contemporary way. Shakespeare and his theater were directed at a particular audience, with particular experiences, backgrounds, expectations and political views. You have to work for the liveliness he achieved with his audience and try to achieve that with your audience. That was the reason for leaving out Hamlet's speech to the First Player, a wonderful speech, very contemporary at the time and with great inner significance for the theater but meaningless nowadays.

Lawrence Guntner: Hamlet's "mirror up to nature" speech was at the very center of Shakespeare appreciation in the GDR. It is as if you had staged *Hamlet* without his "to be or not to be" soliloquy. Were the actors opposed to it?

Weigel: It was not originally planned that way, but Robert Weimann had drawn attention to certain discrepancies between dramatic theory present in Hamlet's speech to the Players and the actions that take place in the play.[1] We found this extremely fascinating and thought we might be able to capture this contradiction; but to defer from understanding Hamlet's speech in terms of a theory of classic theater performance was incredibly difficult. We tried a number of different methods, for example, Hamlet smoking a cigar and propped in a director's chair, giving directions. However, for all his comradery it was still obvious that there was a difference in social standing between Hamlet and the actors, between the prince and people from the fringes of society. It came across well, but it did not correlate with Hamlet's character. He does not have this relaxed air about him. He is always tormented, dark, and complicated. He manages to escape from these depressions only through a cruel stroke of irony.

Hamlet/Maschine, **DIR. Heiner Müller, 1990. Elsinore in the Ice Age. Photo: Wolfhard Theile.**

Guntner: I heard that Müller was playing with the idea of an autistic hero.

Weigel: We even visited an asylum, but Ulrich Mühe who played Hamlet, did not have any outside help. He worked it out by himself and this autism, if you can call it that, became overt. His Hamlet has moments like that, when he becomes oblivious to everything else around him and reacts in a strange and inhibited way. If anything, it could be seen as a symptom of the political and economic situation.

Guntner: Theater changed in the GDR from an interpretive, pedagogical, enlightening force in society to that of an independent institution, free of any social duties. When did this development begin and were there any political reasons for it?

Weigel: The theater has always been influenced by social and political developments. In the GDR leading theater people saw the political aims of the state as identical with those of the theater: to form a new society and to reeducate people to become a new type of human being. My personal reason for joining the theater was to change society and people, to teach them how they could change the world and lead a better life in a socialist-Marxist sense. Parallel to this, however, there was always theater as pure entertainment. On the whole, though, the theater of the fifties and the sixties was a didactic theater. You have to be careful not to simplify matters, but theater did see itself as a living instrument for educating the people, and this was accepted completely within theater circles. The theater was never as important as it was during this period, and it saw itself as part of an entire social process. It assumed responsibility, asked questions, made demands. This invariably led to criticism, disputes, and discussions.

McLean: Where did this criticism come from?

Weigel: The party, from people who really had more important things to do, but because the theater belonged to the public sphere, everyone felt they were entitled to utter their own outlook publicly. Even Walter Ulbricht.

Guntner: Did this have any effect on your work in the theater?

Weigel: It meant that certain plays were not allowed to be performed or taken off the bill. A really insidious example was Peter Hacks's "The Cares and the Sorrows" (*Die Sorgen und die Macht*) that premiered at the Deutsches Theater in 1962 but was taken off the bill after only twenty-two performances. It dealt directly with the reality of life in the GDR, and it provoked a great deal of heated discussion.[2] As a consequence Wolfgang Langhoff, the director, had to step down as head of the Deutsches Theater in the spring of 1963. He was allowed to stay on as director, but he had to give up his post. There were terrible examples of interference. Again in 1968 we were accused of adulterating the "humanistic view of mankind" and the German classics with Dresen's lively, theatrical, folk theater *Faust*. We thought we would put an end to "In the beginning was the deed" once and for all. The party was sensitive about German classicism, which they regarded as the forerunner to our "socialist humanism" and "view of mankind." Walter Ulbricht once said, "Young people should read the *Communist Manifesto* and *Faust*. We are writing *Faust III*." That just about describes the backdrop to our 1968 *Faust* production in which Faust was a small, dark, somewhat unreliable, anarchic being. Fred Düren portrayed Faust as a very unreliable sort of character, whereas Dieter Franke as Mephisto was more the chubby, rolly-polly type. In other words, the types were reversed. We said that Faust should not be like Martin Luther but more in the mold of Thomas Münzer, someone unreliable, vague, and this evoked dreadful discussions. The GDR theater spent a great deal of time reflecting on its own values.

Then theater became increasingly opposed to a society which had stagnated politically and ideologically. Subsequently, it withdrew more and more from its role as a didactic institution and concentrated more on itself. It is in the nature of the theater to experiment and not be just a sounding board for what already exists; to probe and question, not only what is positive and real, but also what could be—the utopian, the world of carnival. This playful nature of the theater at the same time posed problems for representing dependable and pedagogical solutions, since the theater always has an air of the unreliable, a touch of the anarchic.

There were a variety of influences, but overall the theater managed to emancipate itself first and foremost by giving up its idea of behaving as a pedagogical institution. This had a dramatic effect on the nature of the work done in the theater. It allowed the actors the freedom to agitate as independent creative creatures and not just as tools for carrying out the intentions of literature or the text. It allowed the directors the freedom to choose the plays themselves rather than to take the recommendations of the head of the theater into consideration.

The change to a more critical relationship toward the East German state was also due to a change in generations: the younger people had a different relationship from the word go. You could not serve them up a harmless classical production. They wanted to see their own problems reflected in Shakespeare, Schiller, and Goethe. Due to censorship in the GDR, there was no public platform for their political problems.

McLean: How did this censorship work?

Weigel: For instance, new plays had to be registered, but officially there was no censorship, no board of censors. That was particularly annoying because it is easier to deal with a board of censors. In 1913 Carl Sternheim's *Die Hose* (*The Panty Hose*) was scandalous and would not have passed the Kaiser's censor, so Reinhardt renamed it *Der Riese* (*The Giant*), a totally idiotic title. The entire press asked what a "giant" suddenly had to do with a "panty hose," yet he managed to sneak things by the censors with tricks like that. Or if that did not work, he would suddenly announce that the performance was by invitation only. With the purchase of a ticket, you became a club member, so it was no longer a public performance. It is easier to get round clear-cut censorship, whereas with us it was more difficult since there was no official censorship. But the influence of the party was always very strong, and many things were blocked, forbidden, and ruined. For example, they would advise people to understand why a piece could not be performed straightaway, but perhaps next year or in two years time. That is even worse.

The people wanted to see contemporary theater regardless of whether it dealt with Shakespeare or whatever. There was no such thing as the public sphere and social problems, real, concrete problems were not supposed to appear in the press. That is the reason why the theater took on a function that it otherwise never would have had under normal conditions. It became so to speak the public sphere. Productions of *Wilhelm Tell, Faust,* or *Macbeth,* for example, became works that people could relate to their own social situation. In some cases the theater itself could provide the means for this without requiring an updated version of any of the plays. The public was so politically sensitized that they would instantly recognize their own situations. A number of Shakespeare's plays offer basic constellations that were understood as representations of contemporary conflicts in society or in the family, for example, *Romeo and Juliet* or *Hamlet.*

Guntner: How did Alexander Lang's *A Midsummer Night's Dream* [1980] fit into this pattern?

Weigel: Lang was only interested in one aspect of the play, the manipulation of the young people in the woods, something that had to do with a basic feeling many young people had at that time. He simply updated the play in a way in which a lot of young people could empathize: the feeling of having given up one's will, of having become a victim of one's own situation. This feeling was exemplified in the situation of the young lovers Hermia and Lysander, Helena and Demetrius, but it reflected the social situation of a hundred thousand people of all generations. The people in the audience felt that they, too, were entangled in a situation with which they were unable to cope, that they were at the mercy of a higher authority and in danger of losing themselves. Personally, I think Titania and the Fairies and the Mechanicals were given too little attention.

Guntner: Was that perhaps a reaction to the GDR tradition of pushing the Mechanicals into the dramatic foreground?

Weigel: That was part of it, but Lang had this precise feeling for exactly what in this play was important for the people just at that moment. Originally the set designer was Hans Brosch, but during rehearsals he was unexpectedly allowed to travel to Switzerland or West Germany and decided to stay there. We were all very upset at the time, but you have to understand the man. He was a painter and had never been allowed to hold an exhibition here. That was how we lost a number of really good people.

McLean: Who could prevent him from doing it?

Weigel: Exhibitions by individual artists, in private galleries or the like, was extremely rare. There was only the Art Exhibition in Berlin, the jury of which consisted of members from the Union of the Fine Arts and was dominated by the party. They selected what was to be exhibited and his works were not among them, and if they were, then only a few. Without the right setting, hung in a corner somewhere, they lost their individual, somewhat deviant character, and because they were not so realistic, people just stood there and laughed. People like Brosch were being denigrated constantly. Hans Brosch was a personal friend of mine, and when he left, I felt hurt. It was in a way a betrayal of the theater, but I could also understand his motives. We lost another wonderful painter and scenic designer in the same way when Achim Freyer left. He is now a professor at the Academy of Fine Arts in Berlin and a director and scenic designer much in demand. We lost quite a number of stage designers in the eighties. Directors left too, but mainly it was the scenic designers which meant that we lost an entire world of images. The stage for *A Midsummer Night's Dream* was a makeshift job. This red, suffocating stage that seemed like a cauldron was Gero Troike's work—a very good stage designer who also left; it somehow fit Lang's production. It cut across the stage like a machete and contributed to the whole effect of feeling cramped.

McLean: One aspect that fascinates me as an outsider was the whole concept in the GDR of an internal critical debate and dialogue about the nature of the theater that becomes public three or four years later.

Weigel: The discussion about the role of the theater may appear to be more homogenous from the outside than it actually was from the inside. You see important links between certain research and publications in the work of Robert Weimann and certain theater productions which put his theories into practice. There were many influences, and Weimann's *Shakespeare and the Popular Tradition* played a profound role in attaining a more lively and historically sound understanding of Shakespeare. He kept in mind the special conditions of Shakespeare's era, its liveliness and folk traditions. In recent years, theater has not been interested in scholarship; in its development toward independence, theater has come to reject any theories or ideologies. On the one hand, they are tired of theories, on the other, they have become a bit arrogant. Influences and differences in opinion still exist, but they are not so immediately apparent as earlier. In the early years, you used to get yourself a scholar or even better two or three and discuss the matter with them. You tried to find scholars who were not only sound in their research but also had a feeling for the theater and were able to present their material in a lively manner that was usable for the theater. Scholars such as Robert Weimann or Thomas Sorge, for example, were able to relate the happenings on Shakespeare's stage to the concrete social and political situation of the age, and thus we were able to relate it to our own situation.

The reason for the heated controversies about the role of the theater is that we understood ourselves as a critical element in society much more so than was the case in Western countries. When I was young I thought that if we would only do this or that production things would automatically change. We really approached the matter with this enthusiasm and conviction. Later I became more careful and felt that if we reached one hundred people in an audience of six hundred, that would be a great success. Reception processes are very complicated, and only a few think more deeply about a performance and take it with them. In the last years of the GDR, this discussion became more intense. Theater asked itself what kind of role it still had to play in a society which had become increasingly fixed and fossilized, the political calcification that had set in with old age, in a concrete metaphorical sense. The people at the top were seventy and seventy-five, and their underlings lacked independence. After the older fundamental identity had been lost, questions about the role of theater in a society that had become fossilized and looked away from its own reality became more aggravated and fundamental because they were so existential. The old close relationship between politics and the stage had been lost; it was painful but noticeable because it left behind scars. Earlier you could sit down and discuss matters with a politician, but they withdrew more and more until they did not come to the theater at all anymore. We were left to ourselves and had to redefine our role anew. This is surely a discussion that did not take place in Western countries, not to this degree at any rate.

Heiner Müller—an internationally recognized author, even in the West— was often asked why he did not leave for West Germany or the USA since his plays were not performed in the GDR. His answer was that even though he had so many obstacles and difficulties in getting his plays performed, he knew of no other country in which his plays had a comparable social impact. A play that had been suppressed, that had received negative reviews—a play about political issues—was absolutely certain to be a success with the audience here. The audience believed that if the official reviewers criticized it, there must be something good about it. Unfortunately that was not always the case. Nevertheless, East German theater always had an effect upon its audience. Even if the effect was negative, officially it was, nevertheless, an effect. Theater in East Germany was always taken seriously. In fact, we received much more attention than was our due. Six hundred spectators do not rush out of the theater, pick up a pitchfork, and overthrow the government just because they have heard something critical, bad, or even subversive about the state. But those in power seemed to be convinced that this would happen. It was a completely exaggerated estimation of the power of the arts that led, in turn, to their suppression. This receded a bit in the eighties so that it was possible to put on Heiner Müller's *Der Lohndrücker* [*The Scab* 1988], which would have been impossible earlier. The performance contained so many taboos : Stalin and the Workers' Uprising of 17 June, or the fact that the "activists" who were celebrated as "Heroes of Work" had denounced their comrades under the Nazis. They had worked just as hard under the Nazis, their discipline was exactly the same, only the political conditions were different; this yea-saying discipline, this lack of independence, kept causing them trouble. That was cheeky, but they allowed it to be performed and accepted it.

The other side of this calcification was that the party simply got tired of this continual trouble with the arts. In fact, in the end there was not much interference anymore. In the eighties there were many performances which helped to change the way people thought about the state; their attitude toward the state and politics became increasingly critical, and that gave them a stronger voice in their self-determination. In the September 1989 issue of *Theater heute* an interesting piece placed excerpts from Goebbels' diaries side by side with the memories of famous actors and actresses of the time, such as, Marianne Hoppe and Gustav Gründgens. They were unable to remember their own age. They portrayed it as a nice time and recalled how they always dined with Goebbels. What a contradiction! It is important to know these things. When the "Stasi" went after demonstrators on 7–8 October 1989 the people who protested the loudest were from the theater. There was a protest meeting of all the actors and actresses from Berlin as well as from the rest of the country at which they decided to stage a mass demonstration on 4 November. It was a splendid achievement. They saw themselves as responsible citizens and human beings who involved themselves in politics and not, as so often was the case in German history, as "artists" high above politics. Of course, there were others who said that our thing is only the theater. No, I thought the actors and actresses were terrific. Especially the women were strongly involved in committees to organize the demonstration. It was beautiful.

That we were a subsidized and privileged theater far removed from reality also made me stop and think. Even though we had made our contribution to the intellectual climate, nevertheless, we were far removed from the majority of the people. Only 9 percent of our audience were workers. They could not attend performances because they lacked transportation to and back from the theater. There was a great discrepancy between intellectuals and workers, and this discrepancy was kept alive artificially by the state. They knew only too well that when intellectuals and workers get together, theory becomes material force and the masses seize power, just as Marx, to whom they always referred, says.

Guntner: How do you go about selecting which translation to use?

Weigel: When Lang and I were preparing *A Midsummer Night's Dream* we had long discussions about which translation we should use. Lang was set on using Eschenburg's translation [1775–82],[3] but I thought we should use a modern translation. When we did Müller's *Hamlet* I did not concern myself with the translation question, because it is the text of a translator who is simultaneously author and poet. That was enough for us. Müller's translation of the soliloquies in *Hamlet* is brilliant, very rough, strong, and for the theater, full of *gestus*. In addition, he is an established dramatist and poet, so everything fit.

When it comes to a complicated play like *Hamlet,* there is a great danger of getting caught up in details and losing sight of the overall structure of the play. Just as in all of Shakespeare's plays, *Hamlet* contains central images and metaphors, and it is essential that the translation calls forth a picture world that carries the text. We wanted to retain the integrity of the text and not let it be destroyed via interpretation and portrayal on stage. The acting tradition based on interpreting a text, that goes into minute details in an attempt to interpret the text for the audience is a grave danger with a play like *Hamlet.* The great soliloquies require a delicate balance between attention to individual detail and the general sense of it, and that is very difficult. Müller forced Ulrich Mühe, who played Hamlet, to view the soliloquy as a whole. The differentiation in the course of the soliloquy was a touching up that happened later. Normally, actors work on the soliloquies line by line, piece by piece, but Müller left it completely up to Mühe. Ulrich Mühe is a very clever, experienced actor who is able to spring from one situation to another very quickly, but Müller forced him to come to the existential starting point before he could escape into details with his tremendous skills, techniques, and inventiveness. We spent relatively little time on the individual details of the text. Müller tried to accomplish this only via reciting and acting. There are passages, not only soliloquies, which are not acted out but only recited. It is a kind of theater with a relatively static approach to the text.

That, in turn had something to do with the stage decorations that are overpowering and do not allow for a lot of action. The action is employed sparingly and concentrated on Hamlet who, in this respect, moves the most. The king and the queen side of the story was very statuary. Only at the end of the play when every things falls apart and they are caught up in contradictions which they cannot resolve by themselves, when their relationship has been destroyed, is this statuary aspect dissolved, and there is more movement on this side of the dramatic action. This is a way of acting which does not try to repeat the text via the plot, to interpret it, to chew it and spit it out again.

Guntner: When I asked Heiner Müller about his dramaturgical concept for *Hamlet,* he said that it was all in the text.

Weigel: Müller himself as a dramatist has undergone enormous changes. He used to write very traditional plays, with dialogue and real life characters. In more recent plays there are neither any real life characters nor a clearly defined text. He himself has developed a form of drama with a strong tendency toward monologues out of his opposition to traditional theater. He presents masses of text from which the theater has to find something for itself by itself. There is no longer a dramatic structure in the old sense.

The text has its own individual level. That has to do with his own personal opinion that Shakespeare is the great, unattainable ideal and that *Hamlet* is his greatest text, which explains his great respect for the text and his conviction that it is all in the text. An actor should not try to interpret it in the sense of a "doubling," i.e., that you simply repeat what the text says in your portrayal. On the contrary, it is the task of the theater to pass on the text to the audience as clearly and untampered as possible and to add something of its own that may correspond to the script but may also be an interesting contradiction to it. Through this contradiction you sometimes come up with astonishing, odd, foreign, and original stories.

For example, Claudius' confession: "My offense is rank," and Hamlet's reaction: "Now I might do it" [3.3]. First Claudius and Hamlet come together in a kind of dumb show in which Hamlet stabs Claudius: dream fulfillment. Then they separate come back in and sit down on the bed next to each other, and Claudius tells Hamlet the problems he faces. Hamlet listens and consoles him. That is a completely different dramatic situation than what Shakespeare has constructed: the king tries to pray but realizes that he cannot, and then Hamlet says: "Now I'll do it." That is what Hamlet wants to do. One of Hamlet's problems is time, and that was also our problem. This man is called upon to change the world, but at the same time he is also a part of this world. He does not come from outside like Fortinbras; he is a member of the court. After all, he is the prince. Logically he cannot simply just jump into the deed because he himself is a chapter in this story. We tried to make this point. The relationships in Hamlet's family are very complex and complicated. In some ways Claudius is closer to Hamlet than his own father was. Hamlet's father is his biological father but belongs to another age and comes from another world. Claudius, on the other hand, is a part of Hamlet's world, even if he is the other side of the coin. We understood that very well because it can also be found in German drama. For example, Mephisto tells Faust, the great thinker, "You think too much. Just do it."

This contradictory and at the same time inseparable relationship between intellect and power is a very German dilemma. The main idea behind the Dresen Greifswald *Hamlet* was "Buchenwald is near Weimar," that is to say, lofty thinking up in the clouds is always endangered by power and violence. Between intellect and power there exists a dangerous relationship. This is an historical experience for Germany. Today I would not say that "Buchenwald is near Weimar," and Müller is more ready to admit that Claudius is a real crook. Thirty years ago it was performed too simply, e.g., Hans-Dieter Mäde had Hamlet performed as a good man in keeping with our age [Karl-Marx-Stadt, 1964]. Of course, Claudius had to be portrayed as a real theater villain. And that really upset us because we thought that the interesting aspect of the play is that Hamlet is confronted by a man whose methods, he later learns, are violent and to be condemned. Yet his political deeds are doubtless in accord with the present. In other words, Claudius is a character full of contradictions and with a conscience that Shakespeare makes extraordinarily explicit. He is not simply an unscrupulous villain but one who is destroyed by his own deed, and we emphasized that strongly in the performance. Müller had Jörg Gudzuhn play Claudius as a villain and as a man who gets into a situation with which he cannot cope and is then caught up by his own deeds. This development ends with the death of all of the participants. However, the deaths of Claudius and Gertrude are not Hamlet's doing but the result of a process that started long before and are willed by the characters themselves. In fact, they all want to die—at the latest after the closet scene—so that the whole thing can finally come to an end. We have to do with a dying, dried up society. In the end time has simply come to an end. In this sense Claudius does the right thing so that everything is finally over. He takes the chalice and drinks it down greedily.

Guntner: This production of *Hamlet/Maschine* showed that the time for the GDR had come to an end but that the future was indefinite and open. "No hope, no despair."

Weigel: That certainly had something to do with it. No hopes were raised. On the other hand, there was no despair, either; it just happened. Some critics described it as a state funeral, and perhaps it was. Müller often said that it was not his job to give people hope. And if you read Shakespeare closely, he does not either. You can ennoble the ending by saying: "The rest is silence," but that is just as concrete. An age has come to an end. It is only a matter of where you are standing. Of course, I can understand why Hamlet came down to the edge of the forestage thirty years ago, but I still believe that you have to keep your feet on the ground. It is a very realistic play without any hope for the future.

(26 April 1990)

15

Manfred Wekwerth and Robert Weimann: "Brecht and Beyond"

Lawrence Guntner: Would you describe your first meeting with Bertolt Brecht?

Manfred Wekwerth: I have always been plagued by the typical German malady that Goethe describes in *Faust:* two souls in one breast. On the one hand, I am very interested in the natural sciences, and I even started out to take a degree in science; on the other hand, I have always enjoyed theater. In the old form of theater it was impossible to do both, and I would have had to make a decision for one or the other. Brecht brought me to realize that it is possible to combine thinking and acting, and so I brought my interest in science into the theater. I still have not been cured, and I even wrote my dissertation on the topic of "Theater and Science".[1] I still enjoy thinking about the theater and about the problems of the world and their solution. I was able to study this carefully with Brecht, who never pretended to be a philosopher and also enjoyed doing the same thing.

Guntner: What was your life like before you met Brecht?

Wekwerth: At the end of World War II I was still in high school, but I was supposed to report for active military service on May 20, 1945. [The German army surrendered unconditionally on May 8, 1945.] By that time, the Nazis had succeeded in teaching my generation not to think or feel. I had never read anything by Brecht, Lion Feuchtwanger, or Thomas or Heinrich Mann. As for music, I was only familiar with Beethoven, at best, and only with his Ninth Symphony falsified by the Nazis as the "great heroic triumph." I come from Cöthen, a small town in central Germany, and the moment the American army entered our town and toppled the Nazi victory column, a new age began for us. We thought it was a defeat, the end. It was the end of the Third Reich, but it was not the end for us.

In the years immediately following World War II, we tried to rid ourselves of the barbarism of the past. A pastor told us about Kierkegaard's *Sickness Unto Death*, and we performed existential Christmas plays. Christianity has the advantage that you do not have to study it; you can feel it. We were excited about justice and compassion, and one day in 1947–48 I ran across Brecht's play *Die Gewehre der Frau Carrar,* which was my first encounter with Brecht, or anything written by a Marxist for that matter.

I was so excited by the realism, the language, the compactness, and the humanity of this play that I immediately began to rehearse it with my amateur theater group. I was able to talk a real working man into playing the main role of Pedro, even though he himself rejected theater as tomfoolery.

In keeping with the spirit of the times, we were cheeky and bold enough to print an announcement in our local newspaper that *Die Gewehre der Frau Carrar* would be performed by the amateur theater group of Cöthen and beneath it: "The author Bert Brecht will be present." We cut the announcement out and sent it to Brecht in Berlin. We figured that if he were a great man, then he would have sense of humor, and if he did not have a sense of humor, he was not a great man after all. He did not come but sent a bus to Cöthen that brought us to the Chamber Theater of the Deutsches Theater in the Luisenstrasse where the temporary stage of the Berliner Ensemble was located. There we innocently performed our version of *Die Gewehre der Frau Carrar* to an audience that I would have felt differently about had I known who was in attendance: Therese Giehse, Erwin Geschonnek, Helene Weigel, Paul Bienert, Paul Dessau, Hanns Eisler, Hans Rodenberg, Paul Wandel—the best and greatest of theater talent available at the time. The audience applauded enthusiastically because they were moved that people from the provinces would perform political theater.

But Brecht did not like it. He rehearsed with us until late at night, and during the course of the rehearsals, he hired my main actor, Erich Franz, who had not even wanted to act in the play to begin with. Naturally, I was jealous. The next day, just as I was about to leave the theater, I ran into Brecht on the stairway, and in his typically innocuous way of saying something important, he asked me if I would like to learn something because he had seen that I still had a lot to learn. This was in 1951, and it marked the beginning of my work with the Berliner Ensemble. Later I left for awhile, not the least of reasons being that I had different ideas about Shakespeare, but I returned in 1977.

Guntner: What was the significance of Brecht's methods and ideas about drama for your own work, and has your understanding of Brecht changed in the meantime?

Wekwerth: Brecht's understanding of himself was very changeable. I do not know anyone more difficult to pin down in terms of formal style. Some people like to speak of the so-called Brecht style as the gray stage, the clipped manner of speaking, and the spartan gestures, but there was a very good reason for that. When Brecht returned to Berlin in 1948, he had been deprived of a theater for twelve years by the Nazis. *Die Gewehre der Frau*

Carrar had been performed once in Paris in 1936 and later in Scandinavia, but none of the plays he wrote in the United States was ever performed there, except for *Hangmen Also Die,* which is only an average film.

So when Brecht returned from exile, he brought with him a whole suitcase full of plays that had never been performed. He returned to a country that lay in ruins—not only the buildings but also the minds of its people. The theater had been barbarized by what Brecht called "Göring pathos" or "Wagnereanism," the misunderstood, wrong kind of pathos at the base of Nazi performances of *Coriolanus.* Naturally, it was easy for the Nazis to use *Coriolanus.* It begins with a "heil" and ends with the elite personality who is convinced of his own mission and superhuman abilities.

There was no performance tradition left for Brecht to fall back on, neither from Piscator, nor from any other type of political theater, nor from a popular tradition (*Volkstheater*), which had always been disparaged in Germany. Brecht had no money for decorations; furthermore, the actors and actresses he had, such as Therese Giehse and Leonard Steckel, had been in exile, or were very young and had no idea of what theater was about. Nevertheless, he was not going to let this Germania, rotten to the core, forget its political responsibility for what had happened with the help of superficial performances based on the wrong politics. That is why *Mutter Courage,* Brecht's first production [1949], was so rigorously disciplined and simple. It was a withdrawal cure for addicts addicted to the drug of Nazi theater. And like an addict with withdrawal symptoms, the audience missed everything: the opulently colorful stage decorations, the pathetic, meaningless language, the acting style intended only to highlight "great" characters. The great artistic achievement of Brecht's ensemble was that they seemed to perform "artlessly." *Mutter Courage* may seem sparse and devoid of passion for many today, but it evoked terribly strong emotions from the audience in 1949.

Brecht said that you do not need decorations to depict the ruins of war; the ruins were there on the street in front of the theater, so the people imagined them themselves. Strong feelings and emotions were easy to evoke because the people had nothing to eat, were poorly housed, and suffered and struggled just to stay alive. For Brecht, the first task was to destroy the negative feelings, attitudes, ideas, and values in the minds of his audience. This seeming plainness was in reality very strong medicine. The audience protested the half-high curtain, Dessau's music, the empty stage, and that Mother Courage sings for people who have lost something in the war, be it sons, houses, or land. Helene Weigel sang in her squeaky voice: "War is just business, only with lead instead of cheese." The audience exploded. This is what I call the "pedagogical role" of Brecht's theater concept which grew out of the specific German situation after 1945.

The colorfulness of the 1954 production of *The Caucasian Chalk Circle* was just the opposite. The opulent decorations and colorful costumes, inspired by the paintings of Pieter Brueghel and Hieronymus Bosch, were meant to inspire a new kind of heroism that would rescue a child, just as Grusche does. They were meant for a spiritually impoverished country and a people in need of new heroes and modes of behavior. It was performed with great sincerity. Angelika Hurwicz, the actress who played Grusche, was terribly upset after the first performance. She went up to Brecht and said: "I must have acted all wrong. I must have been terrible. People cried." Brecht replied, "If they had not cried, you would have performed the part wrongly. Those who cry because the stepmother rather than the biological mother gets to keep the child are the same people who leave the theater and protest that the Poles now own Silesia, which they still consider to be their private property." That theater was able to arouse the feelings of the audience for the fate of a child was almost a revolution.

Brecht's death in 1956 coincides with when we began to work on Shakespeare. "Alienation" (*Verfremdungseffekt*) means not only breaking familiar things apart, but also taking a fresh look at them. First, we addressed the question of collective guilt and tried to make men and women, who knew nothing of Marx or class conflict, aware that the course of history is not determined by one or two individuals but by groups and classes of people. In *Mann ist Mann*, Brecht says, "A single person is not even worth mentioning. Don't bother with less than two hundred." (*Einer ist keiner, über weniger als zweihundert lohnt es überhaupt nicht zu reden.*) That was Brecht's way of dismantling the so-called autonomous individual. Before his death, Brecht once remarked that it is only when all are on the same social level that we will be able to notice our individual differences. Next we wanted to point out that a society without individuals will become impoverished. After making "collective" discoveries, we decided to turn to the great individuals through Shakespeare since we had noticed similarities between the radical changes in his age and ours. We wanted to encourage people to discover themselves. And *Coriolanus* was the beginning.

Originally, Brecht had planned to produce *Coriolanus, Troilus and Cressida,* and *Timon of Athens,* plays relevant to an age of radical political change. However, we altered Brecht's original concept. Brecht had wanted to show that great leaders were dispensable, and that if the masses join together in collective action, they can do without the Coriolanuses. This was the time of a partial coalition of the Communist, Social Democratic, and Liberal Democratic parties [1949–53]. However, we did not perform *Coriolanus* until 1964, after the death of Stalin. I belonged to the privileged few who did not have to take part in the Stalin cult because Brecht disapproved of it. The people around Brecht recognized Stalin for what he was. I would not claim that we knew of his crimes, but we did not worship him.

Coriolanus, DIR. Wekwerth/Tenschert/choreography Berghaus, 1964. First battle between Romans and Volscians. Photo: Vera Tenschert.

Guntner: Were you suspicious?

Wekwerth: Yes, suspicious. I always much preferred Lenin's politics and still harbor a secret affection for Bukharin's. At any rate, we decided to stage *Coriolanus.* Historians portray Coriolanus as a person who is able to force society to accept his disgraceful behavior for the sake of his special abilities. Coriolanus is the supreme butcher, but the people need him, and the plebeians are hoodwinked by his capture of Corioli. Then he agrees to stand for election as tribune, and the plebeians vote for him, which was just asking for trouble. Without really changing Shakespeare's text, we asked the question of whether a "great leader" is not too expensive for most people. That was our own approach to Brecht and to Shakespeare, that is, we took Brecht one step further with the help of Shakespeare.

Somewhat later I came across *Shakespeare and the Popular Tradition* in which Weimann made a fundamental discovery about the Elizabethan actor's double function: he was both Richard the Third and the Vice. Weimann characterizes the Vice as a social critic and a "corrupter of words" from below, which is exactly what Brecht in his *Organon* was looking for. Brecht was not suggesting that theater in what he called "the age of science," should become scientific (*wissenschaftlich*) but that it should become more "playful" (*spielerisch*), more nonsense theater and clowning. The elements of clowning, playfulness, and "folk theater," when combined with philosophical thoughtfulness, resulted in what Brecht called "philosophical folk theater" (*philosophisches Volkstheater*). That is why we staged *Galilei* [1957] as a folk festival, a production which the Berliner Ensemble continued to show for very many years. With the help of Weimann's book and with his personal assistance with the translation, I staged *Richard the Third* at the Deutsches Theater in 1972. Richard Gloucester was portrayed as a "master player" (*Spielmeister*) who conducts a provocative kind of experiment to see if one can achieve "divine right" without the help of the divinity simply by following a grim kind of human behavior (*menschlich verhält*), that is, by butchering others according to the custom of the age. In 1985 I did *Troilus and Cressida* at the Berliner Ensemble as an ingenious fabrication of philosophical absurdity: "not the demontage of pathos but the pathos of the demontage"—Robert Weimann's formulation by the way. This *Troilus* combined Brecht's ideas with Shakespeare's.

Guntner: Manfred Wekwerth has said that he was strongly influenced by your *Shakespeare and the Popular Tradition*. Robert Weimann, when I read your works, especially those from the sixties, I sensed that you, in turn, were strongly influenced by Brecht. I would like to know if you were influenced by productions by Brecht or Manfred Wekwerth at the Berliner Ensemble.

Robert Weimann: Brecht was a fundamental inspiration in my rethinking of Shakespeare's theater, and that is why I dedicated the English edition of my book to Benno Besson and Manfred Wekwerth and was bold enough to call them, in this dedication, "my friends in the theater who have come closest to a modern Shakespeare in the popular tradition." And that hooks up with what Manfred has just said about a "philosophical folk theater."

Just as he came to Berlin from Cöthen, so too came I to Berlin from the positivistically oriented center of German philology at the University of Halle. In Berlin my first unforgettable impression was Brecht's *The Caucasian Chalk Circle* in the Theater am Schiffsbauerdamm, and the production was a true and lasting eye-opener for me. Here was great theater that not only lavished attention on precise speaking and acting as well on the material of beautifully designed stage props but also evoked a subtle but for all that tremendous response from the audience. The actors broke through the "fourth wall" and carried the play out into the audience. That was an example of how Brecht's "alienation effect" added great dimensions to the East German theater of the day. In a very profound way the Berliner Ensemble confirmed my dissatisfaction with what the German university, contemporary theory and cultural politics, and other influences in the mid-fifties had to offer.

First of all, I was dissatisfied with naturalistic interpretations of Shakespeare. As a student, I had read Tolstoy's rigorous critique of *King Lear* and knew that it was impossible to pass it by as long as the measure of

Shakespeare's poetics was defined in terms of that "reflection of life" that then was at the basis of the postwar expectations of the contemporary spectator or critic. Secondly, in this period of East German history, we tended to accept uncritically anything that came from the Soviet Union, including contemporary uses of the concept of "popularity" (*Volkstümlichkeit*). In nineteenth-century Russian literature, the idea of *narodnosti* had an important and legitimate function. It seemed to me, however, that in the GDR in the fifties, the call for *narodnosti* was terribly inhibiting and normative: so I began more searchingly to explore the sociocultural foundations of the Elizabethan stage, with "special emphasis" (as my dissertation title had it) on *The Knight of the Burning Pestle*. To my delight, it turned out that the popular tradition in Shakespeare's time completely excluded any kind of naturalistic realism. The significance and the implications of this insight was greatly enhanced through the experience of seeing Brecht's plays performed at the Berliner Ensemble. And when, about ten years later [1967], I had finished a special study of the popular tradition in the theater, I sent a copy of the book to Manfred Wekwerth, whom I did not know at that time, with words of appreciation to him and the Berliner Ensemble without whose work my book on the popular tradition would not have been possible.

Guntner: Robert Weimann's book influenced your production of *The Life and Death of Richard the Third*. Did it influence other productions of yours and, if so, how?

Wekwerth: Robert's line of argument approached Shakespeare not from the Roman tragedies but from the English morality plays, and his description of how the roles of Herod and Pilate were performed in the mystery plays was a great discovery and opened up new aspects, not only in Shakespeare. We used this approach with other plays as well. Brecht did this with *Der kaukasische Kreidekreis* in 1954, which he had written in the form of a medieval mystery play and comic interlude, and in 1959 we staged *Arturo Ui* as a farce, as a sideshow spectacle at a fair. Like Shakespeare, Brecht's plays contain an enormous number of elements from the popular tradition. In Germany, however, there is no such thing as a popular tradition. "Folk theater" or "plebeian theater" was always characterized by a cheeky intelligence, the complementary perspective of things from below, even to the point of casting. For example, Brecht loved to cast actors such as Ernst Busch, a proletarian who remained a proletarian even after becoming a great actor, in the role of Frederick the Great or Coriolanus. "Folk theater" was a slightly heretical point of view which enjoyed dismantling false values. That is what real "folk theater" is, the Italian commedia dell'arte, for example, or as Robert has shown, English drama before Shakespeare. With few exceptions, this kind of theater does not exist in Germany. The Bavarians had the good fortune of having had Frank Wedekind and Karl Valentin whose sources lie in the Bavarian folk tradition. In the rarified atmosphere north of Weimar, however, this kind of theater disappeared, and so Robert's book was very welcome because it showed us new ways of staging other plays.

Brecht also talks about this kind of theater in "Volkstümlichkeit und Realismus." *Puntila*, for example, is a "folk play," but this folk play combines the lower and the higher ways of speaking—a stance Brecht also brought to his production of *Urfaust* [1952]. He borrowed a lot from the sideshow—a healthy, naive theatrical materialism—which the audience enjoyed and in which they discovered new things about this Faust cult figure. In the Second World War, German soldiers carried Goethe's *Faust* in their knapsacks and with it the myth of a man who sought only the truth, the idea of the so-called Faustian (*das Faustische*), an idea that Spengler connected with the idea of the so-called German soul (*die deutsche Seele*). This was also an element of Nazi ideology.

Brecht approached *Faust* by asking a few simple questions, and from such questions, he usually came up with some very plebeian ideas of his own. Brecht spoke a wonderful Swabian-Bavarian dialect, and when he said something theoretical in this dialect, it lost any "classical" aura it might have had. With Brecht, it was important to pay attention to his manner and way of speaking and acting—he was a good actor—if you wanted to understand his theoretical ideas. For example, he asked why Faust does not marry Gretchen. If a German teacher were to hear this question, he or she would go crazy. But the question is not so silly after all. In thinking about this, he noticed that in his search for the truth, Faust becomes a rather successful criminal. In *Faust* he commits five murders; in *Urfaust* four. The result was that the classical school of Weimar politically condemned Brecht's production of *Urfaust* as a heretical attack on German culture. Even in 1952, the plebeian point of view, which was the point of view of popular theater, was criticized and rejected in East Germany. Thus, the naive dialectical and materialistic approach to life that Robert describes in detail in *Shakespeare and the Popular Tradition* is the same as Brecht's and applicable to other plays as well.

Weimann: I would like to attempt to clarify the term *Volkstheater*. In Shakespeare, we do not, of course, have anything like a theater of the folk; rather, we see the conjunction of two very different traditions. On the one hand, we see the educated, humanistic tradition drawing on classical antiquity, via Seneca, which is the source of pathos, *decorum*, and eloquence, and on the other we see the plebeian tradition mainly from the morality plays, which continually undercut the pathos of literary representations by irreverently turning things around and upside down. Brecht's mature theater came to fruition at the time when in the GDR cultural energies were bent on retrieving values and forms, together with humanistic traditions lost during the Third Reich. There was, however, the danger that the cultivation of the classics might degenerate into "classicism" and that classical models would indiscriminately be followed in order merely to save a process of political reeducation. An approach to theater like Brecht's, or later Manfred Wekwerth's, was liberating and carried developments a step further. Their's was a theater achieved not through slogans, abstractions, and mere pathos, but through the fullest possible use of the means of the stage, playful, sensuous, and philosophical.

That is why I was fascinated from the beginning by the concept and practical applications of *gestus*. The element of *gestus* is so strong in Shakespeare's plays because they descend from a tradition that foregrounds the type of performance and spectacle in which concrete experience and practical behavior predominate on stage. Brecht said as much in his remarks on the down-to-earth, sensuous quality of Luther's German.[2] As opposed to the German classics, in which the dramatic use of language is distanced from everyday language, Luther's German is very much rooted in everyday practical experience. *Gestus* is an aspect of mimesis not only in the sense of spectacle but also as a vehicle for transporting the down-to-earth, physical dimensions of social stances, contradictions, and projects. As a central part of the Brechtian tradition, awareness of *gestus* can help in the further development of a contemporary vision of Shakespeare on the German stage.

Wekwerth: The word *gestus* is an unusual word invented by Brecht; the word *Verfremdung* was also invented by Brecht. In German we have the words *Befremdung* ["displeasure"], and *Entfremdung* ["estrangement"] but, in this particular formation the *Ver-* prefix did not exist before Brecht.

Guntner: Could you comment on your experience in England with Brecht's approach to Shakespeare?

Wekwerth: When I directed *Coriolanus* at the National Theatre in London in 1974, Christopher Plummer was to play Coriolanus, and we had very different ideas about the role. During the very first rehearsal there was a blow-up. In our version of the play, his mother, Volumnia, tells Coriolanus to turn back in act 5, scene 2. Plummer insisted Volumnia says "Come back," whereas in our version she was supposed to say: "Turn back." At any rate, that is how we had translated it. The conflict was brought to Laurence Olivier, the head of the National Theatre at the time. Olivier himself had played Coriolanus four times, and he affirmed that whenever he had played the role, Volumnia said, "Come back," and, deeply moved, Coriolanus submitted to her. But Olivier said that maybe we had a point, so he had them bring the First Folio and every other edition of Shakespeare he owned. Together with Kenneth Tynan, who was dramaturg at the National

Theatre at the time, he paged through them all, but could not find this "Come back" either.

For Plummer, it was a matter of his contract, which granted him a lot more privileges than the other actors. In fact, he even had the right to choose his own costume, and most of the rehearsal time was to be spent rehearsing with him. He had returned from the Bahamas with a dark suntan and wanted to play Coriolanus in a steel helmet. In one of the rehearsals in which we rehearsed with the plebeians, Plummer became impatient. When we came to the passage where the plebeians refuse to be drafted for the army and stage a sit-down strike—in our production, Coriolanus draws his sword and the plebeians run away before regrouping[3]—Plummer refused to draw his sword because he thought that when Coriolanus appears, the plebeians would flee solely on the strength of his personality. I said, "Please draw your sword." He refused. And then he heard something he had never heard before: "I break [off] the rehearsal." He said nothing for five minutes. The other players smirked, and after about five minutes, he began to brood. We decided to ask Olivier to decide between the Eastern European import and the national monument Plummer. The actors were behind us. They were very interested in our work. The idea that Shakespeare could be developed out of a specific situation, out of a particular *gestus*, was completely new for them. Olivier called the first and only general meeting in the history of the National Theatre, and in the end, he decided for us. Anthony Hopkins then took over the role of Coriolanus, and for three days there were no rehearsals but a general celebration.

Guntner: In Brecht's last directive to the Berliner Ensemble before their 1956 epoch-making tour of Great Britain, he told them not to act pedestrianly (*fussgängerisch*). Are there differences between acting styles in the Berliner Ensemble or other East German ensembles in comparison to the English?

Weimann: Today it is rather difficult to identify a specifically national acting style. A good many English Shakespeare productions are marked by a rhetorical, at times almost statuesque, acting tradition. What became visible in Brecht's theater was the element of *gestus* that brought movement in social relations onto the stage. *Gestus* bound together dramatic language and social identity (and action) so that verbal utterance and the language of the body became interactive. Too often today, we see an opposition or dichotomy between a theater of the body and image (*Körper- und Bildtheater*) and a theater of the spoken word (*Sprechtheater*).

Guntner: Manfred Wekwerth, for all of the productions of Shakespeare you have directed, you have made your own translations. What, in your opinion, is lacking in the many modern German translations of Shakespeare?

Wekwerth: Shakespeare translations comprise an important chapter in German literary history. I began to translate *Richard III* with the help of Elizabeth

Hauptmann and then I persuaded Robert to lend me a hand. Robert's suggestion was that there is a vital shift in the role of Richard between line 13 and 14 of his monologue.[4] In the opening lines, Richard exaggerates his own courtly idiom, the gallant pose, and the pathos, and his shift in lines 13–14 is more than simply a shift in register. At the Deutsches Theater [1972], Richard Gloucester entered with a whole troop of soldiers and drummers to announce the coming of a new age. Then he sent everyone away and climbed down into the audience to chat about the present age in which he did not fit. I tried to approximate this linguistic shift, which also entailed a shift in imagery from the merchant's language to the sailor's language to the lawyer's language, with the help of Robert and Elizabeth.

In *Troilus and Cressida* the element of tension and contrariness associated with "bifold authority" in the play leads to characters changing opinions as easily as their clothes. Troilus curses war in vivid images and then later at the table with his father, Priam, praises war in a way that flatly contradicts his former position (5.2). We tried to show that these ambivalent uses of language signal an element of contingency in that language is basic to the production of ideology in the sense of false consciousness. One way of resolving a problem is to rephrase it. For example, you say "not so nice" instead of "bad," which is what Ulysses does. With the help of a linguistic *salto mortale,* he causes the order of things to evaporate only to be replaced by a magnificent but empty structure.

Guntner: Would you comment on your work in relationship to what we might call "postmodern theater," for example, Heiner Müller's *Hamletmaschine?*

Wekwerth: Theoretically, this play does not appeal to me because too many people appear to lose their heads. In other words, brains and vitality are sacrificed for the sake of a flood of images that, dramatically speaking, no longer function as signs, because they have no signification in terms of theatrical action, and thus convey no meaning. In my opinion, to deny meaning is a blind alley that ends with not taking the audience into account. When you deny meaning as a living force in the theater, when meaning *as such* is made responsible for the sorry state of affairs in which the world is in, then you eliminate reason. This began with Artaud; as long as it had an iconoclastic function, there was a point to it. But then I do not think that you can equate Müller with *Hamletmaschine.* Müller is also *The Scab (Der Lohndrücker), Germania Death in Berlin (Germania Tod in Berlin), The Contract (Der Auftrag)* and his Shakespeare translations. His pessimism is coupled with so much humor and wit that he is always amused at the pompous hermeneutics with which his work is approached, because there is nothing you cannot read into Müller.

What we are trying to achieve is a realism of graphic vitality, in the

Troilus and Cressida, DIR. Wekwerth/Tenschert, 1985. Troilus (Seifert) and Cressida (Harfouch). Photo: Vera Tenschert, courtesy of the Berliner Ensemble.

sense of presenting meaning via the sensuous, the visual, and an exuberant element of play (*Spiel*). For me, theater is a site at which events involving human beings are shown in such a way that the spectators go away with a heightened awareness of their own world because they have been able to reflect upon the course of events, on the plot, on the story, which, for me, remain the heart and soul of the theater. If you argue that the story per se is a lie because it implies a beginning and an end, I would answer that the story may be that there is no story. Absurd theater has proven it, and Beckett has demonstrated that it may even be an exciting dramatic experience. The most delightful thing in the theater is that it is not bound to the story but can provide an alternative version of it. Take *Othello,* for example. If the spectator would ask: "Why does Othello kill Desdemona? Why does he not let her live? Or why does not Faust marry Gretchen? Or why does not Coriolanus bend his knee? Would it not be better for him?" This approach leads to a deeper understanding of Coriolanus because it emancipates the spectator from what happens on stage and allows him to see the events from a distance.

This has to do with the old argument in the GDR about what "realism" really means. For example, does Mother Courage have to learn that she cannot profit from war before the audience can learn this. Brecht's answer was that it was a greater pleasure for the spectator when theater showed the audience something that it could think over for itself. There will always be a kind of theater based on identification and legitimation, but it is more fun and more stimulating if spectators discover for themselves that Mother Courage has not learned anything from her own personal tragedy. But the prerequisite is that the spectator is not dazzled by what happens on the stage but is able to come up with his own alternative version of what happens.

The theater of the future will have an important actor and that will be the spectator. The task of the theater of the future will not be to have the audience and the actors switch places as avant-garde theater does, but to develop a style of acting that provokes the audience to protest, to incite them to alternative plans of action. In other words, spectators can deliver a protest that is enjoyable, not one in which the audience leaves the theater. This is what Brecht's "realism" is all about as opposed to a narrower definition of "realism." It allows us to do more things more often on stage, and without risk, than you can in life. You can probably commit a murder only once, maybe twice, in your life but on the stage you can commit murder again and again, and never be held responsible. The playfulness (*das Spielerische*) of theater, as the most basic of human features, and enjoyment as a constituent element of humanity, is a task for theater more so than film because in theater the actor on stage has a double function. Robert sees Richard Gloucester, for example, as an actor who reflects upon the role of the king and as king who is to be evaluated by the audience, but always from the point of view of the others. This means that there is a conflict between the performer and his role in which, as Weimann argues, lies the power of mimesis. Mimesis is, of course, the great appeal of theater, and this cannot be transferred to another medium. It vanishes the moment the performance is over. One can film it on video, but then it is no longer there. The vanishing of theater in the moment of performance is one of the great poetic and also philosophical elements of the theater.

Weimann: A cooperation between theater and Shakespeare scholarship and theory is only fruitful when the positions are not identical but engage in a dialogue and even contradict each other. As opposed to Manfred, I see theater in this country, including the performance of Shakespeare in the GDR theater, in a state of crisis. As I see it, we find ourselves in a situation of radical historical change. There is, in our theater, especially in Shakespeare productions, a crisis in representation. It is much more difficult, than it was ten years ago, to bring together on the stage the signifier and the signified, a sign and its meaning, in such a way that the audience, actors, directors and politicians, will accept it. Heiner Müller said in his delightfully cryptic manner in Weimar [1987] that "we have not even arrived at our own affairs as long as Shakespeare continues to write our plays." This means that the present generation sees a lot of rupture, gaps, and differences between the work or the works of the past and the concern of the present. It makes no difference whether we speak of postmodernism or not. Today it is difficult to maintain the idea of social progress and the sense of a unified tradition, including the notion of a heritage (*Erbe*) in the theater. Contemporary theater people are sorting out, filtering, and criticizing their debt to the past a lot more than in previous decades. A "rupture" is immanent and that is the sense in which I understand some of the half-baked dramatic experiments, which Manfred criticizes. I am personally grateful for all that I have learned from him and the Berliner Ensemble, and I cannot imagine doing without it, yet I still believe that in future Shakespeare productions in this country we will see new models on the stage that will not necessarily pick up where we left off in the 1970s.

Guntner: What exactly changed in the cooperation between literary scholars and historians and theater people in the last fifteen to twenty years, when did this development set in, and what were the causes?

Weimann: I think it's related to two developments. On the one hand, there is an intensification in the division of interests and predilections in society; on the other hand, both the arts—including the theater—and the sciences have increasingly developed a sense of autonomy so that today it is impossible for us to comprehend art and science as a integral, more or less unified, form of social consciousness as George Lukàcs once did. Scholars recognize that artists, including theater artists, articulate social experience in a very specific, very unique and unconventional way. Often they are more sensitive than scholars because they have a subtle feeling for changes in atmosphere and climate and because they speak a different language and use a different medium. This medium is no longer determined by criteria of rationality, causality or totality as we used to be taught in high school. In this work, artists can set all of these elements aside for the moment or subsume them under entirely different goals, strategies, and effects. The result has been that theater work has begged to differ from scholarship, that it refused to follow a strictly historicizing approach to Shakespeare's stage and age. Theater people are interested in completely different things.

Guntner: When does this development begin?

Weimann: That's hard to pinpoint. It reaches a high point around 1980 with the two productions, both in Berlin, of *A Midsummer Night's Dream* by Alexander Lang and Thomas Langhoff. But the new approach was anticipated by Dresen's 1964 *Hamlet* in Greifswald, a production that was ahead of its time.

(16 January 1989)

Part Three
Women's Voices, Then and Now
(Interviews)

16

Eva Walch: "Gender Makes No Difference"

Lawrence Guntner: Why did so few women direct Shakespeare or become directors in the GDR?

Eva Walch: The obvious answer is that to be a director you have to be authoritarian. For a director who knows what he wants, there is no democracy. He can have colleagues and advisors, and he is well advised if he has contradictory advisors, but in the end there can be only one creative imagination that asserts itself. Someone has to be in command of this huge theatrical apparatus, a material as well as an intellectual and artistic apparatus, that includes organization, administration, and technology. The more definite a picture a director has of what he wants to accomplish, the smoother this process will be. It begins with to whom he assigns which role.

Guntner: Since 1989 and the general change in the political landscape, more women are directing plays in both western Germany and eastern Germany than ever before.

Walch: I think it has something to do with a general emancipation of women, which I feel was further developed in East Germany than in West Germany. Today women are asserting themselves across the board and are entering into professions which were only reserved for men in the past, especially authoritarian professions.

Guntner: With which women directors have you worked?

Walch: Johanna Schall and Katja Paryla.

Guntner: Was that different than working with male directors?

Walch: Johanna Schall is a young director, and I am older and relatively experienced as a dramaturg, so my relationship to her was different than my relationship to Thomas Langhoff with whom I usually work. He is a much more experienced and mature director to whom you can tell less or different things. They are difficult to compare.

Guntner: But was there an especially feminine aspect to your cooperation with Katja Paryla and Johanna Schall?

Walch: Not offhand. I would have to say that it had more to do with the structure of the individual personality, with the way in which they worked with the actors and actresses, and less to do with gender. Generally speaking, I have not observed any really significant differences between male and female directors. The difference between directors is determined by the strength of the individual personality and creative imagination and not by their gender.

Guntner: Were there any female stereotypes often found on the East German stage? The most famous, of course, might be Mother Courage.

Walch: Of course, there was a particular interpretation of women in classical German literature that had to do with the fact that women in East Germany had made a big step forward in their emancipation, more or less voluntarily, yet certainly at some cost. Almost all of the women worked and most of them had children. Today when I mention that I have two children, some Western career women are full of admiration because they say that they were not able to have both. In my own marriage, I can see tremendous changes. I always had a job, but when the children were small I did not have as much time to pursue my career as my husband did to pursue his as a university professor. Later he encouraged me to write a dissertation and that gave me the self-confidence and independence to go my own professional way. Among my East German woman professional friends, I have discovered that they went through a process similar to mine and that the emancipation of women in university circles in the West is much less developed than in the East. Of course, this development had an important influence on the way in which women characters were portrayed on stage, what kind of responsibility one gave them, what kind of self-awareness and confidence, or what kind of influence they had on the course of events in a dramatic action. Shakespeare has many strong roles for women. Viola or Rosalind or Portia are characters who fascinated us with their independence, and with the personal energy and determination with which they went their own way.

Guntner: The plays central to the East German Shakespeare tradition were plays like *Hamlet, Macbeth,* or *A Midsummer Night's Dream,* in which the women do not have an easy time of it, neither in the play nor in the performance: for example, Müller's *Macbeth* at the Volksbühne [1982], or Lang's *A Midsummer Night's Dream* at the Deutsches Theater. Why were plays like *Taming of the Shrew* or *As You Like It,* in which the women play a dominant role, less central?

Walch: There are two answers to that. First of all the situation of women was not central for us. It was not something that had to be continually struggled for, and there was no East German "women's movement" because all of the women here worked and took care of their children. The emancipation of women took place as a part of the general process of economic emancipation. There was no reason to stress women's struggle for liberation on the stage. Other more general questions were in the foreground such as a basic critique of the system. Second, Lang's production of *A Midsummer Night's Dream*, which made a longer-lasting impression on me than perhaps any other Shakespeare performance I have ever seen, did say that things were not so good for women in the GDR. It was a direct critique of still dominant patriarchal behavior patterns. Lang alienated [*verfremdet*] the character of Titania by making her into a symbol of male fantasies à la Marilyn Monroe by using a blond wig, makeup, synthetic red coat, and high heeled shoes. At the same time Titania is alienated [*entfremdet*] from her own true self. This performance showed that once she puts these accessories aside she will discover her true self.

Tragedies like *Macbeth* and *Hamlet* are more immediately political than the comedies. East German theater was probably more attracted to the tragedies because it was always an immanently political theater and was always on the lookout for material.

Guntner: Are there any women in the theater, who serve as examples for you?

Walch: The dramaturg, Ilse Galfert. She could be ruthless and inconsiderate of others as well as of her own person when it came to pursuing her goals. When my work becomes tough, I remember the single-minded rigor with which she boxed through what she thought was important for a performance, for the intensity and complete submission of everything in her life for the benefit of the theater. On the other hand, I am grateful that I do not have to be that single-minded because I have a wonderful family and do not need the theater as a replacement for them. Galfert was also legendary as a "director maker." Dresen and Lang, for example, were "developed" by her. She was able to hold her own even with very determined directors like Dresen. Really good directors look for contradictions, and they rub themselves smooth on them. And that I believe is the function of the dramaturg. There must be some person in the production to whom the director can open himself up. The dramaturg serves as an important shield for the actors and actresses if at some point the director does not know exactly what he wants; a feeling of insecurity by the director calls forth a feeling of insecurity in the actors. A director needs to give his actors and actresses a feeling of trust in what he is doing and for which he is responsible. On the other hand, the director needs someone to whom he can admit his own insecurities, and with whom he can discuss questions, or turn things upside down behind closed doors without disclosing it to his cast.

Guntner: Was there censorship of theater in the GDR?

Walch: Of course, even if it was not completely effective. There was also an internalized self-censorship at work that conditioned theater people as to how far they could go before they would endanger a production completely. There were a number of examples, even here at the Deutsches Theater, that could be mentioned. But censorship existed in all shapes and forms. It was possible to prohibit a particular play when it was proposed by the general director. Or it was possible to take a play off the bill during rehearsal, or after the dress rehearsal, or after the premiere, or after the tenth performance, via various institutions backed by various ministries or via an official theater critique. For example, I wrote reports on plays for the Henschel Verlag. Twice I recommended plays which could have been understood as sharply critical of the GDR. On the basis of my recommendation, one of the plays was translated. The head lector of the publisher could not read English, and on the basis of the translation he dropped it. The money for the translation was for nought, and I was reproached for the waste of money and for my political shortsightedness. I should have known that this play could not be performed in the GDR. Those were the kind of experiences you internalized. You knew exactly how far you could go. You could go into rehearsals, knowing that if someone objected during the dress rehearsal, you could cut a few sentences so that the premiere could take place. But inside you sensed that somewhere along the line you were going to run into trouble. And these were the internalized, self-regulating control mechanisms that functioned as self-censorship. The good people, politically interested people, pushed things to the edge and a little bit further, otherwise we could not have gone as far as we did.

Guntner: Shakespeare is perhaps most political when you let his text speak for itself and the political interpretation is constructed by the audience in a particular context, without the performers' intention.

Walch: In a theater performance, nothing is done unintentionally. The actors know exactly what they are doing. That all kinds of unplanned effects and meanings may come about is possible.

Guntner: Was there a kind of conspiracy between the director and the players against the regime?

Walch: Not at all. To be in theater was a responsible job; it also entailed artistic responsibility. All artists had a large portion of self-confidence, especially in regards to the special position they held in the GDR. The politically aware and engaged theater artists simply pulled the rest along with them. Of course, there were those who simply withdrew and concentrated on their "art," but they were embedded in a context which was politically determined.

Guntner: What changed during the seventies and under Honecker?

Walch: It was the period when the GDR was receiving international recognition. On the one hand, it meant certain liberties and international exchanges took place on various levels. On the other hand, this opening up meant the slow undermining of the system, its economic and ideological downfall, and finally the fall of the Wall. Conservatism set in, a societal fossilization, and people were robbed of their illusion that the system would be able to develop dynamically by itself. However, I personally benefitted from the political recognition of the GDR. After twenty years of teaching English I was finally able to travel to England for the first time.

Guntner: How did you feel?

Walch: Fantastic! It was like the Berlin Wall coming down. I was allowed to go to England in 1981 after nineteen years of professional experience. I taught German for four months at a college in High Wycombe and felt very comfortable there. I had close contacts with the dramatist Arnold Wesker. I spent two days a week with his family at their home in London and got to know a lot of people. I was so happy to experience something like a European identity. There was a common ground, and I did not feel like someone from "the East" or from another culture. I never experienced this feeling again with my own West Germans, who ostensibly come from the same cultural background.

(24 May 1994)

17

Johanna Schall: "The Audiences Now Smell Different"

Lawrence Guntner: What does Shakespeare mean to you?

Johanna Schall: I love him. Because he is illogical, poetic, and full of contradictions. He is so human. He is one of the very few playwrights, male or female, who wrote about human beings and not about the ideas he had about human beings. Human beings can behave irrationally and strangely and not according to the expectations you have of them. There is a tendency in drama to confine people within very small boundaries, but great authors are able to bring together all kinds of possibilities that are in human beings and let them be.

Guntner: Where did you learn to speak English so well?

Schall: My mother, Barbara Brecht-Schall,[1] grew up in America, but I did not grow up bilingually. I used to look at old Hollywood films a lot, and I wanted to read Shakespeare in the original so I decided to speak English. Although I come from a theater family, I never really intended to become an actress, but one day I just knew I had to become an actress. I did not go to acting school, but the Deutsches Theater agreed to accept me, and Alexander Lang agreed to train me. I played Hippolyta in Lang's production of *A Midsummer Night's Dream* while I was still in training. It was only my second role on stage.

Guntner: How did you feel as Hippolyta?

Schall: It must have been a terrible situation for a woman who was accustomed to being her own person, and a queen, captured by this terrible Theseus. Now she had to behave according to his dictates. He is in power, but she hates him, and she knows that she will have to live with this for a long time. It is hard to know how she feels because she does not say a lot. Alex pushed me in the directions of why she does not say much. Her reactions were in contradiction to Theseus's most of the time, but how can you perform this without resorting to a bad pantomime?

Guntner: Is this a particularly female situation? In Lang's production the women did not say much, and after act 4, they did not say anything at all.

Schall: Hippolyta is the only woman still talking while being continually fondled. For Hippolyta it is not simply talking, but screaming and trying to put up with being sexually abused.

Guntner: Could you call Alexander Lang's production of *Dream* "antifeminist"?

Schall: It is a fact that women are made into objects very often, so why should this production be antifeminist if it shows this fact? If you show a basic fact of life, like the oppression of women, on stage, you are a "realist" and not an antifeminist. In the past and still today, women are viewed as objects most of the time. It is hard to change yourself into somebody who is doing something and not to whom something is being done.

Guntner: Do you have any women who have influenced or helped you?

Schall: I had never even thought about these issues until I directed David Mamet's *Oleanna* [Deutsches Theater]. It was new to me to separate my experience into male and female. I am distrustful of questions about "the female point of view," and I am not very much into personal examples.

Guntner: As an actress?

Schall: Katja Paryla. When she started, she helped me a lot. During rehearsals she would tell me to pay attention to my breathing, or think from one end of the sentence to the other and not stop in the middle. Very practical things. She told me that when you go on stage there must be a certain tension, as if your buttocks were screwed together. I also like the way she acts: very strange, crazy.

Guntner: Are there any kinds of stereotypes of women at work on the stage?

Schall: The victim, the sufferer. "Stereotypes" is too easy. Most people simply have little boxes that they want to put people into. Most plays were written by men, and women were required to be inactive, at least not active, in politics or society.

Guntner: If you were to direct *A Midsummer Night's Dream*, would you do it differently than Lang did?

Schall: I suppose so, but I loved that production exactly because it was not about sentimental dancing in the wood. Everyone became passionate and was transformed completely because they were in the woods. But if you look at the play itself, it is a horrible experience. You wake up in the woods, and you are not loved anymore by someone whom you loved passionately. Helena even says, "treat me as your spaniel." It is a terrible situation for a woman, and normally it is glazed over with a lot of romanticism. Nightmares have a double quality: on the one hand, they are frightening, but on the other, they force you to face things that you would normally ignore. You might normally say, "Have a nice day," but in your dreams you would like to kill this person or make passionate love to him. Nightmares sometimes come very close to the truth, but who likes to look at the truth?

One more thing about Hippolyta: after act 4 when the young lovers woke up, it dawned on Hippolyta that something had gone wrong. One of the women still had flowers in her hair and she would never be right again. Hippolyta was the only one who at least made a small attempt to do something about it. This was unusual, because normally women on stage are depicted as passive from the beginning to the end, and in this production she was not. Hippolyta noticed that something was wrong and tried to help, but Theseus grabbed her and shoved her off the stage. She was not supposed to meddle. In act 5 she was again the only one who cried out that something had gone terribly wrong. She realized that she was going to end up as the young women had, as a victim.

Guntner: One of the basic rights of East German socialist society was equal rights for each sex.

Schall: Theoretically, yes. Ninety percent of the women had a job. The government provided nursery schools and kindergartens for your children during the day and that was better than what we have now.

Guntner: What has changed?

Schall: Many nursery schools and kindergartens have been closed, high unemployment among women, abortion rights have been curtailed, and women have to pay for oral contraceptives. So in some respects, things have become worse. On the other hand, I do not believe in equality; I believe in difference, in the equal right to be as different as you want to. Women did not have equal rights in the GDR because the largest part of the household rested on their shoulders, including the children. And just look at the government. There were only three or four women in it.

Guntner: Any reasons for the few women directors and general directors of theater in the GDR? Helene Weigel and Ruth Berghaus were the exception. If women were supposed to have the right to work, why were they not given work at a high level in the theater?

Schall: It is a question of being used to things. Everybody is used to seeing men in leading positions, and this is also a problem for women. When I started to direct about two years ago—Strindberg's *The Pelican*—it was a strange experience as a woman to be in a position of making the decisions. You tend to apologize a lot and tend to strive for harmony. If you are strong and decisive as a woman, they say you are harsh and hard. It is hard to decide that you do not care about what others think or say. It is something you have to learn. Of course, I like people to like me. The cliches are not only put on women by men, but women do it to themselves, so you behave accordingly.

Guntner: You are going to have a difficult time of it as a director if you like to be liked.

Schall: But on the other hand, it helps to be friendly. I think people in this theater like to work with me because I usually know what I want, and I do not think that screaming helps. I like to work in a friendly way because I like to be treated that way myself. The point is that you yourself have to decide, and that is something I really like, to be the person who makes the final decision. That is one of the reasons I wanted to become a director.

Guntner: There has been a whole spate of women directors in the West as well as the East since 1989: What has happened?

Schall: I do not know. I had wanted to direct for a very long time, but I was not ready. Then one day I knew that I was ready, and I was lucky. I found actors who would work with me, I had the possibility to do it.

Guntner: Would you describe yourself as a feminist?

Schall: It is important that women are treated fairly in society, but there are so many individual, very different problems that I could not say that I am a feminist. I do not really know what a feminist is. The question is what is more important at a particular time and how to bring about political change. Some of those "political correctness" things seem to me as if they were trying to put women back into the Victorian age. I think you can only relate on a personal level, but you cannot do it with rules.

Because of directing Mamet's *Oleanna,* I noticed that some people do not see theater as telling stories but they look at it with ideology in their minds. Two days before we opened I got a call from a male colleague who said: "You've got to stop this production. It is so antifeminist." And I said: "What? If I were doing *Richard III,* would I ever be accused of being "anti-male?" He said, "Of course not." So I said: "So why are you worried about *Oleanna?* Because it is a play about a woman?" "But she is lying," was his reply, so I said: "Of course she is lying, but why is she lying? That is the point of interest." The other night we came to the point in the performance where he beats her up, and one group started to clap and another group shouted them down. I like that because the performance forced them to confront each other. People do not look at the performance as the story of a certain woman who is dealing with a certain man, in a certain social environment, but they file the play in a feminist or antifeminist pigeonhole, and that is very sad. It is like the people who do not like fairy tales because there is violence in them, as if life were not violent.

Guntner: What is your favorite Shakespeare play?

Schall: It changes about every two years, but at the moment it is *The Taming of the Shrew.* For me, it is a play about political correctness. Katherina is saying that she will not behave according to the rules. To see the kind of strength she has, the enthusiasm for what she is doing, makes it one of the saddest stories I have ever read. It is very depressing to see that these two people, who I think are a perfect match—strong, clever, and terribly attracted to one another—can't become a couple because of rules, because Petruchio has to have someone under his thumb.

Guntner: Do you see Katherina's final speech as straightforward, or to be played with a wink?

Schall: There is not one wink in the entire play. I think it is even worse. I think she embodies a danger for all of the other women. In the end the widow and Bianca show tendencies of being rebellious, but she puts them down and becomes an enemy of the other women. I would cast a woman as Baptista to show that her mother is in cahoots with society in demanding that her daughter be submissive, socially adjusted, and pleasant. She is no better than a man. On the other hand, there are so few women's roles in the play that I would like to work with more women.

Guntner: What do you like about working with women?

Schall: Women are more willing to take risks.

Guntner: What has changed since 1989?

Schall: The audience smells different. Our audience is made up to a great extent of West Germans, and there is more perfume and aftershave in the air. They want entertainment. East German actors had to learn the behavioral patterns and performance codes to which West German audiences were accustomed: in the GDR we had no Yuppies, no frustrated suburban housewives, no ex-hippies. Today anything goes; you can say anything you want to. Theater is no longer the place to say the forbidden, so the spoken word no longer has the same effect on the audience. The East German audience was much more political than the West German audience. They were trained to listen very carefully to what was being said and they even tried hard to discover ambiguities. For example, "Pyramus and Thisbe" in *A Midsummer Night's Dream* is played through a wall, so it was taken by our audience to refer to the Berlin Wall even if it was not. There is also the problem of government subsidies, which puts the theater under pressure to fill the house. This means that theaters are reluctant to produce something an audience might not want to see.

(25 May 1994)

18

Katja Paryla: "Titania à la Marilyn Monroe"

Lawrence Guntner: Do you have any female role models as an actress?

Katja Paryla: That's really hard to say. Like Johanna Schall I come from a theater family, and I grew up with actors around me all the time. I suppose I never had an exaggerated reverence for them. I have had the good fortune to have met and worked with so many good people, male and female, that I am really unable to be more precise. I enjoy being a woman very much and want to be understood as such, but Fritz Kortner was probably more influential than many women. For me it is simply a matter of whether someone does good work or not.

Guntner: How long have you been directing?

Paryla: I started when I was still going to acting school and started working with other actors, just like Johanna. With a group from the theater in Schwedt I did Goldoni's *The Cafe,* then Ionesco's *The Bald Soprano* at the Deutsches Theater [1989], which is still on the bill. Then I did Shakespeare's *Henry VI* in the Chamber Theater in 1991.

Guntner: Why *Henry VI?*

Paryla: When I went to directing school as an acting student I did some scenes with other students from *Henry VI.* We had so much fun with the absurdity, the insanity, with which this man created a montage of stories and situations that I fell in love with this play. In the midst of the events that led up to the so-called Wende I remembered this play. It suddenly became so exciting, because if there is any play that shows us the perverseness of power structures it is this one. Jan Kott, in *Shakespeare Our Contemporary,* points out that everyone of these characters who assumes a position of power is stained with blood the moment he appears on the scene. For me it also has something to do with the utopia of socialism and everything connected with it. Despite all the good and beautiful ideas, the moment someone even thinks about imposing power over others, these power structures already exist. The same is true for religion, especially Christianity. You already have distrust, and when there is distrust, you have hate, and death is not far behind. And this perversion in the course of history, occurs in this play in such rapid succession and in such detail and

253

was so fascinating to me that I decided to compress these three evenings into a single performance—a two-and-one-half-hour "Reader's Digest *Henry the Sixth*," as one critic called it. I used the Schlegel-Tieck translation and then borrowed some passages from Eschenberg. His language is beautifully concrete and not so monotonously regular in the rhythm as Schlegel's. Eschenberg has more poetic power behind it. Nevertheless, I stuck with Schlegel, because Eschenberg's rendition was so coarse. Since this play was so chuck full of coarse brutality, I could use Schlegel's smoothness in the translation to work against this.

Guntner: You staged the death of Jeanne d'Arc as *The Muppet Show*?

Paryla: All of the scenes which had to do with France—up on the walls, down from the walls—detracted from the main thrust of the Wars of the Roses, and the only thing I retained was the story of Jeanne d'Arc. I staged it as *The Muppet Show*, not because I wanted to ridicule it, but to show that in terms of the power struggle underlying the Wars of the Roses, the events in France were a nice story but only secondary.

Guntner: Did you try to bring a particularly female aspect to this production?

Paryla: The character who interested me most was Henry VI. If we want to talk about a female principle we can associate with reconciliation, or to approach a situation through tolerance, then the young Henry VI embodies this. So Henry was not a ridiculous figure but someone who was born ahead of his time. What I learned during rehearsals was that this attempt to take one step backward, to attempt to influence others in the direction of reconciliation, to act from a position of understanding for others, will be misunderstood by others. In the end Henry winds up as a greater killer than the others. I had a woman play the young Henry in an attempt to show that this longing for harmony, the books which he had read as a child, something I like very much about him, is something he retains all of his life. Although Henry, and all of us get older, he, and we all remain little children in our minds. I tried to show that this child Henry was still present in all of these situations so that Henry was continually confronted by his own childhood, by his utopian vision, by his own softness. And that is why I had an actress play the role of the young Henry.

Guntner: You played Titania in Lang's *A Midsummer Night's Dream*. How did you see Titania as a feminine being?

Paryla: She played the child-woman role à la Marilyn Monroe, the wish fulfillment of some men. But in the confrontation between Oberon and Titania we see that Oberon treats her the way many men want to treat women and he does this all evening. And that is why we played Oberon's vision of the woman as a kind of pinup. What we realized during rehearsals is that what comes out during the very first confrontation between Titania and Oberon is very up to date. Titania describes how the power struggle between the mighty of the world is destroying the natural environment: the rivers are drying up, the animals are dying. I realized that Shakespeare's accusation on behalf of the natural environment was so poetic and so relevant to our world today, that this became a point of departure for approaching Titania. She was not simply a child-woman. The moment she removed her wig and fell in love with Bottom, she stood naked and vulnerable. That she falls in love with the donkey, Bottom, is not something to laugh about. And she was not ashamed that she had slept with him after she was awakened from her dream. She had to be pulled away from him forcibly. She suffered from being separated from the human being she had come to know and love.

Guntner: Was this your idea or Lang's?

Paryla: It is hard to say. It was an insight and an approach to the character of Titania that developed during rehearsals. The dramaturgical concept was seen as a reply to Peter Brook's *Dream*. The days of the flower children had passed and they had been replaced by hard drugs and people were desperate, so this was the counterpoint to Brook's production. We showed that seduction through drugs is murder. This was not the case with Brook's production, which was light and merry. The production also had to do with the situation of the young people in the audience, who had been seduced by ideology, and with the situation of actors whose work no longer interested those in power.

Guntner: What has changed since 1989?

Paryla: The security offered by the ensembles in the GDR was, on the one hand, boring but, on the other hand, in the case of the Deutsches Theater, made it possible for a wonderfully homogeneous theater to develop. In West Berlin, for example, in the Schiller Theater, an actor would have a contract for two or three years, and in this time, he would have to make it or leave. So he did not think about whether he was telling a story with a political content, or whether he was telling a story or not, but mainly thought about himself. That was the main difference to the GDR. West German actors and actresses thought more about themselves than about the story they were telling. East German actors and actresses saw themselves as members of a theater ensemble who were telling a story with this or that intent. They thought more about what they were trying to say with this story and not only about simply acting. You had a feeling with the director that you were telling a story from a point of view that had something to do with the world in which you lived with which you may not have been in agreement. Even if one were the protagonist and at the center of the story, you still thought about how you could tell this story together. Another difference was that the GDR actor was not so prone to internalizing a story but willing to experiment pragmatically with ways of telling it.

Guntner: The heads of theaters were expected to submit their repertoire proposal for the coming season to the regional party headquarters for approval.

Paryla: It would not have been possible for us to do Ionesco's *The Bald Soprano* before 1989. The play was not allowed beforehand. The point is that in this country it was preached that everything that happened took place to make the world a better place to live, but empty slogans like "We work hard today to live well tomorrow" were absolutely absurd. The state tried to explain everything in terms of sociology, that every failure was in reality a step towards a better future. Then you had playwrights like Beckett or Ionesco who said that the moment my life begins, in effect, the moment my own death begins. Or Camus says why wait for tomorrow when tomorrow I will be a day older. The government said that such an attitude despised reality, and was in opposition to the socialist view of humanity (*das sozialistisches Menschenbild*): someone who was good, had a profession, who put himself at the service of the community and led a moral life. It was like the Catholic Church and the Ten Commandments. There were also the Ten Commandments of socialism; they were very similar, a confession of faith, a dogma.

(25 May 1994)

19

Ursula Karusseit: "Politically Minded People"

Lawrence Guntner: You played the "sad" Gertrude separated from her beloved Hamlet in Benno Besson's famous 1977 production of *Hamlet* at the Volksbühne.

Ursula Karusseit: My "sadness" had to do with my personal situation at the time. Gertrude was my first Shakespeare role in many years. I played Isabella in *Measure for Measure* at the Deutsches Theater in 1966, Olivia in *Twelfth Night* at the Volksbühne, and then various roles in Heiner Müller's *Macbeth*, again at the Volksbühne, in 1982.

But back to *Hamlet*. Before the curtain went up for the premiere, we all sat on stage in our costumes. Besson gave a long speech, and still the performance did not go well. Two days later we traveled to Weimar for the annual meeting of the German Shakespeare Society with all of those Shakespeare experts and people who we were afraid would be critical of our approach. We were absolutely convinced that they would tear us apart. However, the performance went well, until the scene when Ophelia entered in a bloody nightshirt on the verge of insanity. Ophelia was played by Heide Kipp, who was just one year older than me. In fact, we sometimes switched roles. When she came out some men up in the second balcony started to groan and whistle because you could see a bit of her bosom. Then Heide went down front to the ramp of the stage and tore open her gown so that both breasts were entirely visible. It was her way of throwing down a gauntlet to the audience. She continued to recite her text and in a thrice it was absolutely still up there. The performance turned out to be a huge success.

Guntner: Anna-Christin Naumann has said that Kipp's dramatic gesture was an expression of the contradiction between the patriarchal discourse of the dramatic text Ophelia is forced to speak for her father Polonius and the frustrated female emotions expressed by her body language. The revolt of the female body, so to speak, against the corset imposed on her by a patriarchal society, in the play and in the GDR.

Karusseit: Naumann may have smelled that out, but that was not Heide's intention. Her struggle was directed against the audience, for the play, for her role, and for the performance.

Guntner: Theater as an institution has always been the domain of men. The power structures in the theater have been traditionally dominated by men, and the stereotypical portrayal of women on stage has been determined by men as well.

Karusseit: Absolutely. That is why I applied for the position of Head at the Volksbühne when the GDR still existed, then again in Potsdam and in Cottbus. I simply wanted to see what would happen when a woman headed up a theater. Earlier I never gave it much thought, but in the course of the years I have come to realize what a dirty deal actresses often get. Whenever people talk about *Hamlet,* for example, it is always Hamlet, Hamlet, Hamlet. No one ever says Gertrude or Ophelia. Right from the beginning the women's parts are pushed aside, and I would like to know why. Why not let a woman direct *Hamlet*?

Guntner: What you have directed to date?

Karusseit: My debut was supposed to be Rudi Strahl's *Der blaue vom Himmel* (*The Blue in the Sky*), a part of a *Spektakel* at the Volksbühne in the early eighties. The whole theater was to be transformed into a stage and performances were to take place all over the building. For reasons of cultural policy, the performance was not allowed. All of the writers in the GDR had been called upon to write something against the stationing of new atomic rockets in Europe, and Strahl, who writes comedies, wrote a comedy that takes place in heaven. A young girl comes to heaven and asks God to return laughter to earth because no one in her village is laughing anymore, and she is afraid that there will be a war. Of course, she did not meet up with the boss because he was behind closed doors trying to construct a new human being out of electrical transistors. Instead she runs into the archangels Michael and Gabriel, both in uniform. One is a general and the other is a colonel. Somehow the National People's Army got their hands on the script and vetoed the play. That was possible in the GDR. The play had to be handed into the Ministry of Culture for approval. The army was a state within the state and could veto anything that they felt went against their interests.

Guntner: You mean the head of the Volksbühne had to submit his play or his repertoire for official approval?

Karusseit: First there was the level of the local municipal administration to be passed. In the local party, there was someone responsible for culture. They made a preliminary decision. Often things never even reached the Ministry of Culture.

Guntner: Who was the party official in Berlin at that time?

Karusseit: Konrad Naumann, the general secretary of the Socialist Unity Party in Berlin [1971–85], a very unpopular man who was removed by Honecker himself. This was the kind of person who had the say so. Then it was passed on to the Ministry of Culture, and we received a directive from the ministry that we could not perform the play since it was insulting to the army.

Guntner: What role did Kurt Hager play in this?

Karusseit: Hager was the head of ideology and had the final say so, but often things never got that far. Decisions were made at a lower level.

Guntner: There was a degree of arbitrariness in all this.

Karusseit: One day a woman came and drew a slip of paper out of her purse and read the directive of the Ministry of Culture outloud for all to hear. Next to her sat the head of the theater, but he had never seen this document before. She announced that the uniforms in the play were an insult to the National People's Army, even though we had completely different uniforms on during rehearsal—exaggerated uniforms bearing no resemblance to those of the army. What she was saying was absolutely absurd; I told her that she was treating us like infants in a kindergarten and that she should at least let the audience decide for itself. I was furious, and afterwards we all got terribly drunk; we had completed over forty rehearsals. Then the head of the dramatic repertoire asked me if I still had the strength to do something else so that the young ensemble did not have to hang around for six months. I discovered Synge's *Playboy of the Western World.* The papers called it the most successful directing debut since Alexander Lang. Then I directed Frederike Roth's *Der Ritt auf die Wartburg* in Osnabrück, a play about women who go to East Germany to look for some excitement since there is none at home, and then a Christmas fairy tale, *The Prince of Portugal,* at the Volksbühne. Then I directed Brecht's *Puntila* and later I did Shakespeare's *Measure for Measure* in Dessau. I just finished doing Brecht's *The Good Person of Szechwan* in Dresden, and now I am going with Besson to Finland to do Carlos Gozzi's *König Hirsch.*

Guntner: If you were to become head of the Deutsches Theater, what would you as a woman do differently?

Karusseit: The women actresses at the Deutsches Theater are so good that all I would have to do would be to pick out enough plays that would give them all something to do. But I would not presume to be able to head up the Deutsches Theater. The finances are so tight that there is no space to experiment. Everything has to be a success right from the start. I would be satisfied with a small theater.

Guntner: What female elements are lacking in eastern German theater today?

Karusseit: I notice that every actor or actress needs a papa or a mama. The actors have a need to be able to go to the head of the theater with their worries without being told that he has no time for them or has too many other things to do. Most heads of theaters go to receptions and are rarely present in their own theaters. Today theaters are run by bureaucrats from the administration. I would develop my dramatic repertoire completely around the actors and actresses available to me. I would not select plays according to my own personal preference but see to it that everyone advanced a little bit in his or her profession.

Guntner: Any particular themes or topics?

Karusseit: Plenty, but I still have to begin with the ensemble. I cannot perform a play with a lot of women's roles if I do not have any actresses at my disposal. I cannot perform *Hamlet* if I do not have an actor to play Hamlet. I was in Cologne, and Manfred Karge, who played Hamlet at the Volksbühne, said to me that he had always wanted to do *Mother Courage* but never had the actress for the role. You can do it, he said, so I played Mother Courage in Cologne. I was never allowed to play Courage at the Volksbühne because the Berliner Ensemble turned its thumb down on any Brecht productions in East Germany.

In the GDR, money did not play an important role in theater, but now we are living in the era of the bean counter, and every penny is turned over ten times before it is spent. We even have the barbarism of theaters being shut down as was the Schiller Theater in Berlin. They did not save any money because they still had to pay the people for the rest of the year anyway, and in that time they could have continued to perform and come up with a new concept as well as proposed some reasonable budget cuts to be able to maintain the theater. Now they are doing Broadway musicals, and dramatic theater performance has come to an end. Someone from America prophesied there would be no dramatic performances as we know them within the not so distant future. The trend is to do musicals, even in western Germany where new theaters are being built just for particular shows.

Guntner: The tradition of "going to the theater" may, indeed, be replaced by the musical, but I am still convinced that drama, perhaps in another form, will still be performed.

Karusseit: Castorf is the only head in all Berlin who continues to charge the same admission at the Volksbühne as before 1990, and that is the reason why his theater is full. He can do this only if he has those privileges that other theaters do not have. They cannot continue to charge the same admission. He has the unemployed, students, and homeless people in his audience. The homeless have set up their cardboard houses and their grills next to the theater. It always smells like charcoal. His actors love him because he does not rehearse so much. He lays down certain guidelines and lets them do their thing. He does not come to the theater until around noon, but no one dare come *after* him. He can come too late but no one else. I cannot recognize the plays anymore. Now the rest of the pack imitate him and poorly.

Guntner: Was there a specifically "GDR approach" to roles determined by ideology or politics or worldview?

Karusseit: No, not in our approach to a role. But the East German actor thought politically, or at least we thought of ourselves as politically minded people, even if we were against the regime and its system. We saw politics in all the plays, and we intentionally played to the secret partner in the audience. Hidden political messages were a characteristic of GDR theater performances, not like in cabaret in which everything is expressed more or less directly but insinuations artistically packed so that the audience understood. For example, in Besson's legendary production of Jewgeni Schwarz's anti-Stalinist parable *The Dragon* [Deutsches Theater, 1965], there is a scene in which the people want to look up in the sky to watch Lancelot's struggle with the dragon. Then the mayor of the town comes and tells them that it is forbidden to look up in the sky, so the people take out their mirrors and watch the fight without looking up. The audience roared with laughter. We opened up a safety valve for them to laugh. In Besson's production of Hacks's *Die schöne Helena* [Deutsches Theater, 1964], the audience could not keep still for laughter. There is a scene in which Agamemnon gives a long speech in which he says: "We have everything: painters, brick layers, critics. What is lacking are men with brains. But there must be some somewhere. They exist in other countries, even among the barbarians to the east. And I tell you, they exist here, too." It brought the house down.

Guntner: The East German audience paid much more attention to what was being said.

Karusseit: And we performed in this direction, especially Besson's productions, even though Wolf Biermann and Müller claim that Besson's productions were the downfall of political theater in the GDR.[1] Müller criticized him for having performed Schwarz's political satire as a fairy tale for adults, but the audience loved it. I acted in it almost five hundred times before I left the Deutsches Theater for the Volksbühne, and then they performed it another 500 times and always to full houses. The performance was packed with hidden political messages, and the audience understood exactly what was meant. You do not have to make things obvious. This performance was an international success and it won first prize at the 1966 Théâtre des Nations Festival in Paris. As actors, we always thought politically, on a different political level than was dominant in West Germany. The success with which East German actors have been able to assert themselves on the West German market has a lot to do with the fact that we had better training and approached things more concretely. West German colleagues will tell you that themselves. What the East Germans did not understand immediately after the fall of the Wall was that they worked for much lower wages than they should have just to get some work.

Guntner: Would you say that there were any stereotypes of women peculiar to the East German stage?

Karusseit: No, but I was always willing to experiment. In Müller's *Macbeth* I played one of the bald-headed witches painted blue who waltzed around the three Macbeths to the tune of "The Blue Danube." My first entrance was not as a witch but as the bleeding sergeant who reports the course of the battle to Duncan, and in Müller's version this takes a long time. I had my witch's gown under my uniform. Then I played the porter with dark motorcycle goggles, bald head, and leather jacket. I only had one arm and a crippled leg, on one foot a lady's shoe, on the other a sneaker so that my posture stood out. It was a lot of fun to portray various types in one character. Heiner said these people will do anything. The witches are the soldiers and the murderers. Evil does not have a particular face, and we were never so disguised that the audience could not recognize us as witches.

Guntner: How did Lady Macbeth die?

Karusseit: There was a loud thump, which signaled that she had jumped out the window. Lady MacDuff is stabbed in a telephone booth by two of the Macbeths. Then she slumped down dead in the booth. During the rehearsals I sat in the third row and watched and told Heiner that one could not see or hear her. The people in the third row paid twelve marks to get in, the highest price in the house in GDR, and they deserved to see something. And Heiner replied, they did not have to. You do not understand everything in life, either. Heiner was not interested in making things transparent. What was not understood, was not understood. Although the roles were foreign to me, I enjoyed this performance very much. I never really did conventional theater because I was always fascinated by bizarre costumes and roles. I simply love to act.

For me it does not matter whether the director is a man or a woman as long as a director knows what he or she is doing. Gender does not play a role for me with a director.

Guntner: Do you have any female role models in the theater?

Karusseit: Therese Giehse [(1898–1975), who with Helene Weigel, is recognized as the greatest female interpreter of Brecht's work]. I once had the good fortune to meet her personally. In 1974 Besson was directing *Die heilige Johanna der Schlachthöfe* in Munich, and I played Johanna Dark. Joachim Kaiser, then the most important critic in Munich, called the play "antiquated" and had nothing good to say about the performance. The audience's reaction was mixed, so at Easter time in 1974 I was very down. Giehse was doing a Brecht evening in the Theater Workshop in the same building. I parked my old Russian car in the lot across from the theater, and she came over to me, introduced herself, and congratulated me on the performance. She had been to the dress rehearsal and told me that she had liked it very much. In her broad Bavarian accent she told me not to be depressed by the critics and that we were good. That Therese Giehse would say that to me pepped me up. We entered the theater together, and someone had left a small bouquet of violets for her at the door. She gave them to me. Ten minutes later she came to my dressing room to wish me good luck, and then the woman from the wardrobe brought me a little bag of fennel lozenges for my throat. I was touched. I had seen her many times at the Berliner Ensemble, and she still remains my role model. She was always unbelievably concrete in her performances. You could always follow exactly what she was doing.

Guntner: Let us come back to the situation of women in East Germany.

Karusseit: In 1968 I played a woman called Gertrud Habersaath in the film *Wege übers Land* which caused a bit of excitement in the GDR. The Deutsches Theater sent me as a delegate to a National Women's Conference headed up by Lotte Ulbricht with women from The Alliance of Democratic German Women (*Demokratischer Frauenbund Deutschlands*), the Central Committee, and other women in official functions. They discovered me in the back of the auditorium and asked me to give a speech. All of the prepared speeches had to be handed in ahead of time for approval. I quickly jotted down some notes in stenography and gave them to a secretary to type up, but there were no copies for the people in the audience. My speech contained a lot of criticism of the working conditions, primitive equipment, and transportation. I even spoke about abortion. Then I asked why men were paid higher wages than women in the theater. I said that I delivered the same quality that an actor did and that I ought be paid the same. All the forewomen from the factories who had spoken before me kept repeating the same slogan: "The same wage for the same work." But I said that did not seem to be the case in the theater. I questioned the validity of their claim and that really upset them. The whole conference was filmed and shown during the television news. I was shown giving autographs, then the woman who spoke before me was shown, but when it was time for my speech, they gave the weather report. They had cut me out. The next day a colleague from the Deutsches Theater told me that because of me they had decided to cut his speech for "lack of time." All of these official "women" were upset that I criticized something in this wonderful atmosphere in which you were only supposed to talk about successes. The women in attendance were enthusiastic but not the women of the presidium: Lotte Ulbricht, the wife of Walter Ulbricht, Inge Lange, secretary of the

Central Committee and head of the Commission on Women, as well as officials and members from the Frauenbund.

Guntner: Did anything change for the better for the women when Honecker took power in May 1971? What about in the theater?

Karusseit: Ulbricht is the only one who ever went to the theater. Honecker never went to the theater. The Ulbrichts came to see *Der Drache* and brought their own wine because they were afraid that someone might try to poison them. They sat up in their box, and Lotte Ulbricht said to Besson: "It's wonderful! Finally an evening when I don't have to think about anything." When they came to see *Die Schöne Helena* she said the same thing, so Besson asked: "What do you mean?" "No guidelines or slogans to remember." (The press and television always delivered the guidelines and slogans one was supposed to have in mind.) "Everything is so clear and straightforward in the theater," she said.

Guntner: Someone has said that the Brecht tradition left little space for women to develop in.

Karusseit: I do not agree. There is a lot of space, and Brecht created some great roles for women, but too few and only the same plays were performed. We had the problem of Brecht's heirs. Helene Weigel played Mother Courage and that became definitive and exemplary for the way the role was to be portrayed. Her daughter insisted that every Mother Courage was to perform the role in the same way, but you cannot play the role that way today.

Guntner: What has changed since 1990?

Karusseit: A lot. There is a lot more movement in everything. You can say anything you want, complain about anything or insult anyone you want, but there is no longer a homogeneous audience, so you cannot predict a reaction. There is no longer a monopoly on certain plays by certain directors. The cultural treaty between East and West Berlin is no longer in existence. For example, Stein's production of Chekhov's *Three Sisters* could not be performed in what was then East Berlin, even though it was in Weimar. There are fewer financial means at our disposal. Theater outside Berlin has improved. It is no longer the case that only third-rate talent goes to the provinces. The old ensembles do not exist in the same form, even though they have begun to stabilize themselves. The advantage of the ensembles was that it was possible to work continuously over a long period of time, but when actors became civil servants in the sixties, it was no longer possible to get rid of them; there was no space for new young talent unless someone died. And there are more women directing plays, including Shakespeare.

(24 May 1994)

Notes

Frequently Used Abbreviations

SJH	*Shakespeare Jahrbuch* (Bochum)
SJW	*Shakespeare Jahrbuch* (Weimar)
ShS	*Shakespeare Survey*
SQ	*Shakespeare Quarterly*
SzT	*Bertolt Brecht,Schriften zum Theater* (Frankfurt/M.: Suhrkamp, 1963).
ThdZ	*Theater der Zeit*
ThH	*Theater heute*

Preface

1. On the *Umsiedlerin* affair, which was to become one of the most notorious theater scandals in the history of the East German stage, see the interview with Müller and Tragelehn in this volume, "Der Fall Heiner Müller—Dokument zur *Umsiedlerin*," *Sinn und Form* 3 (1991): 429–86, and Heiner Müller, *Krieg ohne Schlacht* (Berlin, 1992), especially pp. 160–87. For a thorough documentation and discussion of the role of the Socialist Unity Party, the state police and the Cultural Ministry in causing this scandal, see Matthias Braun, *Drama um eine Komödie* (Berlin: Ch.Links, 1995).

2. *See* interview with Adolf Dresen in this volume.

3. *Krieg ohne Schlacht. Leben in zwei Diktaturen* (Cologne: Kiepenheur & Witsch, 1992), 112.

4. *See* interview with Weigel in this volume.

5. *See* Traute Schölling, "On with the Show? The Transition to Post-Structuralist Theatre in Eastern Germany," *Theatre Journal* 45 (1993): 21–33, as well as other essays in this special issue on "German Theatre After the F/Wall.

6. *See* "Shakespeare. Eine Differenz," *SJW* 125 (1989): 21f.; unless otherwise indicated, all translations are by J. Lawrence Guntner.

Introduction: Shakespeare in East Germany

1. For an account of their careers and fates, see Ulrich Liebe, *verehrt verfolgt vergessen. Schauspieler als Naziopfer* (Weinheim/Berlin: Beltz/Quadriga, 1992), and Beate Lause and Renate Wiens, *Theater Leben. Schauspieler erzählen von Exil und Rückkehr* (Frankfurt/M.: Hain, 1991).

2. *See* Peter Brook's description of his experiences in Germany in 1946 in *The Empty Space* (1968; London: Penguin, 1972), 48–49. By the 1947/48 theater season, 419 theaters had opened in Germany, 116 in the Soviet Occupational Zone, and 42

alone in Berlin; see Manfred Berger, et al., eds., *Theater in der Zeitenwende* (Berlin: Henschel, 1972), vol. 2, 26.

3. In his speech to the Pan-German Cultural Congress in Leipzig in 1951, Bertolt Brecht said, "neither the actors nor the audience seemed to be aware of the extent of the destruction. . . . [T]he damage was even more extensive than only construction could repair. . . . [T]he means of artistic expression had been completely destroyed. . . . [P]oetry had become declamation, the artistry had become artifice. . . . [I]nstead of the exemplary we had the representative, instead of passion we had temperament." Berliner Ensemble/Helene Weigel, eds., *Theaterarbeit* (Dresden: VVV Dresden Verlag, 1952), 7–8.

4. *See*, for example, *Theater in der Zeitenwende*, vol. 1, 24–27.

5. *See* Friedrich Wolf, "Das Drama als Waffe und Werkzeug," in *Gesammelte Werke*, vol. 16 (Berlin and Weimar: Aufbau, 1968), 248–51.

6. The resolution "About the Repertory of Drama Theaters and Measures for its Improvement" was adopted on 26 August 1946 by the Central Committee of the Communist Party of the Soviet Union. Quoted by Marc Slonim, *Russian Theater from the Empire to the Soviets* (New York, 1962), 364.

7. *See* Werner Mittenzwei, "Der Methodenstreit—Brecht oder Stanislawski?" in *Theater in der Zeitenwende*, vol. 1, 347–361.

8. *See* Armin-Gerd Kuckhoff, *Das Drama William Shakespeares* (Berlin, 1964), 695–696, and his essay in this volume. Kuckhoff served as dramaturg for Wangenheim and was involved in this production.

9. Wangenheim, himself once a member of the Reinhardt ensemble, had started and led the successful Communist agitprop "Truppe 31," famous for their play "The Mousetrap," which begins with an interlude with characters from *Hamlet:* Rosencrantz, Guildenstern, and Hamlet himself. Text in Gustav von Wangenheim, *'Da liegt der Hund begraben' und andere Stücke* (Reinbek: Rowohlt Taschenbuch, 1974), 23–111.

10. Gustav von Wangenheim, "Uber meine *Hamlet*-Inszenierung. Ansprache an die jugendlichen Zuschauer," reprinted in *Shakespeare Jubiläum* (Weimar: Hermann Böhlaus Nachfolger, 1964), 62.

11. *See* Friedrich Ebert Stiftung/Kautsky-Bernstein Kreis e.V., eds. *Der alte Streit: Freiwilliger Zusammenschluss oder Zwangsvereinigung* (Berlin, 1996). For a personal account of this merger, the reasons behind it, as well as its consequences, see Hans Mayer, *Der Turm von Babel. Erinnerung an eine Deutsche Demokratische Republik* (Frankfurt/M.: Suhrkamp, 1991), 18–27.

12. *See* especially Walter Ulbricht's "Questions Regarding the Development of a Socialist Literature" (*Fragen der Entwicklung der sozialistischen Literatur*) in *"Greif zur Feder Kumpel."* Protokol der Autorenkonferenz des mitteldeutschen Verlages Halle (Saale) am 24. April 1959 im Kulturpalast des Elektrochemischen Kombinats Bitterfeld (Halle/Saale, 1959), 98f.

13. Betriebsparteiorganisation Autoren Berlin, "Offener Brief an das Deutsche Theater," *Neues Deutschland*, 11 February 1959, quoted and translated by H. G. Huettich, *Theater in the Planned Society. Contemporary Drama in the GDR in its Historical, Political, and Cultural Context* (Chapel Hill: University of North Carolina Press, 1978), 82.

14. *See* interview with Thomas Langhoff in this volume.

15. *See* "Blutarmes Theater" *Neues Deutschland*, 1 June 1957, quoted by Manfred Nössig in *Theater in der Zeitenwende*, vol. 2, 438; he discusses the performance on 207ff.

16. *See*, for example, Armin-Gerd Kuckhoff, *Das Drama William Shakespeares*

(1964), or Anselm Schlösser, *Shakespeare, Analysen und Interpretationen* (Berlin and Weimar: Aufbau, 1977).

17. *See* Abusch, *Shakespeare—Realist und Humanist, Genius der Weltliteratur* (Berlin: Aufbau, 1964), 19ff., and Robert Weimann's essay in this volume.

18. English translation by Carl Weber, *Performing Arts Journal* 35/36 (1990): 32.

19. *See* Armin-Gerd Kuckhoff, "Shakespeare auf den Bühnen der DDR in den Jahren 1963 und 1965," *SJW* 103 (1967), who cites 46 productions, with 1351 performances for 747,166 spectators.

20. *See* Hans-Dieter Mäde, "*Hamlet* und das Problem des Ideals," *SJW* 102 (1966): 7–23, and Georg Seehase, "Zum Problem der geschichtlichen Perspektive des Stückschlüsses in *Hamlet*," *SJW* 102 (1966): 74–81. Cf. criticism in Klaus-Peter Steiger, *Die Geschichte der Shakespeare-Rezeption* (Stuttgart: Kohlhammer, 1987), 155–59.

21. *See* Manfred Nössig and Hans-Gerald Otto in *Theater-Bilanz 1945-1969* (Berlin: Henschel, 1971), 29.

22. *See*, for example, Fritz Rödel in *Theater der Zeitenwende*, 2.322.

23. Cf. Brecht in "Kleines Organon," no. 68, *SzT* 8:52.

24. On Dresen's ideas on the production, *see* "Alte Stucke lesen," in *Siegfrieds Vergessen* (Berlin: Ch. Links, 1992), 9–17, and interview with him in this volume. See also Thomas Sorge, "Unsere Shakespeares—Nachdenken über einen Wegbereiter," *SJW* 126 (1990): 24–40, and his article in this volume. The most complete study is Katarina Stein, "Hamlet, Prince of Greifswald: Negotiating Shakespeare in the GDR" (Master's thesis, Freie Universität Berlin, 1995).

25. "Der Sündenfall des Geistes, der viele Opfer fordert," quoted by Willi Schrader, "Shakespeare-Rezeption in der DDR im Lichte der Shakespeare-Tage in Weimar," *SJH* (1989): 80.

26. "Hamlet hatte in seiner Zeit keinen Ausweg. Uns, die wir die Macht haben, den Verstand zu handhaben, würde keine Zeit entschüldigen." The quote is from the program, see ibid., p. 80.

27. "Overweight and out of breath" and "fat and asthmatic" is how Brecht saw the actor (Richard Burbage) who portrayed Hamlet for Shakespeare; *see* Brecht's "Das Theater des Shakespeare" in "Der Messingkauf," *SzT* 5:123, and "Die Heiterkeit der Kunst" in "Uber das alte Theater," in *SzT* 1:108.

28. "Artistische und zugleich naturalistische Spielweise, realistische und zugleich gehobene Spielweisel" as quoted in *Theaterarbeit*, p. 13.

29. The exceptions were Alexander Weigel's reviews "Von der Schwierigkeit der Realisierung," *ThdZ* 19:8 (1964): 20–22, and "Von der Realisierung des Ideals," *ThdZ* 19:15 (1964): 8–10, that praised the Greifswald performance and pointed out the contradictions in the Karl-Marx-Stadt performance.

30. "Der neue deutsche Shakespeare" was scheduled to be published in 1989 by Henschelverlag; Müller's translations are collected in *Shakespeare Factory*, 2 vols. (Berlin: Rotbuch, 1985–89); on Tragelehn's translations, *see* Rainer Priebs, "Syntaktische Abweichung als Wirkungsmittel in der Shakespeare-Übersetzung B. K. Tragelehns," *SJW* 114 (1978): 131–141. On the issue of the specificity of East German Shakespeare translations, *see* "Shakespeare in heutiger Bearbeitung. Maik Hamburger, Heiner Müller, and B. K. Tragelehn im Gesprach mit Eva Walch," *ThdZ* 25:7 (1970): 7–11, and "Shakespeares Texte sind komplexer als jede Aneignung—man braucht zu verschiedenen Zeiten verschiedene Übersetzungen. Maik Hamburger, Heiner Müller, B. K. Tragelehn im Gespräch mit Christoph Müller," *ThH* 16, no. 7 (1975): 32–37. Eva Walch, "Zur Praxis und Kritik der Shakespeare-Übersetzung in der DDR" (Ph.D. diss., Humboldt Universität, 1978), her "Zur Praxis und Kritik der

Shakespeare-Übersetzung in der DDR," *SJW* 113 (1977): 168–77, and her "Zwei neue deutsche Übersetzungen von Shakespeares *The Tempest*," *SJW* 116 (1980): 101–19.

31. *Shakespeare Jubiläum 1964*, 63–100, and *SJW* 102 (1966): 60–96.

32. Published in a revised English translation by Johns Hopkins University Press in 1978. The full German title is *Shakespeare und die Tradition des Volkstheaters. Soziologie, Dramaturgie, Gestaltung* (Berlin: Aufbau, 1967).

33. In his dissertation, published as *Drama und Wirklichkeit in der Shakespearezeit* (Halle, 1958), especially pp. 13–180. He took this approach one step further in "The Soul of the Age: Towards an Historical Approach to Shakespeare," in Arnold Kettle, ed., *Shakespeare in a Changing World* (London, 1964), 17–24.

34. On the "complementary perspective," see *Shakespeare and the Popular Tradition*, 237–46.

35. On theoretical issues at stake in terms of official cultural policy, *see* Weimann's article in this volume.

36. Many of Weimann's contributions to symposia in the 1980s have been collected in *Shakespeare und die Macht der Mimesis* (Berlin and Weimar: Aufbau, 1988); a revised English-language edition entitled *Authority and Representation* in *Early Modern Discourse* was published by Johns Hopkins University Press in 1996. For an eloquent and insistent brief for a rethinking of fundamental theoretical questions and how a new approach to mimesis in Shakespeare as both appropriation and representation could function as a fruitful beginning, *see* Weimann's "Mimesis zwischen Zeichen und Macht," *Zeitschrift für Germanistik* 9, no. 2 (1988): 133–55.

37. *See* interview with Adolf Dresen in this volume.

38. "Address at the Fourth Plenary Conference of the Central Committee of the SED," reprinted in *Neues Deutschland*, 18 December 1971, quoted by H. G. Huettich, *Theater in the Planned Society* (Chapel Hill: University of North Carolina Press, 1978), 151.

39. *See* "Prologue," n.1 for the *Umsiedlerin* scandal. Tragelehn and Einar Schleef were awarded the Fritz Kortner Prize in 1990 for their work in the seventies at the Berliner Ensemble: Frank Wedekind's *Frühlings Erwachen* (1974) and August Strindberg's *Fräulein Julie* (1975).

40. *See* Maik Hamburger, "New Concepts of Staging *A Midsummer Night's Dream*," *ShS* 40 (1988): 51–61.

41. On Wekwerth's production of *Richard III*, *see* Lawrence Guntner, "Brecht and Beyond: Shakespeare on the East German Stage," in *Foreign Shakespeare*, ed. Dennis Kennedy (Cambridge: Cambridge University Press, 1993), 118f.

42. On Besson's staging of *Hamlet*, see Robert Weimann, "Eigenes und Fremdes in *Hamlet*. Zur Inszenierung der Berliner Volksbühne," *SJW* 114 (1978): 87–91, Christa Neubert-Herwig/Lily Leder, "Benno Bessons Versuche mit Shakespeare," *SJW* 114 (1978): 81–86, Armin-Gerd Kuckhoff, "Shakespeare auf den Bühnen der DDR im Jahre 1976," *SJW* 114 (1978): 152f., and Volker Canaris, "*Hamlet*—ein Clown, ein Zeitgenosse," *ThH* 18, no. 6 (June 1977): 6–8.

43. *See* Anna Christin Naumann's essay in this volume, her "Sprache und Körperaktion: Subjekterfahrung durch den theatralischen Diskurs mit Shakespeare-Texten," *SJW* 126 (1990): 160–63, and her "Untersuchungen zu Struktur und Funktion des Wechsels zwischen Vers und Prosa in *Hamlet* und *Ein Sommernachtstraum* an ausgewählten Inszenierungen in der DDR unter besonderer Berücksichtigung des Verhältnisses von Sprache und Körpersprache der Schauspieler" (Ph.D. diss., Humboldt University, 1989).

44. Müller's often praised and frequently performed rendition was so close to the Hamburger-Dresen translation that it raised the question of plagiarism, a disagree-

ment which had to be settled in court. Gregor Gysi, Müller's lawyer, succeeded in having the case thrown out of court in Leipzig.

45. As a gag, Lang and Langhoff originally planned to appear in roles in performances directed by the other; on the performances, see Dieter Kranz, ed., *Berliner Theater* (Berlin: Henschel Verlag, 1990), 320–25, and interview with Thomas Langhoff in this volume.

46. See interviews with Alexander Lang, Johanna Schall, and Katja Paryla in this volume. On the production, see Maik Hamburger, n. 40, Martin Linzer, "*A Midsummer Night's Dream* in Germany," *The Drama Review* 25:2 (summer 1981): 48–54, Martin Linzer, ed., *Alexander Lang. Abenteuer Theater* (Berlin: Henschel Verlag, 1983), 69–100, and Kranz, *Berliner Theater,* 317–19.

47. See Robert Weimann, "Autorität der Zeichen versus Zeichen der Autorität. Statussymbol und Repräsentationsproblematik in *König Lear*," *Orbis Litterarum* 42 (1987): 221–35, and *Macht der Mimesis,* 195–218.

48. See "Die Welt hat keinen Ausgang als zum Schinder. Ein Diskussionsbeitrag zu Heiner Müllers *Macbeth*," *ThdZ* August 27:8 (1972): 46–47.

49. Wolfgang Harich, "Der entlaufene Dingo, das vergessene Floß," *Sinn und Form* 25:1 (1973): 189–218; for Müller's account, see *Krieg ohne Schlacht,* 260–65.

50. On Müller adaptation, see Günther Klotz's essay in this volume and the documentation compiled by Lily Leder and Angela Kuberski, *MACBETH von Heiner Müller nach Shakespeare.* Theaterarbeit in der DDR (Berlin: Verband der Theaterschaffenden der DDR, 1982); Bernhard Greiner, "Explosion einer Erinnerung," *SJH* (1989): 91f. and Roland Petersohn, *Heiner Müllers Shakespeare-Rezeption. Texte und Kontexte* (Frankfurt/M.: Peter Lang, 1993). For a description of the performance and Müller's comments on it, see Kranz, *Berliner Theater,* 358–363; also Hans-Thies Lehmann, "Das Ende der Macht—auf dem Theater: Heiner Müllers *Macbeth*—Text 1972: Inszenierung 1982," *ThH* (December, 1982): 16–25.

51. "Ruth Berghaus und Heiner Müller im Gespräch," in Heiner Müller, *Gesammelte Irrtümer 2,* eds. Gregor Edelman and Renate Ziemer (Franfurt/M: Verlag der Autoren, 1990), 75.

52. "Nur ein Entschluß! Aufsteht die Bahn— / Tritt in die Schranken kühn und dreist."

53. "So oder anders du mußtest fallen Hamlet du taugtest nicht für das leben / glaubtest an die kristallbegriffe und nicht an den menschlichen lehm. German translation from Zbigniew Herbert, *Gedichte aus zehn Jahren* (Frankfurt/M.: Suhrkamp, 1967); German translation by Karl Dedecius.

54. Maik Hamburger in "Theaterschau," *SJW* 127 (1991): 162.

55. On the production, see Hamburger, ibid., and Andreas Höfele, "A Theater of Exhaustion? 'Posthistoire' in Recent German Shakespeare Productions," *SQ* 43, no. 1 (1992): 84f. and Lawrence Guntner, "Brecht and Beyond," 130–34.

56. On the relationship between Shakespeare's *Hamlet* and Müller's *Hamletmaschine, see* Roland Petersohn, *Heiner Müllers Shakespeare-Rezeption* (Frankfurt/M.: Peter Lang, 1993), 81f., and Bernhard Greiner, "Explosion einer Erinnerung in einer abgestorbenen dramatischen Struktur: Heiner Müllers *Shakespeare Factory*," *SJH* (1989): 99f.

57. In *Shakespeare. Man of the Theatre,* ed. Kenneth Muir (Newark: University of Delaware Press, 1983), 182–99.

58. "Shakespeare und Luther. Von neuzeitlicher Autorität und Autor-Funktion," *SJW* 120 (1984): 7–24.

59. "Umschauen, umdenken . . ." *SJW* 124 (1988): 7–22.

60. "Shakespeare-Adaptionen in der DDR," *SJW* 124 (1988): 223–34.

61. Reprinted as "Unsere Shakespeares—Nachdenken über einen Wegbereiter," *SJW* 126 (1990): 24–40.

62. "Vernunft und Chaos bei Shakespeare," *SJW* 128 (1992): 7–20; Walch had proposed the topic as early as 1986, but it was rejected by the program committee.

63. *See* the interview with Johanna Schall in this volume.

64. The only theater which has maintained the old prices is the Volksbühne under Frank Castorf. As a consequence it attracts the younger generation and those with lower incomes as well as artists and intellectuals from nearby Prenzlauer Berg.

65. The lack of a clear profile in Shakespeare productions that concentrates on the virtues of theater as an art form as opposed to a media culture seems to be the dilemma in theaters in both western and eastern Germany. See the "Theaterschau" for 1992/93 in *SJH* (1994): 158–228.

66. *See* the interview with Ursula Karusseit in this volume; on the lack of orientation and distinct east-west profile in Shakespeare performance in both eastern and western Germany, see Maik Hamburger's "Theaterschau" in *Shakespeare Jahrbuch* since 1992.

67. On the difficulties women directors face in general, *see* the interviews with Eva Walch, Johanna Schall, and Ursula Karusseit in this volume.

68. Robert Weimann's *Authority and Representation in Early Modern Discourse, Leonard Goldstein, The Social and Cultural Roots of Linear Perspective* (Minneapolis: University of Minnesota Press, 1988), Thomas Sorge, *Gespielte Geschichte. Die ausgestellte Fiktion in Morus' 'Utopia' und Shakespeares englische Historienspiele* (Frankfurt/M.: Peter Lang, 1992), Günter Walch's work on the history plays, or Maik Hamburger's chapters on East German Shakespeare performance in Wilhelm Hortmann's *Shakespeare on the German Stage. Vol. 2 (1914–1990)* (Cambridge University Press, 1997), and his "'Are you a party in this business.' Consolidation and Subversion in East German Shakespeare Productions," *ShS* 48 (1995): 171–84.

Chapter 1. National History and Theater Performance

1. I do not differentiate between the "Soviet Occupational Zone," and the German Democratic Republic, which was founded in 1949.

2. Wangenheim fell back on Gervinius who saw parallels between Hamlet and the lethargy of German citizenry before the revolutions of 1848. *See* G. G. Gervinius, *Shakespeare*, vol. 3 (Leipzig, 1849/59), 240ff., and Ferdinand Freiligrath's poem "Deutschland ist Hamlet" also written in the aftermath of the revolutions of 1848. Also Manfred Pfister, "Hamlet und der deutsche Geist: Die Geschichte einer politischen Interpretation," *SJH* (1992): 13–38.

3. *See* Hans-Dieter Mäde, "Hamlet und das Problem des Ideals," *SJW* 102 (1966): 12f.

4. *See* also Gustav von Wangenheim, "Über meine *Hamlet*-Inszenierung. Ansprache an die jugendlichen Zuschauer," in *Shakespeare Jubiläum 1964*, ed. Anselm Schlösser (Weimar: Böhlaus Nachfolger, 1964), 45–62, and Kuckhoff, "Shakespeare-Rezeption auf den Bühnen der DDR 1945–1980," *SJW* 118 (1982): 110, and "Anlässe, Shakespeare zu spielen," *SJW* 119 (1983): 12f.

5. For a description of the "feeling" and atmosphere of this period, *see* Hans Mayer, *Der Turm von Babel. Erinnerungen an eine Deutsche Demokratische Republik* (Frankfurt/M.: Suhrkamp, 1991).

6. On the cultural politics of postwar Berlin, which had a military commander and a well-funded "cultural officer" in each of the four occupational zones, see Henning Müller, *Theater der Restauration* (Berlin, 1981), 34f.

7. The "theory of reflection" (*Widerspiegelungstheorie*) was one of the central elements of the Stalinistic idea of "soviet realism" as developed by Zhdanov. It had a detrimental influence on the aesthetic premises of the "socialist culture" in the GDR because it severely narrowed the free space available for performance, especially as it was coupled with the idea of "engagement" (*Parteilichkeit*). This concept defined the point of view of historical reality and the form it could or should take in the arts, namely, "social progress." Both of these categories were the determinants of the idea of "realism," the "progressive antecedent" of "Soviet realism," the "true reflection" of our age in art. In reality, this meant that the "true reflection" of an age was that which was in accordance with the party line of the Socialist Unity Party (*Sozialistische Einheitspartei*). Fortunately this played a minor role in the practical work of theater performance, but, nevertheless, it provided the ideological tools to attack a production, or even have it taken off the bill, e.g., *Hamlet* directed by Adolf Dresen in Greifswald (1964) or Heiner Müller's *Die Umsiedlerin* directed by B. K. Tragelehn in Berlin-Karlshorst (1961). By the beginning of the seventies the concept had become discredited.

8. See *Sämtliche Werke*, Jubiläumsausgabe, vol. 86 (Stuttgart/Berlin, n.d.), 149–152, or *Annalen* vol. 30, 3,7, and Eckermann, *Gespräche mit Goethe* (Leipzig, 1948), 77f.

9. See for example A.-G. Kuckhoff, "Theaterschau," *SJW* 118 (1982): 142.

10. A more convincing portrayal of the craftsmen as folk characters, because it was more differentiated, contradictory, and emotional, was the 1970 production of *A Midsummer Night's Dream* at the Deutsches National Theater in Weimar, directed by Fritz Bennewitz. See a discussion in *SJW* 106 (1970): 17, 211.

11. For example, H. G. Werner, "Zur Interpretation von Werken der Vergangenheit," *ThdZ* 37, no. 1 (1982): 31f.; G. Mieth, "Nutzt ein 'magisches' Begriffspaar?" *ThdZ* 37, no. 3 (1982): 8f., and A.-G. Kuckhoff, "Theaterschau," *SJW* 119 (1983): 137–140.

12. For more details, see Kuckhoff, "Theaterschau," *SJW* 118 (1982): 142–51.

13. Meiningen is a small county seat of about 26,000 people. At the end of the nineteenth century, the theater under the patronage of Duke George II, made a name for itself throughout Europe for its Shakespeare productions. For a description of the performance, see *SJW* 120 (1984): 167–68.

14. For more details, see *SJW* 121 (1985): 179–82.

15. It is hard to assess the exact influence of Western theater productions, especially those in West Germany, on developments in East Germany. However, the internationalization of theater performance made possible via the media certainly played some role.

16. For example, the work of Heiner Müller, Alexander Lang, Wolfgang Engel, and Frank Castorf. See Thomas Sorge, "Vom Chaos des Spiels und der Ganzheitlichkeit. Zu Frank Castorfs *Hamlet*-Inszenierung in Köln," *SJW* 128 (1992): 147–56, and Doris Perl, "'A Document in Madness?' Zu Heiner Müllers Umdeutung in der klassischen Character in der *Hamletmaschine*," *SJW* 128 (1992): 157–70.

17. For example, Benno Bessons "Theaterspektakel" at the Volksbühne, including a production of *Hamlet* in a translation by Heiner Müller and Matthias Langhoff. Peter Stein's *Shakespeare Memory* (1976) and *As You Like It* (1977) at the West Berlin Schaubühne (1976) suggest that this development was not limited to East Germany.

18. See Jan Kerber, "Shakespeare und der dritte Zweck. *Troilus and Cressida* als Probe im Theaterwürfel," *SJW* 123 (1987): 165–70.

19. See Günther Klotz's essay in this volume, and Willy Schrader, "Shakespeare-Rezeption in der DDR im Lichte der Shakespeare-Tage in Weimar, *SJH* (1988): 68–87.

20. On Müllers *Hamlet/Maschine*, see Martin Linzer, "Die Welt ist aus den Fugen," *ThdZ* (May 1990), Maik Hamburger, "Theaterschau," *SJW* 127 (1991): 161ff., and Andreas Höfele, "A Theater of Exhaustion? Posthistoire' in Recent German Shakespeare Productions," *SQ* 43, no. 1 (1992): 84f., and Lawrence Guntner, "Brecht and Beyond: Shakespeare on the East German Stage," *Foreign Shakespeare,* ed. Dennis Kennedy (Cambridge: Cambridge University Press, 1993), 130–34.

21. *See* Robert Weimann, *Shakespeare and the Popular Tradition* (Baltimore: Johns Hopkins, 1979), 237ff. for a discussion of the "complementary perspective" provided by the minor characters.

22. *See* Kuckhoff, "Umschauen, Umdenken . . . ," *SJW* 124 (1978): 7–13.

23. Christoph Schroth in the program notes. *See also* the interview with Schroth in this volume.

24. For a description of the performance of *Romeo and Juliet* and *A Winter's Tale,* see "Theaterschau," *SJW* 124 (1988): 243–46.

Chapter 2. From Goethe to *Gestus*

1. Johann Peter Eckermann, *Gespräche mit Goethe,* ed. Fritz Bergmann (Leipzig: Insel, 1968). German texts in this essay are translated by me.

2. Heinrich Heine, *Die romantische Schule* in *Gesammelte Werke,* ed. Wolfgang Harich, vol. 5 (Berlin: Aufbau, 1951), 54.

3. Bertolt Brecht, *Schriften zur Literatur und Kunst,* ed. Werner Hecht, vol. 2 (Berlin and Weimar: Aufbau, 1966), 163f.

4. Martin Luther's remarks in his *Sendbrief vom Dolmetschen* (1530) are condensed in the familar quotation, "Dem Volk aufs Maul schauen." In his own revisions of the Bible up to the last edition of 1546, Luther modified passages in favor of a more literary diction, thus inaugurating a redeparture from popular speech. Cf. Maik Hamburger, "Anmerkung zur gestischen Sprache in der Luther-Bibel," *SJW* 120 (1984): 138–42.

5. "Die Ungeschicklichkeit der deutschen Sprache für den Handgebrauch bei enormer Leichtigkeit in der Behandlung der schwierigsten Themata." Karl Marx and Friedrich Engels, *Über Sprache, Stil und Übersetzung* (Berlin: Dietz, 1974), 401.

6. "Die deutsche Sprache ist die tiefste, die deutsche Rede die seichteste," in *Aphorismen und Gedichte. Auswahl 1903–1933,* vol. 3 (Berlin: Verlag Volk und Welt, 1984), 161.

7. Ute Baum, *Bertolt Brechts Verhältnis zu Shakespeare* (Berlin: Brecht Zentrum der DDR, 1981). For Brecht's view of Shakespeare the playwright, see Margot Heinemann, "How Brecht Read Shakespeare" in *Political Shakespeare,* eds. Jonathan Dollimore and Alan Sinfield (Manchester: Manchester University Press, 1985), 202–31.

8. The genesis of the "DJ" (*dialektischer Jambus*), as he calls it, is described by Peter Hacks in "Uber den Vers in Müllers *Umsiedlerin*-Fragment," *ThdZ* 16:5 (1961): 13–15. Interestingly, he begins by saying: "The history of the realistic play in Germany is the history of the appropriation [*Aneignung*] of Shakespeare."

9. Brecht, *Schriften zum Theater* 3:139.

10. J. W. Goethe, *Berliner Ausgabe,* vol. 7 (Berlin, 1963), 644.

11. *Mass für Mass,* trans. Wolf Heinrich Graf Baudissin (Leipzig: Reclam, 1948).

12. *Shakespeares sämtliche dramatische Werke,* trans. A. Böttger, H. Döring, A. Fischer, et al., vol. 5 (Leipzig: Reclam, n.d.), 113.

13. Johann Heinrich Voss, Heinrich Voss and Abraham Voss, *Shakespeares Schauspiele,* vol. 2 (Leipzig: Brockhaus, 1818), 131.

14. Acting text (Berlin: Deutsches Theater, 1996); published as playscript (Berlin: Henschel, 1983).

15. Playscript (Berlin: Henschel, 1974).

16. *Shakespeares Werke*, trans. and ed. Rudolf Schaller (Weimar: Arion, 1961).

17. Acting text (Greifswald: Theater, 1966); published as playscript (Berlin: Henschel, 1973).

18. Weimann, *Shakespeare und die Tradition des Volkstheaters* (Berlin, 1967), rev. English ed., *Shakespeare and the Popular Tradition* (1978).

19. Goethe, *Berliner Ausgabe*, 18:632.

20. Cited from Walter Benjamin, "Die Aufgabe des Übersetzers," in *Gesammelte Schriften*, vol. 4, part 1 (Frankfurt/M.: Suhrkamp, 1972), 4.

21. Fritz Kortner, *Aller Tage Abend* (Munich: Kindler, 1959).

Chapter 3. Shakespeare Contemporized

1. Cf. Kenneth Muir, "The Pursuit of Relevance," in *Essays and Studies*, n.s. 26 (1973): 20–34; referred to by Horst Prießnitz, ed., *Anglo-amerikanische Shakespeare-Bearbeitungen des 20. Jahrhunderts* (Darmstadt, 1980), 2.

2. "Ich denke, wir können den Shakespeare ändern, wenn wir ihn ändern können," in "Die Dialektik auf dem Theater. 1. Studium des ersten Auftritts in Shakespeares *Coriolan*," in Brecht's *Schriften zum Theater* vol. 3 (Berlin and Weimar, 1964), 253.

3. "Der Messingkauf," *SzT* 5:138.

4. "Anmerkungen zu 'Winterschlacht'," *SzT* 5:138.

5. Käthe Rülicke-Weiler's "Postscript" in Johannes R. Becher, *Dramatische Dichtungen. Gesammelte Werke*, vol. 8 (Berlin and Weimar, 1971), 829.

6. "Stückwahl," *SzT* 6:264.

7. "Kölner Rundfunkgespräch," *SzT* 1:130.

8. Brecht in a manuscript note, quoted by Käthe Rülicke-Weiler in her comprehensive study *Die Dramaturgie Brechts* (Berlin, 1968), 147.

9. "Fragen zum ersten Auftritt. Zu *Coriolan von Shakespeare*," *SzT* 6.335.

10. Ibid, 334.

11. In *Shakespeare-Märchen* (Berlin, 1967).

12. Cf. Heiner Müller, *Gesammelte Irrtümer, Interviews und Gespräche*, (Frankfurt/M.: Verlag der Autoren, 1986), 102.

13. Ibid.

14. Jürgen Habermas, *Der philosophische Diskurs der Moderne. Zwölf Vorlesungen* (Frankfurt/M.: Suhrkamp, 1985), 7.

15. Müller, *Gesammelte Irrtümer*, 54.

16. Ibid, 72.

17. "Wir sind bei uns nicht angekommen, solange Shakespeare unsere Stücke schreibt," in "Shakespeare eine Differenz," *SJW* 125 (1989): 21.

18. Müller, *Shakespeare Factory* (Berlin: Rotbuch, 1989), 2.224.

Chapter 4. The Sixties

1. *ThdZ* 19, no. 6 (1964):3.

2. C. U. Wiesner, "Theater-Eule," *Der Eulenspiegel* 15, no. 30 (1964): 6.

3. C. U. Wiesner, *Eulenspiegel* 15, no. 17 (1964):6.

4. "Was lesen Sie denn so am liebsten?" *Eulenspiegel* 15, no. 15 (1964): 8f.

5. "Lehrer über vier Jahrhunderte," *ThdZ* 19, no. 6 (1964): 6.

6. *Protokoll der Verhandlungen des V. Parteitages der SED, 10–16 July 1958* (Berlin 1959), 2:1401.

7. "Shakespeare contra Kofferheule," *Eulenspiegel* 14, no. 17 (1963): 6f.

8. *Protokoll der Verhandlungen* 1: 182.

9. *Kulturkonferenz* (Berlin, 1960), 40.

10. Ibid.

11. Ibid., 45.

12. Ibid., 56f.

13. Ibid., 55.

14. Hans-Rainer John, "Gespräch vor Bitterfeld," *ThdZ* 19, no. 8 (1964): 5.

15. Franz Hentschel, "15 Jahre DDR: Von nationaler Repräsentanz und Verantwortung," *ThdZ,* 19, no. 19 (1964): 5.

16. "Theaterschau," *SJW* 103 (1967): 206.

17. "Hamlet heute hier. Ein Gespräch über fünf Inszenierungen," *ThdZ,* 19, no. 17 (1964): 6.

18. Walter Ulbricht, "Uber die Entwicklung einer volksverbundenen sozialistischen Nationalkultur," in *Zweite Bitterfelder Konferenz 1964* (Berlin 1964), 82f.

19. Ibid., 38.

20. "Warum und zu welchem Ende," *ThdZ* 19, no. 8 (1964): 10.

21. Manfred Nössig, "Von Spaß und Ernst. Nach der 2. Bitterfelder Konferenz," *ThdZ* 19, no. 11 (1964): 4.

22. Hoffmeier, *ThdZ* 19, no. 7 (1964).

23. "*Hamlet* in der Diskussion. II," *ThdZ* 19, no. 13 (1964): 13.

24. *SJW* 102 (1966): 18f.

25. Christoph Funke, "Hamlet in der Diskussion. I," *ThdZ* 19, no. 12 (1964): 9.

26. Horst Gebhardt, "Hamlet heute hier," *ThdZ* 19, no. 17 (1964): 10.

27. Mäde, 16.

28. "Von der Schwierigkeit der Realisierung," *ThdZ* 19, no. 8 (1964): 21.

29. Ulf Keyn, "Hamlet unser Zeitgenosse," *ThdZ* 19, no. 8 (1964): 17.

Chapter 5. Dramatic Text and Body Language

1. This essay is a summary of my dissertation "Untersuchungen zu Struktur und Funktion des Wechsels zwischen Vers und Prosa in *Hamlet* und *Ein Sommernachtstraum* an ausgewählten Inszenierungen in der DDR unter besonderer Berücksichtigung des Verhältnisses von Sprache und Körperaktion der Schauspieler" (Zentralinstitut für Literaturgeschichte der Akademie der Wissenschaften der DDR, 1989).

2. For his dramaturgical concept Besson borrowed ideas from Robert Weimann's *Shakespeare and the Popular Tradition in the Theater* (Baltimore: Johns Hopkins, 1978; German edition, 1967).

3. From my interview with Besson on 17 November 1987 in the Akademie der Künste der DDR.

4. *See* Besson's remarks on his staging of *Hamlet*, in the archives of the Volksbühne.

5. *See* Lang's remarks on his staging of *Ein Sommernachtstraum*, in the archives of the Akademie der Künste der DDR. All quotes from Lang are from this discussion.

6. *See* Langhoff's remarks on his staging of *Ein Sommernachtstraum*, in the archives of the Verband der Theaterschaffenden der DDR. All quotes are from this discussion.

7. Michel Foucault, in Axel Honneth, ed. *Postmoderne oder der Kampf um die Zukunft* (Frankfurt/Main: Suhrkamp, 1988), 138.

Chapter 6. Shakespeare Redefined

1. Ruth Freifrau von Ledebur, *Deutsche Shakespeare-Rezeption seit 1945* (Frankfurt/M.: Akademische Verlagsgesellschaft, 1974), especially pp. 280–312, also Manfred Pfister, "Hamlet und der deutsche Geist: Die Geschichte einer politischen Interpretation," *SJH* (1992): 13–38, and "Hamlets Made in Germany, East and West" in Michael Hattaway, Boika Sokolova and Derek Roper, eds. *Shakespeare in the New Europe* (Sheffield: Sheffield Academic Press, 1994), 76–91.

2. *See,* for example, Armin-Gerd Kuckhoff's essay in this volume.

3. The *Shakespeare Jahrbuch* (Weimar) contains most of the contributions to the Weimar Shakespeare conferences. The above reference to my own work is to a long paper ("Shakespeare und das Volkstheater seiner Zeit. Redekonventionen und publikumsnahe Gestalten im Lichte der Platform-Buhne," *SJW* 100/101 (1964/1965): 72–134) read at the 1964 reinauguration conference—a piece that formed the conceptual kernel to my *Shakespeare and the Popular Tradition in the Theater* (German ed., 1967). This was followed up by more than a dozen papers and lectures read at Weimar conferences and printed in the *Shakespeare Jahrbuch* between 1964 and 1994.

4. See Alexander Abusch, *Shakespeare, Realist und Humanist, Genius der Weltliteratur* (Berlin and Weimar: Aufbau Verlag, 1964), 19–21.

5. As in Mäde's production of the play in Karl-Marx-Stadt; *see* Hans-Dieter Mäde, "Hamlet und das Problem des Ideals," *SJW* 102 (1962): 7–23.

6. See Schlösser, "Über das Herangehen an *Hamlet*," *SJW* 120 (1984): 111–112.

7. "The Function of Criticism," in *Selected Essays, 1917–1932* (London: Faber, 1932), 27.

8. Ibid., 29; Eliot's italics.

9. *See* the essays by Maik Hamburger and Thomas Sorge and the interview with Adolf Dresen in this volume.

10. *See* "Gegenwart und Vergangenheit in der Literaturgeschichte," reprinted in *Methoden der deutschen Literaturgeschichte. Eine Dokumentation,* ed. Viktor Zmegac (Frankfurt: Athenaeum, 1971), 340–74. For an English version, see "Past Significance and Present Meaning," *New Directions in Literary History,* ed. Ralph Cohen (London: Routledge, 1974), 43–62 (first published in *New Literary History* 1, no. 1 (1969): 91–109).

11. *See* my *Structure and Society in Literary History* (1984), 49.

12. *See* the interview with Frank Castorf in this volume; Thomas Sorge, "Das Chaos des Spiels und der Ganzheitlichkeit. Zu Frank Castorfs Hamlet-Inszenierung," *SJW* 128 (1922): 147–56, and Lawrence Guntner, "Brecht and Beyond," in Dennis Kennedy, ed. *Foreign Shakespeare* (Cambridge: Cambridge U.P., 1993), 134–35.

13. *Shakespeare in a Changing World,* ed. Arnold Kettle (London: Lawrence and Wishart, 1964), 10.

14. *See* "Die Moderne—ein unvollendetes Projekt," in Jürgen Habermas, *Kleine politische Schriften I–IV* (Frankfurt/M.: Suhrkamp, 1981), 444–64.

15. For an early critical dialogue with both historians, *see* my *Drama und Wirklichkeit in der Shakespearezeit* (Halle: Niemeyer, 1958), 26–27 and 54–55. Cf. von Ledebur, *Deutsche Shakespeare-Rezeption seit 1945,* 89 (citing Joachim Krehayn): "To view Shakespeare's position as between . . . the classes must be rejected as non-Marxist."

16. Full documentation of this "mingle-mangle" (John Lyly's phrase, from his prologue to *Midas*) was central to the thesis of my dissertation, *Drama und Wirklichkeit*, 13–180.

17. *See* my contribution to this discussion, "Eigenes und Fremdes in *Hamlet*," *SJW* 114 (1978): 87–91.

18. I first drew attention to the need for coming to terms with the challenge of poststructuralism in "Der Poststrukuturalismus und das Produktionsproblem in fiktiven Texten," *Weimarer Beiträge* 31 (1985): 1061–99; "Text und Tätigkeit in *Hamlet*," *SJW* 121 (1985): 30–43; "Mimesis zwischen Zeichen und Macht. Neue Perspektiven (am Beispiel Shakespeares)," *Zeitschrift für Germanistik* 9 (1988): 133–55. These studies at least in part prepared the way, critically and conceptually, for a series of international conferences in Weimar (1985, 1987, 1989, 1991), which sought to come to terms with the new paradigm in Shakespeare studies. The history of the assimilation of poststructuralism in (East) Germany has scarcely begun to be studied, except in such pioneering essays as that by Utz Riese, "Postmodern Culture: Symptom, Critique or Solution to the Crisis of Modernity? An East German Perspective," *New German Critique* 57 (Fall 1992): 157–69. In what follows, I have used, revised, and augmented a subsection I contributed to *Shakespeare and National Culture*, ed. John Joughin (Manchester: Manchester University Press, forthcoming).

19. Translated by Gayatri C. Spivak (Baltimore: Johns Hopkins University Press, 1976), xxxi.

20. Alexander Weigel, "Das Erbe und das Theater der Schauspieler von heute," *SJW* 119 (1983): 67–68.

21. Among the panelists and contributors were Susan Bassnett, Walter Cohen, Marion O'Connor, John Drakakis, Stephen Greenblatt, Graham Holderness, Zdenek Stríbrny, Henryk Zbiersky, Kiernan Ryan and others.

22. The representative was Willi Schrader without whose cooperation (and integrity) this conference would have been inconceivable.

23. Lisa Jardine, *Still Harping on Daughters* (New York, 1989), viii. Among many other voices, see Jean Howard, "Cross-dressing, the Theatre and Gender Struggle in Early Modern England," *SQ* 39 (winter 1988): 435.

24. *Die Zeit*, 12 May 1978; see *Dokumente zur Kunst-, Literatur- und Kulturpolitik der SED, 1975–1980*, ed. Peter Lübbe (Stuttgart, 1984), 543.

25. For an early outline of the problem, *see* my "Shakespeare and the Uses of Authority," in *Shakespeare, Man of the Theatre. Proceedings of the Second Congress of the ISA, 1981*, eds. Kenneth Muir, et al. (Newark: University of Delaware Press, 1983), 183–99.

26. Cf. my 1983 *Festvortrag*, "Shakespeare und Luther: Von neuzeitlicher Autorität und Autor-Funktion," *SJW* 120 (1984): 7–24.

27. John Foxe, *Acts and Monuments*, ed. S. R. Cattley, 4th ed., rev. by J. Pratt, vol. 6 (London: Seeley and Burnside, 1877), 31 and 40.

28. "Autorität der Zeichen versus Zeichen der Autorität. Statussymbol und Repräsentationsproblematik in *König Lear*," *Orbis Litterarum* 42 (1987): 221–35. There is an English translation, "The Authority of Emblems versus the Emblems of Authority in *King Lear*," *Aligarh Critical Miscellany* 3, no. 1 (1990): 1–16. Cf. my *Shakespeare und die Macht der Mimesis* where "The power of representation" throughout is shown both to engage and disengage the representation of power.

Chapter 8. Adolf Dresen

1. See Adolf Dresen, "Alte Stücke lesen," in *Siegfrieds Vergessen* (Berlin: Ch.Links, 1992), 9–17.

2. For a description of this important production, *see* Spencer Golub, "Between the Curtain and the Grave: The Taganka in the *Hamlet* Gulag," in *Foreign Shakespeare,* ed. Dennis Kennedy (Cambridge: Cambridge University Press, 1992), 158–77.

3. For a fascinating study of the performance and the following scandal, *see* Katarina Stein, "Hamlet, Prince of Griefswald: Negotiating Shakespeare in the GDR," Master's thesis (Freie Universität Berlin, 1995).

4. Wolf Biermann, singer, song writer, and cabaret artist, was expatriated from the GDR in 1976. Many of the artists, intellectuals, actors, and actresses who protested publicly were censored, jailed, or left the country. *See* Manfred Krug, *Abgehauen* (Düsseldorf: Econ Verlag, 1996).

5. See also "Goethes schwache Schlüsse," a lecture at the Technical University in West Berlin, 13 December 1979, in *Siegfrieds Vergessen,* 22–45.

Chapter 9. Alexander Lang

1. See Martin Linzer, ed. *Alexander Lang Abenteuer Theater* (Berlin: Henschel Verlag, 1983), 19–29.

Chapter 11. Heiner Müller

1. As he reveals in this interview and elsewhere, Heiner Müller has been fascinated by Shakespeare all of his life. Other remarks on Shakespeare can be found in his *Gesammelte Irrtümer. Interviews und Gespräche,* 2 vols. (Frankfurt/M: Verlag der Autoren, 1986/1990), and *Krieg ohne Schlacht. Leben in zwei Diktaturen* (Cologne: Kiepenheuer & Witsch, 1992).

2. Text in Heiner Müller, *Shakespeare Factory,* vol. 1 (Berlin: Rotbuch, 1985), 99–181; stagescript and stills in Theo Girshausen, ed. *B. K. Tragelehn. Theater Arbeiten. Shakespeare/Molière* (Berlin: edition hentrich, 1988), 38–57.

3. Text in *Shakespeare Factory,* 1.189–243. See also Lily Leder and Angela Kuberski, eds. *"Macbeth" von Heiner Müller nach Shakespeare. Volksbühne Berlin 1982,* and Wolfgang Storch, ed. *Explosion of a Memory* (Berlin: edition hentrich, 1988), 38–57. On the scandal surrounding the production, *see Krieg ohne Schlacht,* 260–265.

4. The revised text published as "Die Bauern" (1964) in *Die Umsiedlerin oder das Leben auf dem Lande* (Berlin: Rotbuch/Verlag der Autoren, 1988). On the scandal see *Krieg ohne Schlacht,* 160–87; B. K. Tragelehn, "Zeig mir ein Mausloch und ich fick die Welt," in *Explosion of a Memory,* 240–43, and "Der Fall Heiner Müller— Dokumente zur Umsiedlerin," *Sinn und Form* 3 (1991): 429–86; Matthias Braun, *Drama um eine komiödie* (Berlin: Ch.Links, 1995).

Chapter 12. B. K. Tragelehn

1. *See* "Man braucht zu verschiedenen Zeiten verschiedenen Übersetzungen. Maik Hamburger, Heiner Müller, B. K. Tragelehn im Gespräch mit Christoph Müller," *ThH* 16, no. 7 (1975): 32–37, and Eva Walch, "Shakespeare in heutiger Bearbeitung. Maik Hamburger, Heiner Müller, B. K. Tragelehn im Gespräch mit Eva Walch," *ThdZ* 25, no. 7 (1970): 7–11.

2. *See* Rainer Priebs, "Syntaktische Abweichungen als Wirkungsmittel in den Shakespeare-Übersetzungen B. K. Tragelehns," *SJW* 114 (1978): 131–41.

3. On which *see* B. K. Tragelehn, "Shakespeares Zeitgenossen," *ThdZ* 27, no. 3

(1972); reprinted in Theo Girshausen, ed. *B. K. Tragelehn. Theater Arbeiten* (Berlin: edition hentrich, 1988), 228f.

4. Text, photos, and an interview with Tragelehn from 1976 reprinted in Girshausen, 8–42.

5. Text, photos, and an interview with Tragelehn, reprinted in Girshausen, 43–72.

6. Excerpts from Tragelehn's translations of Marlowe and Ford in Girshausen, 230–42.

Chapter 13. Frank Castorf

1. For a discussion of Castorf's Cologne *Hamlet* (1989), *see* Lawrence Guntner, "Brecht and Beyond," 134–35, and Thomas Sorge, "Vom Chaos des Spiels und der Ganzheitlichkeit. Zu Frank Castorfs *Hamlet*—Inzenierung in Köln." *SJW* 128 (1992):147–150.

2. For a description of the performance that was taken off the bill after the premiere, see Siegfried Wilzopolski, *Theater des Augenblicks. Die Theaterarbeit Frank Castorfs* (Berlin: Zentrum für Theaterdokumentation und -information, 1992), 31–36.

Chapter 14. Alexander Weigel

1. *See* especially "Mimesis in *Hamlet*," in *Shakespeare and the Question of Theory*, eds. Patricia Parker and Geoffrey Hartmann (London: Methuen, 1985), 275–91, and "Mimesis in *Hamlet*: Spiegel und Wirklichkeit," in *Shakespeare und die Macht der Mimesis* (Berlin, 1988), 229f.

2. Kurt Hager, chief ideologue of the party, denounced the play for "distorting our socialist reality" in the official party newspaper *Neues Deutschland,* 30 March 1963.

3. Johann Joachim Eschenburg's prose translation of Shakespeare was the first complete translation into German.

Chapter 15. Manfred Wekwerth and Robert Weimann

1. *Theater und Wissenschaft. Überlegungen für eine Theorie des Theaters* (Dissertation, Humboldt Universität Berlin, 1970); second edition in *Schriften. Arbeit mit Brecht* (Berlin: Henschel Verlag, 1975), 393–525.

2. *See* "Über reimlose Lyrik mit unregelmäßigen Rhythmen," in *Schriften zur Literatur und Kunst,* vol. 2 (Berlin/Weimar: Aufbau Verlag, 1966), 163ff.

3. Cf. Brecht, "First Scene of *Coriolanus*," in John Willet, trans., *Brecht on Theater* (New York: Wang and Hill, 1964), 252–65.

4. See Weimann, *Shakespeare and the Popular Tradition* (Baltimore: Johns Hopkins U.P., 1978), 159–60.

Chapter 17. Johanna Schall

1. Johanna Schall is the granddaughter of Bertolt Brecht, and the daughter of Barbara Brecht-Schall and Ekkehard Schall.

Chapter 19. Ursula Karusseit

1. See *Krieg ohne Schlacht,* 206–7.

Bibliography

Abusch, Alexander. *Shakespeare—Realist und Humanist, Genius der Weltliteratur.* Berlin and Weimar: Aufbau, 1964.

Barker, Clive. "Theater in East Germany." In *The German Theater. A Symposium,* edited by Ronald Hayman, 188–200. London: Wolf, 1975.

Baum, Ute. *Brechts Verhältnis zu Shakespeare.* Edited by Brecht-Zentrum der DDR. Berlin: Buchhandlung Brecht, 1971.

Berger, Manfred, et al., eds. *Theater in der Zeitenwende. Zur Geschichte des Dramas und des Schauspieltheaters in der Deutschen Demokratischen Republik.* 2 vols. Berlin: Henschel Verlag, 1972.

Braun Matthias. *Drama um eine Komödie* Berlin: Ch. Links Verlag, 1995.

Brecht, Bertolt. "Study of the First Scene of *Coriolanus.*" In *Brecht on Theater,* edited by John Willet, 252–65. New York: Hill and Wang, 1964.

———. *Schriften zum Theater.* 7 vols. Frankfurt/M.: Suhrkamp, 1963.

Calandra, Denis. *New German Dramatists.* New York: Grove Press, 1983.

"Das Werk Shakespeares: Interpretation—Adaption—Bearbeitung—Neuschöpfung. Rundtischgespräch mit Anselm Schlösser, Fritz Bennewitz, Rolf Rohmer, Robert Weimann, Armin-Gerd Kuckhoff; Leitung: Johanna Rudolph." *SJW* 110 (1974): 10–33.

Deutsches Theater Berlin. *100 Jahre Deutsches Theater Berlin 1883–1983.* Berlin: Henschel Verlag, 1983.

Dresen, Adolf. "Das Theater ist die Herstellung der Polis." In *Regie und Interpretation. Gespräche mit Regisseuren,* edited by Herbert Mainusch, 49–58. Munich: Wilhelm Fink, 1985.

———. "Alte Stücke lesen." In *Siegfrieds Vergessen. Kultur zwischen Konsens und Konflikt,* 9–17. Berlin: Ch. Links Verlag, 1992.

———. "Schule des Individuums: Über die Krise und Chance des Theaters." *SJW* 131 (1995): 11–32.

Funke, Christoph, Daniel Hoffmann-Ostwald, and Hans-Gerd Otto, eds. *Theater-Bilanz 1945–1969.* Berlin: Henschel Verlag, 1971.

Funke, Christoph and Wolfgang Jansen. *Theater am Schiffbauerdamm. Die Geschichte einer Berliner Bühne.* Berlin: Ch. Links Verlag, 1992.

Gebhardt, Peter. "Brechts *Coriolan*-Bearbeitung." *SJH* (1972): 113–135.

Girshausen, Theo., ed. *B. K. Tragelehn. Theater Arbeiten.* Berlin: Hentrich, 1988.

Greiner, Bernhard. "Explosion einer Erinnerung in einer abgestorbenen Struktur: Heiner Müllers *Shakespeare Factory.*" *SJH* (1989): 88–112.

Guntner, Lawrence. "Brecht and Beyond: Shakespeare on the East German Stage." In *Foreign Shakespeare,* edited by Dennis Kennedy, 109–39. Cambridge: Cambridge University Press, 1993.

Hamburger, Maik. "'Are you a party in this business?' Consolidation and Subversion in East German Shakespeare Productions." *ShS* 48 (1995): 171–84.

———. "Das Subjekt auf der Bühne." *SJW* 126 (1990): 140–44.

———. "*Gestus* and the Popular Theater." *Science and Society* 41 (Spring 1977): 36–42.

———. "*Hamlet* at World's End: Heiner Müller's Production in East Berlin." In *Shakespeare and Cultural Traditions,* edited by Tetsuo Kishi, Roger Pringle, and Stanley Wells, 280–84. The Selected Proceedings of the International Shakespeare Association World Congress. Newark: University of Delaware Press, 1994.

———. "New Concepts of Staging *A Midsummer Night's Dream.*" *ShS* 40 (1988): 51–61.

———. "Shakespeare in East Germany." In *Shakespeare on the German Stage,* edited by Wilhelm Hortman. Vol. 2 (1914–1990) Cambridge: Cambridge University Press, forthcoming.

———. "A Spate of *Twelfth Nights:* Illyria Rediscovered." In *Images of Shakespeare,* edited by Werner Habicht, D. J. Palmer, and Roger Pringle, 236–44. Newark: University of Delaware Press, 1988.

Hasche, Christa, Traute Schölling, and Joachim Fiebach, eds. *Theater in der DDR. Chronik und Positionen.* Berlin: Henschel Verlag, 1994.

Höfele, Andreas. "A Theater of Exhaustion? 'Posthistoire' in Recent German Shakespeare Productions." *SQ* 43, no. 1 (1992), 80–85.

Hofmann, Jürgen. "Mauerschau: Ost-Berlin." In *Theaterbuch Berlin,* edited by Jürgen Hofmann, 335–80. Berlin: Klaus Guhl, 1985.

Hohendahl, Peter Uwe, and Patricia Herminghouse, eds. *Literatur und Literaturtheorie in der DDR.* Frankfurt/M: Suhrkamp, 1976.

Heinemann, Margot. "How Brecht Read Shakespeare." In *Political Shakespeare,* edited by Jonathan Dollimore and Alan Sinfield, 202–31. Manchester: Manchester University Press, 1985.

Hörnigk, Frank, ed. *Heiner Müller Material.* Leipzig: Reclam, 1989.

Huettich, H. G. *Theater in the Planned Society: Contemporary Drama in the GDR in its Historical, Political and Cultural Context.* Chapel Hill: University of North Carloina Press, 1978.

Joughin, John, ed. *Shakespeare and National Culture.* Manchester: Manchester University Press, 1997.

Klotz, Günther. "Shakespeare-Adaptionen in der DDR." *SJW* 124 (1988): 223–235.

Kranz, Dieter, ed. *Berliner Theater. 100 Aufführungen aus drei Jahrzehnten.* Berlin: Henschel Verlag, 1990.

Kuberski, Angela, ed. *Wir treten aus unseren Rollen heraus. Dokumente des Aufbruchs Herbst '89.* Theaterarbeit in der DDR, no. 19. Berlin: Zentrum für Theaterdokumentation und -information, 1990.

Kuckhoff, Armin-Gerd. *Das Drama William Shakespeares.* Berlin: Henschel Verlag, 1964.

———. "Anlässe. Shakespeare zu spielen." *SJW* 119 (1983): 9–30.

———. "Erbe—Gegenwart—Prognose." *SJW* 106 (1970): 29–62.

———. "Shakespeare auf den Bühnen der DDR, 1963/1964 und 1965/1965." *SJW* 103 (1967): 217–25.

———. "Shakespeare auf den Bühnen der DDR (1945–1980)." *SJW* 118 (1982): 107–119.

——. "Umschauen. Umdenken . . .," *SJW* 124 (1988): 7–22.

Lang, Alexander and Thomas Langhoff. *"Ein Sommernachtstraum* (Deutsches Theater) / *Ein Sommernachtstraum* (Maxim Gorki Theater). Gespräch mit Alexander Lang und Thomas Langhoff." In *Berliner Theater,* edited by D. Kranz. Berlin: Henschel Verlag, 1990, 317–25.

Ledebur, Ruth Freifrau von. *Shakespeare in Deutschland seit 1945.* Frankfurt/M.: Akademische Verlagsgesellschaft, 1974.

Lennartz, Klaus. *Vom Aufbruch zur Wende. Theater in der DDR.* Seelze: Ehrhard Friedrich Verlag Velber, 1992.

Linzer, Martin, ed. "A Midsummer Night's Dream." In *Alexander Lang. Abenteuer Theater,* 69–100. Berlin: Henschel Verlag, 1983/1987.

——. "*A Midsummer Night's Dream* in East Germany." *The Drama Review* 25 (summer 1981): 48–54.

Linzer, Martin and Peter Ullrich, eds. *Regie: Heiner Müller.* Berlin: Zentrum für Theaterdokumentation und -information, 1993.

Mäde, Hans-Dieter. "Hamlet und das Problem des Ideals." *SJW* 102 (1966): 7–23.

Mayer, Hans. *Der Turm zu Babel. Erinnerungen an eine Deutsche Demokratische Republik.* Frankfurt/M.: Suhrkamp, 1991.

Müller, André. *Der Regisseur Benno Besson.* Berlin: Henschel Verlag, 1966.

Müller, Christoph. "Shakespeares Stücke sind komplexer als jede Aneignung—man bracht zu verschiedenen Zeiten verschiedene Ubersetzungen. Maik Hamburger, Heiner Müller, B. K. Tragelehn im Gespräch mit Christoph Müller." *ThH* 16:7 (1975): 32–37.

Müller, Heiner. *Shakespeare Factory.* 2 vols. Berlin: Rotbuch, 1985/89. [Vol. 1: *Bildschreibung, Wie es Euch gefällt, Waldstück, Macbeth, Wolokolamsker Chaussee I;* Vol. 2: *Hamlet, Anatomie Titus Fall of Rome, Wolokolamsker Chaussee II–V,* and *Materialien.*]

——. *Die Hamletmaschine. Heiner Müllers Endspiel.* Cologne: Prometh, 1978. Translated and edited by Carl Weber, *Hamletmachine and Other Texts for the Stage.* New York: PAJ Publications, 1984. [Includes *Hamletmachine, Quartet, Correction, The Task, Despoiled Shore,* and *Gundling's Life.*]

——. *Gesammelte Irrtümer: Interviews und Gespräche.* Frankfurt/M.: Verlag der Autoren, 1986.

——. *Gesammelte Irrtümer 2. Interviews und Gespräche.* Edited by Gregor Edelman, and Renate Ziemer. Frankfurt: Verlag der Autoren, 1990.

——. *Krieg ohne Schlacht.* Cologne: Kiepenheuer und Witsch, 1992.

——. "*Macbeth von Heiner (nach Shakespeare).* Gespräch mit Heiner Müller." In *Berliner Theater,* edited by D. Kranz, 358–363.

——. *Macbeth von Heiner Müller nach Shakespeare.* Edited by Verband der Theaterschaffenden der DDR. Theaterarbeit in der DDR, no. 17. Berlin: Verband der Theaterschaffenden der DDR, 1989.

——. "Shakespeare eine Differenz." *SJW* 125 (1989): 21–23; translated by Carl Weber, *Performing Arts Journal* 35/36 (1990): 31–33.

Müller, Heiner, and Weimann, Robert. "Gleichzeitigkeit und Repräsentation. Ein Gespräch." In *Postmoderne-globale Differenz,* edited by Robert Weimann and Hans Ulrich Gumbrecht, 182–107. Frankfurt/M.: Suhrkamp, 1991.

Müller, Henning. *Theater der Restauration.* Berlin: Aufbau, 1981.

Neef, Sigrid. "Auf verlorenen Posten und doch siegreich. Die Choreographie der Schlacht-Szene im *Coriolan* 1964 am Berliner Ensemble." In *Das Theater der Ruth Berghaus*, 17–25. Frankfurt/M.: Fischer Verlag, 1989.

Parker, R. B. "Dramaturgy in Shakespeare and Brecht." *University of Toronto Quarterly* 32 (1963): 229–246.

Patterson, Michael. *German Theater Today. Post-War Theater in West and East Germany, Austria, and Northern Switzerland.* London: Pitman, 1976.

Perl, Doris. "'A Document in Madness'? Zu Heiner Müllers Umdeutung der klassischen Charaktere in der *Hamletmaschine*." *SJW* 128 (1992): 157–170.

Petersohn, Roland. *Heiner Müllers Shakespeare-Rezeption.* Frankfurt/M: Peter Lang, 1993.

Pfister, Manfred. "Hamlet und der deutsche Geist: Die Geschichte einer politischen Interpretation." *SJH* (1992): 13–38.

———. "Hamlets Made in Germany, East and West." In *Shakespeare in the New Europe*, edited by Michael Hattaway et al., 76–91. Sheffield: Sheffield Academic Press, 1994.

Pietzsch, Ingeborg, et al. ed. *Bild und Szene. Bühnenbilder der DDR.* Berlin: Henschel Verlag, 1988.

———. *Thomas Langhoff. Schauspieler Regiesseur Intendant.* Berlin: Henschel Verlag, 1993.

Priebs, Rainer. "Syntaktische Abweichungen als Wirkungsmittel in den Shakespeare-Übersetzungen B. K. Tragelehns." *SJW* 114 (1978): 131–41.

Profitlich, Ulrich, ed. *Dramatik der DDR.* Frankfurt/M.: Suhrkamp, 1987.

Rouse, John. "Heiner Müller and the Politics of Memory." *Theater Journal* 45 (March 1993): 65–74.

Rudolph, Johanna. *Lebendiges Erbe.* Leipzig: Reclam, 1972.

Schneider, Rolf. *Theater in einem besiegten Land. Dramaturgie der Nachkriegszeit 1945–1949.* Frankfurt/M. and Berlin: Ullstein, 1989.

Schrader, Willi. "Shakespeare Rezeption in der DDR im Lichte der Shakespeare-Tage in Weimar." *SJH* (1989): 68–87.

Schivelbusch, Wolfgang. *Sozialistiches Drama nach Brecht: Drei Modelle, Peter Hacks, Heiner Müller, Hartmut Lange.* Darmstadt: Luchterhand, 1974.

Schlösser, Anselm. *Shakespeare. Analysen und Interpretationen.* Berlin and Weimar: Aufbau, 1977.

———. "Über das Herangehen an *Hamlet*." *SJW* 120 (1984): 103–13.

Schölling, Traute. "On with the Show? The Transition to Post-Structuralist Theater in Eastern Germany." *Theater Journal* 45 (March 1993): 21–33.

———. "Buridan's ass between two performances of *A Midsummer Night's Dream*, or Bottom's *telos* in the GDR and after." In *Shakespeare and the New Europe*, edited by Michael Hattaway, Boika Sokolova, and Derek Roper. Sheffield: Sheffield Academic Press, 1994, 54–75.

Sorge Thomas. "Hamlet und die Totengraber." *SJW* 111 (1975): 67–80.

———. "Tradition and modernization: some thoughts on Shakespeare criticism in the new Europe." In *Shakespeare and the New Europe*, edited by Michael Hattaway, Boika Sokolova, and Derek Roper. Sheffield: Sheffield Academic Press, 1994, 321–27.

———. "Unsere Shakespeares—Nachdenken über einen Wegbereiter." *SJW* 126 (1990): 24–40.

———. *Gespielte Geschichte. Die ausgestellte Fiktion in Morus' Utopia und in Shakespeares englischen Historienspiele*. Bremer Beiträge zur Literatur-und Ideengeschicte. Bd. 11 (1992).

Stein, Katarina. "Hamlet, Prince of Greifswald: Negotiating Shakespeare in the GDR." Master's thesis, Freie Universität Berlin, 1995.

Storch, Wolfgang, ed. *Explosion of a Memory Heiner Müller DDR. Ein Arbeitsbuch*. Berlin: Hentrich, 1989.

Subiotto, Arrigo. "Coriolan" in *Bertolt Brecht's Adaptations for the Berliner Ensemble*. London: Modern Humanities Research Association, 1975. pp. 147–90.

Symington, Rodney T.K. *Brecht und Shakespeare*. Bonn: Bouvier, 1970.

Teraoka, Arlen A. *The Silence of Entrophy or Universal Discourse: The Postmodernist Poetics of Heiner Müller*. New York: Peter Lang, 1985.

Trilse-Finkelstein, J. C., and Klaus Hammer, eds. *Lexikon Theater International*. Berlin: Henschel, 1995.

Ulrich, Peter. "Erinnerungen an Hamlet." *SJH* (1994): 143–48.

Ullrich, Renate. *Mein Kapital bin ich selber. Gespräche mit Theaterfrauen in Berlin-O 1990/1991*. Berlin: Zentrum für Theaterdokumentation und -information, 1991.

Walch, Eva. "Shakespeare in heutiger Bearbeitung. Maik Hamburger, Heiner Müller, B. K. Tragelehn im Gespräch mit Eva Walch." *TdZ* 25:7 (1970): 7–11.

———. "Zur Praxis und Kritik der Shakespeare-Übersetzung in der DDR." *SJW* 113 (1977): 168–77.

———. "Zur Praxis und Kritik der Shakespeare-Übersetzungen in der DDR (1952–1978)." Ph.D. dissertation, Humboldt Universität, 1978.

———. "Zwei neue deutsche Übersetzungen von Shakespeares *The Tempest*." *SJW* 116 (1980): 101–19.

Walch, Günter. "*Henry V* as Working-House of Ideology." *ShS* 40 (1988): 63–68.

———."Shakespeare's *König Heinrich V*. Ein realistisches Historienspiel." *Weimarer Beiträge* 32 (1986): 68–88.

———. "Tudor Legende und Geschichtsbewegung in *The Life of King Henry V*: Zur Rezeptionslenkung durch den Chorus." *SJW* 122 (1986): 34–66.

———. "Vernunft und Ordnung bei Shakespeares." *SJW* 128 (1992): 7–20.

Wangenheim, Gustav von. "Uber meine *Hamlet*-Inszenierung. Ansprache an die jugendlichen Zuschauer." In *Shakespeare Jubiläum*, edited by Anselm Schlösser, 45–62. Weimar: Böhlaus-Nachfolger, 1964.

Weber, Carl. "Crossing the Footbridge Again Or: A Semi-Sentimental Journey." *Theater Journal* 45 (March 1993): 75–89.

Weigel, Alexander. "Von der Idealisierung des Ideals." *ThdZ* 19, no. 15 (1964): 8–10.

———. "Von der Schwierigkeit der Realisierung " *ThdZ* 19, no. 8 (1964): 20–22.

Weimann, Robert. "Appropriation and Modern History in Renaissance Prose Narrative." *New Literary History* 14 (spring 1983): 459–95.

———. *Authority and Representation in Early Modern Discourse*. Baltimore: Johns Hopkins, 1996.

———. "Bi-fold Authority in Shakespeare's Theatre." *SQ* 39 (1988): 401–17.

———. *Drama und Wirklichkeit in der Shakespearezeit*. Halle and Saale: Niemeyer, 1958.

———. "History and the Issue of Authroity in Representation: The Elizabethan Theater and the Reformation." *New Literary History* 17 (1985/86): 449–76.

————. "History, Appropriation, and the Uses of Representation in Modern Narrative." In *The Aims of Representation: Subject/Text/History*, edited by Murray Krieger, 175–215. New York: Columbia University Press, 1987.

————. "Mimesis in *Hamlet*." In *Shakespeare and the Question of Theory*, edited by Patricia Parker and Geoffrey Hartman, 275–92. New York: Methuen, 1985.

————. "Shakespeare and the Uses of Authority." In *Shakespeare. Man of the Theatre. Proceedings of the Second Congress of the ISA*, edited by Kenneth Muir et al., 183–99. Newark: University of Delaware Press, 1983.

————. "Shakespeare on the Modern Stage: Past Significance and Present Meaning." *ShS* 20 (1967): 113–20.

————. *Shakespeare und die Tradition des Volkstheater*. Berlin, 1967. Translated as *Shakespeare and the Popular Tradition: Studies in the Social Dimension of Dramatic Form and Function*, edited by Robert Schwartz. Baltimore: Johns Hopkins University Press, 1978.

————. *Shakespeare und die Macht der Mimesis: Autorität und Repräsentation im elisabethanischen Theater*. Berlin: Aufbau, 1988.

————. "The Soul of the Age: Towards an Historical Approach to Shakespeare." In *Shakespeare in a Changing World*, edited by Arnold Kettle, 17–24. London, 1964.

Wekwerth, Manfred. "*Leben und Tod Richard des Dritten*. Ein Gespräch mit Manfred Wekwerth." In *Berliner Theater*, edited by D. Kranz. Berlin Henschel Verlag, 1990, 176–79.

————. *Notate über die Arbeit des Berliner Ensembles 1956 bis 1967*. Frankfurt/M: Suhrkamp, 1967.

————. *Schriften. Arbeit mit Brecht*. Berlin: Henschel Verlag, 1975.

————. *Theater in Diskussion*. Berlin: Henschel Verlag, 1982.

Wichner, Ernest and Herbert Wiesner, eds. *"Literaturentwicklungsprozesse". Die Zensur der Literatur in der DDR*. Frankfurt/M.: Suhrkamp, 1993.

Wilzopolski, Siegfried. *Theater des Augenblicks. Die Theaterarbeit Frank Castorfs*. Berlin: Zentrum für Theaterdokumentation und -information, 1992.

Zipes, Jack. "Bertolt Brecht oder Friedrich Wolf? Zur Tradition des Dramas in der DDR." In *Literatur und Literaturtheorie in der DDR*, edited by Peter Uwe Hohendahl and Patricia Herminghouse, 191–240. Frankfurt/M.: Suhrkamp, 1976.

Contributors

FRANK CASTORF, head of the Volksbühne since 1992, has directed *Othello* (1992), *Hamlet* (1989), and *King Lear* (1992). In 1993 the Volksbühne was selected as German Language Theater of the Year by *Theater heute.* The interview was conducted at the Deutsches Theater on 16 November 1989.

ADOLF DRESEN's productions of *Hamlet* (1964), *Measure for Measure* (1966), and *Faust* (1968) attracted much critical discussion within the GDR. Dresen's theater essays are collected in *Siegfrieds Vergessen. Kultur zwischen Konsens und Konflikt* (1992). The interview was conducted in Hamburg on 4 December 1990.

J. LAWRENCE GUNTNER teaches at the Technical University at Braunschweig and has written on Shakespeare on film and on East German Shakespeare productions.

MAIK HAMBURGER, a dramaturg at Berlin's Deutsches Theater, has translated Shakespeare, Donne, and modern dramatists and written numerous articles on the theater and on translating Shakespeare. He has directed *Much Ado About Nothing* (1969) and *Twelfth Night* (1985). Since 1988 he has been theater reviewer for *Shakespeare Jahrbuch.*

URSULA KARUSSEIT is a popular actress who played Isabella in Dresen's *Measure for Measure* (1966), Emilia in the Karge/Langhoff *Othello* (1972), and Gertrude in Besson's *Hamlet* (1977). She also directed *Measure for Measure* (1994), among other plays. The interview was conducted in Senzig near Berlin on 24 May 1994.

GÜNTHER KLOTZ has written numerous articles on English and American literature, three books on modern British drama, and was coeditor of *Shakespeare Jahrbuch.*

ARMIN-GERD KUCKHOFF was head of the Theater Academy "Hans Otto" in Leipzig, coeditor of the *Shakespeare Jahrbuch* (1963–90), theater reviewer for *Shakespeare Jahrbuch* (1963–88), and he has written *Das Drama der Antike* (1963) and *Das Drama William Shakespeares* (1964).

ALEXANDER LANG, actor and director, is sometimes referred to as "the Peter Stein of the GDR." His *A Midsummer Night's Dream* (1980) was a milestone and high point in GDR Shakespeare performance. The interview was conducted at the Schiller Theater in (West) Berlin on 31 October 1990.

THOMAS LANGHOFF, actor and director, has been head of the Deutsches Theater Berlin since 1991. He directed *A Midsummer Night's Dream* (1980), *The Merchant of Venice* (1985), and *Henry IV* (1996). In 1991 and 1992 the Deutsches Theater was selected as German Language Theater of the Year by *Theater heute*. The interview was conducted at the Deutsches Theater on 25 April 1990.

ANDREW M. McLEAN teaches at the University of Wisconsin-Parkside, and has written about teaching Shakespeare, Shakespeare on film, and on the relationship between literature and history.

HEINER MÜLLER (1929–1995) was a playwright, translator, and director and arguably the most important German dramatist since Brecht. Among his translations are *As You Like It, Hamlet, Macbeth,* and *Titus Andronicus.* He directed *Macbeth* (1982) and *Hamlet/Maschine* (1990). The interview was conducted in Berlin on 29 April 1990.

ANNA NAUMANN wrote her dissertation on the tension between dramatic verse and body language in selected East German Shakespeare performances.

KATJA PARYLA, a popular actress, played Titania/Hippolyta in Lang's *A Midsummer Night's Dream* (1980) and directed *Henry VI* (1991). She is presently head of dramatic performance at the Deutsches Nationaltheater in Weimar. The interview was conducted at the Deutsches Theater on 25 May 1994.

JOHANNA SCHALL played Hippolyta in Lang's *A Midsummer Night's Dream* (1980) and Jeanne d'Arc in Paryla's *Henry VI* (1991). She directed *The Taming of the Shrew* (1996). The interview was conducted at the Deutsches Theater on 25 May 1994.

CHRISTOPH SCHROTH, the director and head of the theater in Schwerin (1988–1991), now heads the theater in Cottbus. He directed *A Midsummer Night's Dream* (1971), *Romeo and Juliet* (1986), *A Winter's Tale* (1987), and *Othello* (1993). The interview was conducted at the Berliner Ensemble on 25 April 1990.

THOMAS SORGE has written articles on Shakespeare and *Gespielte Geschichte. Die ausgestellte Fiktion in Morus' 'Utopia' und in Shakespeares englischen*

Historienspielen (1992). An earlier version of this essay appeared in *Litteraria Pragensis. Studies in Literature and Culture.*

B. K. TRAGELEHN, director and translator, was awarded the 1990 Kortner Prize for his work at the Berliner Ensemble during the seventies. He has translated Shakespeare as well as plays by Jonson, Ford, and Webster. He directed *Measure for Measure* (1966) and *As You Like It* (1969) in the GDR and five Shakespeare productions in West Germany: *Measure for Measure* (1977), *Macbeth* (1984), *Hamlet* (1986); *Twelfth Night* (1987), and *Tempest* (1988). The interview was conducted in Berlin on 29 April 1990.

EVA WALCH is a dramaturg and translator of Shakespeare. The interview was conducted at the Deutsches Theater on 24 May 1994.

ALEXANDER WEIGEL is a dramaturg at the Deutsches Theater and was an editor and theater critic for *Theater der Zeit.* The interview was conducted at the Deutsches Theater on 26 April 1990.

ROBERT WEIMANN, now Professor of Drama and Performance Theory at the University of California-Irvine, served as president of the German Shakespeare Society, Weimar (1985–93). Among his numerous writings on Shakespeare are *Shakespeare and the Popular Tradition in the Theater* (German ed., 1967; 1978) and *Shakespeare und die Macht der Mimesis* (1988). His most recent project following up and developing further the 1988 German book is *Authority and Representation in Early Modern Discourse* (1996) and *Shakespeare and the Power of Performance* (forthcoming).

MANFRED WEKWERTH, Brecht's pupil, was the chief director (1960–69) and later head of the Berliner Ensemble (1977–1991). He served as President of the Academy of the Arts of the GDR (1982–1990). He has written numerous articles and books on theater theory, translated Shakespeare for the stage, and directed *Coriolan* (1964), *Richard III* (1972), and *Troilus and Cressida* (1985). The interview was conducted at the Academy of the Arts of the GDR in Berlin on 16 January 1989.

Index

Abusch, Alexander, 35, 98, 106, 123, 267
Ah Q. See Hein, Christoph
alienation effect (*Verfremdungseffekt*).
See Brecht, Bertolt
appropriation. *See* socialism
authority, 136, 158, 205, 236

Bartoczewski, Bernd, 51
Baudissin, Wolfgang Graf von, translator
of Shakespeare, 73
Baum, Ute, 76
Becher, Johannes, 85–87, 184
Bennewitz, Fritz, 42–43, 129
Berghaus, Ruth, 52, 202, 250
Berlin Wall, 34, 42, 55, 65, 149, 194, 247
Berliner Ensemble, 31, 41, 87, 154, 157,
163, 192, 200, 203, 227, 232
Besson, Benno, 43, 47–50, 52, 111–14,
130, 152, 163, 179–81, 192, 196, 206,
210, 231, 259, 261
Beyer, Frank, 98
Beyer, Hermann, 52
Biermann, Wolf, 43, 45, 135, 155, 169,
261, 277 n
Bitterfeld Conference: First (1959), 34,
102; Second (1964), 36, 43, 106
Bloch, Ernst, 159
Brandt, Willy, 51
Brasch, Thomas, 57, 170
Braun, Volker, 43, 66, 77, 142
Brecht, Bertolt, 29, 35, 41, 74, 84–89, 92,
129, 150, 155–57, 163, 165, 179, 185,
192, 200, 203, 207, 210, 226; and alien-
ation effect (*Verfremdsungseffekt*), 31,
50, 229, 231. Works: *The Caucasian
Chalk Circle,* 228, 231; *Coriolanus,* 36,
39, 87, 196, 229; *Fear and Misery of
the Third Reich,* 87, 156; *The Good
Person of Szechwan,* 259; *The Life of
Galileo,* 203, 231; *A Little Organum for
the Theater,* 88; *A Man's a Man,* 191,
229; *Mother Courage and Her Chil-*
dren, 196, 228, 238, 260; *Puntila and
Matti,* 233, 259; *The Resistible Rise of
Arturo Ui,* 87, 232; *See also* Berliner
Ensemble, *Gestus*
Brook, Peter, 114, 154, 156, 164, 181,
206, 255
Brosch, Hans, 168, 219
Buchenwald, 38, 132, 152, 155, 166
Büchner, Georg, 75, 201
Bulgakov, Michael, 210
Bunge, Hans, 196
Burghardt, Max, 86

Castorf, Frank, 57, 97, 127, 150, 181, 191,
208–14, 260
censorship, 34, 152, 160, 193–95, 200–
202, 217–19, 245, 256, 258
cinema, 20, 203, 209, 228, 263. *See also*
Monroe, Marilyn; Marx Brothers
complementary perspective, 70

deconstruction, 54, 56
Deicke, Günther, 89–90
Derrida, Jacques, 132, 137
Dessau, Paul, 200, 202, 227
Deutsches Theater Berlin, 50, 56, 157,
162, 227, 259
Döring, Heinrich, translator of Shake-
speare, 79
Dresen, Adolf, 37–77, 124, 130, 144, 151–
62, 179, 195, 200, 217, 224, 240, 245
Düren, Fred, 217
Dürrenmatt, Friedrich, 152

Eisler, Hanns, 193, 227
Engel, Wolfgang, 52, 97, 121
Engels, Friedrich, 75
Erpenbek, Fritz, 35
Eschenburg, Johann Joachim, translator
of Shakespeare, 114, 164, 222
Eulenspiegel, Der, 99

289